£20-9?

REFUGEE CHILDREN IN THE UK

STANDARD LOAN

University of Chichester
Bognor Regis Campus
Upper Bognor Road, Bognor Regis
West Sussex PO21 1HR

D1339267

371.
8
RUT

Education in an Urbanised Society

Series Editors: Gerald Grace, Meg Maguire and Ian Menter

Education continues to face a range of problems, crises, issues and challenges. Often, although not exclusively, those experiencing the most severe problems are working within an urban context. Such schools face very particular challenges – high ethnic minority intake, pupil underachievement, problems of teacher recruitment and retention, social deprivation and other factors. Teachers themselves need to be prepared for classes with a rapid turnover of pupils, pupils from homeless and refugee families, and pupils with English as an additional language.

This series is intended to help education professionals and academics gain a broader understanding of the challenges faced. It examines the problems facing teachers and learners working in challenging and difficult circumstances, with a view to overcoming disadvantage in contemporary education in the UK and Ireland. It explores social and educational developments and provides educational practitioners, academics and policy makers with focused analyses of key issues facing schools in an urban society, examining the interaction between theory and practice. It offers insights into the linkage between education development and wider social, cultural and economic needs and thus contributes to the achievement of social justice in and through education.

Current titles

Mel Ainscow and Mel West: *Improving Urban Schools*

Pat Broadhead and Chrissy Meleady: *Children, Families and Communities*

Meg Maguire, Tim Woodridge and Simon Pratt-Adams: *The Urban Primary School*

REFUGEE CHILDREN IN THE UK

JILL RUTTER

Open University Press

Open University Press
McGraw-Hill Education
McGraw-Hill House
Shoppenhangers Road
Maidenhead
Berkshire
England
SL6 2QL

email: enquiries@openup.co.uk
world wide web: www.openup.co.uk

and Two Penn Plaza, New York, NY 10121–2289, USA

First published 1999
Copyright © The Editors and Contributors 2006

All rights reserved. Except for the quotation of short passages for the purposes of
criticism and review, no part of this publication may be reproduced, stored in a
retrieval system, or transmitted, in any form, or by any means, electronic,
mechanical, photocopying, recording or otherwise, without the prior permission
of the publisher or a licence from the Copyright Licensing Agency Limited. Details
of such licences (for reprographic reproduction) may be obtained from the
Copyright Licensing Agency Ltd of 90 Tottenham Court Road, London, W1T 4LP.

A catalogue record of this book is available from the British Library

ISBN 10: 0 335 21373 1 (pb) 0 335 21374 X (hb)
ISBN 13: 978 0 335 21373 3 (pb) 978 0 335 21374 0

Library of Congress Cataloging-in-Publication Data
CIP data applied for

Typeset by YHT Ltd, London
Printed in Poland by OZ Graf. S.A.
www.polskabook.pl

CONTENTS

SERIES PREFACE

The Open University Press has been the leading publisher of urban education studies in this country. With early texts such as *Cities, Communities and the Young: Readings in Urban Education* (1973a) and *Equality and City Schools: Readings in Urban Education* (1973b), the Press gave a considerable impetus to urban education study, research and policy discussion in Britain.

This publication initiative was taken because it was recognised that teaching and learning in urban schools constituted distinctive challenges which required close analysis and imaginative and radical responses. It was also recognised that educational and social policy aspirations for equality of opportunity, social justice and community regeneration faced their greatest tests in the context of urban schooling in major cities and in large working class estates on the margins of such cities.

In England, the Department of Education and Skills' publications, *The London Challenge* (2003) and *London Schools: Rising to the Challenge* (2005) demonstrate that teaching and learning in urban contexts are still high on the policy agenda. While the particular focus upon London has current priority, similar reports could be produced for Birmingham, Glasgow, Liverpool, Manchester, Belfast, Cardiff, Newcastle and other major centres. The urban education question has continuing relevance for policy and practice and it involves national and international dimensions.

It was for these reasons that we suggested to the Open University Press/ McGraw-Hill publishing team that a new series on teaching and learning in urban contexts would be very timely and professionally valuable. We were pleased that this proposal received such a positive response, not only from the publishers but also from our colleagues who will be the contributors to the series.

The series is designed to be a resource for:

• students undertaking initial teacher education

- students following programmes of Educational Studies
- serving teachers and headteachers undertaking advanced courses of study and professional development such as NPQH
- education policy professionals and administrators
- citizens who want to be actively involved in the improvement of educational services such as parents and school governors.

The challenge we have set for the contributors to the series is to write texts that will engage with these various constituencies. To do this, we believe that such texts must locate the issue under examination in an appropriate theoretical, historical and cultural context; report relevant research studies; adopt a mode of analysis expected from 'reflective practitioners' – and keep all of this grounded in the realities of urban professional experience and work settings, expressed in an accessible style.

Gerald Grace, Ian Menter and Meg Maguire

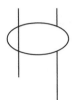

EDITOR'S PREFACE

There are few aspects of education in urbanised societies such as the United Kingdom that demonstrate better the challenges, opportunities and contradictions facing contemporary educators and policy makers than the questions raised by the presence of refugees. Their migration certainly demonstrates the global nature of our society, the mobility of peoples, the linguistic diversity of many communities and the tensions and animosities that are all too often manifested in and around schools. But of course the presence of refugees also provides a broader cultural base for schools, a broader pool of talent and skill and an opportunity for a 'tolerant' and 'civilised' society, such as this one is claimed to be by many politicians, to demonstrate its support for human rights, social justice and diversity.

Jill Rutter is outstandingly well-qualified to write this book. She has worked in a variety of situations which have given her an unparalleled range of experiences with migrant and refugee populations in the UK and overseas. A former London school teacher, she moved to work as Education Adviser for the Refugee Council in 1988. Here she kept a diary of her experiences, which is one of several sources she draws upon in this volume. In 2001 she moved to the Education Department of London Metropolitan University. As well as preparing student teachers in the subject of citizenship, she has undertaken a number of research projects relating to refugee and migrant children, most recently a study of the educational implications of the asylum–migration nexus.

As editors of this series on Education in Urbanised Societies we are delighted that such a pre-eminent scholar in the field has contributed this book to the series. We are certain that it will be of enormous value to a wide range of interested parties, including teachers, voluntary sector workers, campaigning groups and policy makers. Jill offers a thorough historical account of the history of refugee and asylum policy and provision in the UK and draws attention to the varying governmental and community responses to different phases of migration.

Her distinctive contribution to the field is to urge the adoption of what she describes as an ecological mode of analysis. Such analysis enables us to consider and understand the experiences of refugees and the appropriate educational responses to their needs in a much more holistic way than many other approaches. She points out the dangers of adopting the popular and sometimes populist 'traumatisation' approach which, while reflecting the experiences of some refugee families, tends to pathologise them in such a way that they continue to be seen as 'victims' even after arrival and settlement in this country. Such discourses nevertheless have sometimes been important in developing appropriate media and political support for refugees, leading to the allocation of much-needed resources. Nor does she deny – indeed she draws our attention to – the appalling ways in which refugees have sometimes been turned into the new scapegoats for economic ills, or poor race relations, in some sections of the media.

In short, Jill deals with the complexity of these matters and their educational implications in a sophisticated yet highly readable way. She sets some real challenges to all of those working in the field. The book is a wonderful example of emancipatory critical social research. It is work explicitly based on a commitment to social justice that simultaneously leads the way towards action.

Ian Menter
University of Glasgow

ACKNOWLEDGEMENTS

Refugee Children in the UK uses the findings of a number of research projects that I have undertaken. These include my doctoral research, as well as projects on Congolese and Somali children's school experiences. I am grateful to the funders of this research and to Diana Leonard and Crispin Jones, my academic supervisors at the University of London's Institute of Education.

Many other people assisted me in the preparation of this book, and its publication would not have been possible without the contributions of those teachers, refugee adults and children who assisted me in research visits to schools. I am grateful to those whose academic work on forced migration has influenced my research and writing. They include Barbara Harrell-Bond as well as Effie Voutiria, Frederick Ahearn, Nira Yuval-Davis, Roger Zetter and David Griffiths. Within education, I am indebted to my colleagues Louise Archer and Becky Francis, as well as Richard Hamilton and Dennis Moore who encouraged me to revisit child development theories. Others have made comments on the text or provided me with material. I would like to thank Richard Lumley, Bill Bolloten, Tim Spafford, Joe Flynn, Prakash Ross, Workneh Dechasa, Khalid Koser, Nick Van Hear, Nick Mai, Richard Stanton and the demographers at the Greater London Authority, Richard Williams, Martyn Pendergast, David Davies and Giorgia Dona. I would also like to thank Ian Menter and Meg Maguire, and the editors and production staff at the Open University Press for their work. Finally, my family deserves special thanks, for tolerating my absences. Love and a special thank you to my parents and to Emil, Isador and Guy.

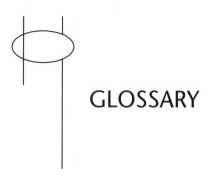

GLOSSARY

A-Levels: national academic examinations in England, Northern Ireland and Wales. Young people usually take two or three A-Levels at 18 years. There is a different examination system in Scotland.

Asylum-seeker: a person who has applied for political asylum in another country.

Bilingual student: a student who has access to, or needs to use, two or more languages at home and school. It does not imply fluency in the languages and includes students who are beginning to learn English.

Department for Education: the English central government department with responsibility for education, child protection and welfare. During the period 1989–2005 the Department for Education was variously named the Department for Education and Science (DES), the Department for Education (DfE) the Department for Education and Employment (DfEE) and most recently the Department for Education and Skills (DfES).

EAL: English as an additional language.

English Language Acquisition Stages: a four-stage assessment model that shows children's fluency in English. Stage One English language learners are beginners, while Stage Two English language learners have some oral fluency but limited writing skills. Stage Four language learners approach the fluency of a native speaker. Recently, English central government has promoted a new English, language assessment system, although this is still not widely used (QCA, 2000).

EMAG: the Ethnic Minority Achievement Grant. This is monies available from the Department for Education and Skills in England to fund EAL and refugee support, *inter alia*. (EMAG was known as the Ethnic Minority and Traveller Education Grant between 1999 and 2000, when the Traveller Education Fund was temporarily merged with it.)

Forced migration: the movements of refugees and internally displaced people (people displaced by conflicts) as well as people displaced by natural or environmental disasters, chemical or nuclear disasters, famine or development projects.

GCSE: General Certificate of Secondary Education, a national academic examination in England, Northern Ireland and Wales. It is usually taken at 16 years at the end of compulsory education. There is a different examination system in Scotland.

Irregular migration: international migrants who enter and remain in their new countries outside regular migration pathways. They include clandestine entrants, those who overstay their visas, and people who work in contravention of their visa requirements.

NASS: National Asylum Support Service, the section of the Immigration and Nationality Directorate of the Home Office that now administers support for asylum-seekers in the UK.

NGO: non-governmental organisation.

OFSTED: the Office for Standards in Education. This is a non-departmental government body responsible for inspecting all schools in England, as well as teacher education, local education authorities, youthwork, 16–19 education and early years education including child minders. Its has equivalent bodies in Scotland and Wales: Her Majesty's Inspectorate of Education in Scotland and Estyn (the Office of Her Majesty's Chief Inspector of Education and Training in Wales).

PTSD: post-traumatic stress disorder.

Pupil mobility: pupil mobility per year = ((new pupils entering outside normal times of new enrolment – pupils leaving)/total school roll) × 100.

Refugee: the term has a legal meaning, as a person who has been given full refugee status, according to the provisions of the 1951 UN Convention and 1967 UN Protocol Relating to the Status of Refugees, after having been judged to have fled from his or her home country, or be unable to return to it, 'owing to a well-founded fear of being persecuted for reasons of race, religion, nationality, membership of a particular social group or political opinion'. The term refugee is often used generally in many texts, including this book, to describe forced migrants.

Special educational needs: conditions that impede a child's learning and are generally grouped as (i) communication and interaction difficulties, which include language and literacy problems; (ii) cognition and learning difficulties, including specific difficulties, such as dyslexia, as well as more generalized learning difficulties; (iii) behavioural, emotional and social difficulties; and (iv) sensory, physical or medical difficulties. Children with English as an additional language are not considered to have special educational needs.

PART ONE:
SETTING THE SCENE

AN INTRODUCTION

I am Kurdish. I speak Turkish and I understand Kurdish but I can't read or write them. I came to London from Turkey when I was eight. In Turkey we start school when we are seven so I didn't know much about school when I came to London.

I've been in six schools in four years and lived in five different houses. Each time I changed schools I had to make new friends which was very hard. My little brother used to cry because it was so hard for him to get used to a new school. I used to get really hurt when other children teased me and made me look stupid because I didn't know English. When you're new you get picked on a lot. It sometimes happens even now.

We came to London because of the political situation in Turkey. People were always harassing and terrorising Kurdish people. I wish people understood more about refugees and had more respect for people's different backgrounds.

I interpret a lot at the doctor's, solicitor's and job centres. I don't take as much time off school as I used to. My mother is learning English and my brother can help now too.

I'd like to be an interpreter, a teacher in a junior school or a computer operator. I also want to travel to visit my relatives in Cyprus, France and Germany.
                                                                    Mahmut, aged 12.

Mahmut is a Kurdish refugee now living in the UK. He is also one among millions of forced migrants in today's world, such a movement of people being of concern to governments, international agencies and non-governmental organisations alike. The 1990s saw an increase in the numbers of asylum-seekers entering western Europe in comparison with the previous decade. Migration, in particular asylum, has emerged as a political 'problem' throughout western Europe and an issue on which elections are fought.

Although demographic data are imprecise, it is likely that there are at least 60,000 'refugee' children of compulsory school age residing in the UK. In Greater London some 6.5 per cent of all school children are asylum-seekers, refugees or other groups of forced migrants (Rutter, 2003b). Every day, in this global metropolis, those employed in education, healthcare and welfare provision meet these children in the course of their work. Other British towns and cities have seen the growth of refugee communities since the dispersal of asylum-seekers away from London and the South East after 1997.

This book examines the experiences of refugee children within British secondary schools. The motivations for writing this book were concerns about the negative school experiences of many refugee children and their failure to make progress within UK schools. I focus on secondary schools because these institutions seemed least able to meet the holistic needs of refugee children. It is at this level, too, where the gaps in children's progress open up.

In this introductory chapter, I describe the political context in which the book has been written, as well as my explanations of the complex causes of refugee children's lack of progress. The book draws on my research, as well as observations made while I was employed as Education Adviser at the Refugee Council. However, I could not have written the book without being able to stand aside from such an advocacy role. Researching *Refugee Children in the UK* made me critically examine the discourses that I had previously articulated while at the Refugee Council.

Labelling of refugee children

The key message of *Refugee Children in the UK* is that the differential educational progress of refugee children has complex causes that often relate to their different pre-migration and post-migration experiences. The book argues that educational support for refugees needs to be ecological in its approach. But it seldom is, the reasons being:

- Present UK education policy, dominated by the school effectiveness movement, places little emphasis on out-of-school social factors that influence children's progress.
- Policy text presents refugees as being a homogeneous group, preventing detailed examination of the different pre-migration and post-migration factors.
- The dominance of trauma discourses in research and policy text also prevents analysis of other pre-migration or post-migration factors that influence children's progress.

Research literature about refugee children is dominated by studies that examine the traumatic experiences of refugee children and their psychological adaptation in exile. (Around 76 per cent of the material included in my literature review on refugee children comprised psychological research monographs about trauma.) A trauma or traumatic stressor might be defined as 'an overwhelming event, resulting in helplessness in the face of intolerable danger, anxiety and instinctual arousal' (Eth and Pynoos, 1985). Until the late

19th century, trauma was understood as a physical reaction to injury, but as the psychiatric and psychotherapeutic professions began to emerge, the notion of trauma was extended to include the psychological sequelae of distressing events (Young, 1995). During the 1970s, epidemiological and psychometric studies, mostly conducted in the USA[1], generated a new condition: post-traumatic stress disorder (PTSD).

Research conducted since the mid-1980s suggests that PTSD is a condition to which refugees, including children, seem particularly vulnerable (see, for example, Arroyo, 1985; Chimienti *et al.*, 1989; Espino, 1991; Fazel and Stein, 2002; Hodes, 2000). One study suggested that 40 per cent of refugee children in the UK manifest psychiatric disorder (Hodes, 2000). The dominance of psychological research about refugee children has meant that these children's life experiences are equated with trauma in a manner that labels and homogenises them.

In comparison with the volume of studies on the traumatic experiences of refugee children there is little research about refugee children's educational experiences. Indeed, most of the existing text about refugee children's education is reflective practice – focusing on what comprises 'good' practice in schools (see, for example, Bolloten and Spafford, 1998; Camden, London Borough of, 1996; Enfield, London Borough of, 1999; Refugee Council, 2000; Rutter, 2003a). Three discourses have dominated this good practice literature, namely:

- the importance of a welcoming environment, free of racism
- the need to meet refugee children's psychosocial needs, particularly if they have had traumatic prior experiences
- ensuring that refugee children's linguistic needs are met, primarily by assisting their learning of English.

The implication of much practice literature is that refugee children will not make progress if schools do not implement its recommendations. This has a certain truth, but over the past ten years I have begun to see that the story is much more complicated. It was not just the failures of individual schools that led to refugee children's lack of progress, but a much more complex set of factors, many of which related to children's pre-migration and post-migration experiences. But the social construction of the refugee child in most policy text – public documents outlining practice or political statements of intent – is very narrow. The hegemonic construction of the refugee child assumes homogeneity, yet the refugee children that I met came from many different countries and had very different pre-migration and post-migration experiences. I also felt their construction as 'traumatised' impeded a real analysis of their backgrounds and experiences as well as masking the significance of post-migration experiences such as poverty, isolation, racism and uncertain immigration status.

Refugee Children in the UK argues that a range of ecological factors influence refugee children's educational progress. As such, the book draws on ecological

---

[1] Some of these studies were conducted among servicemen newly returned from the Vietnam War.

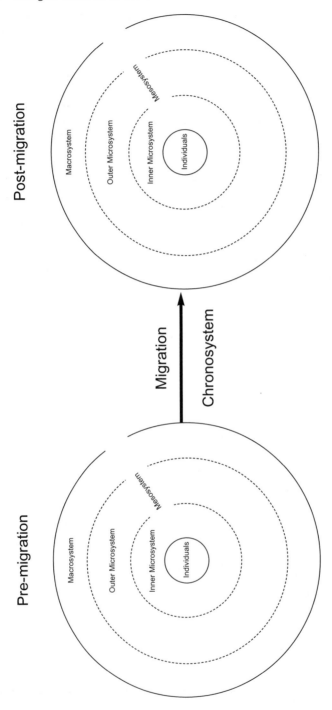

Figure 1.1 An ecological model of factors that may influence refugee children's education progress
Adapted from Hamilton and Moore, 2000.

models of child development, particularly the work of Bronfenbrenner, and Hamilton and Moore (Anderson, 2004; Bronfenbrenner, 1992; Brooks-Gunn, 2001; Hamilton and Moore, 2004). As well as individual factors, children's development is influenced by events within their inner microsystem (the family environment) and their outer microsystem (their school and neighbourhood). Children's development is also influenced by national contexts (the macrosystem) as well as the mesosystem. The latter comprises interactions between the microsystem and macrosystem – as outlined in Figure 1.1.

Refugee children will have experienced other microsystems, mesosystems and macrosystems before arriving in the UK. Pre-migration ecological factors will have influenced their development, as well as post-migration ecology. Such ecological models of child development also relate to psychological conceptualisations of resilience and vulnerability, which have emerged as an alternative theoretical basis for understanding the adaptation of refugee children in exile.

The context of the research

The book has been written at a time of major change in asylum policy and education policy, as well as conceptualisations of 'race'. From the mid-1980s onwards, European and British governance has viewed the asylum-seeker as an inconvenient 'problem' and a challenge to the powers of the State. EU and national asylum policy has converged and moved towards a course of action where greater and greater hurdles have been put in front of the would-be asylum-seeker.

Media discourses have partially driven asylum policy. The need to play to the hostile media has resulted in asylum legislation and policy being symbolic in its action, or drafted with little consideration for its broader social consequences. One example of this has been the ending of asylum-seekers' right to work. This has forced some to work 'off the books', in conditions that can be dangerous (Anderson and Rogaly, 2005).

Moral panics sell newspapers – a panic that has been targeted at the 'asylum-seeker', rather than the 'refugee', with the tabloid print media rarely using the latter term. While media hostility has been constant since the early 1990s, the themes have changed. In 1991–3, during the passage of the Asylum and Immigration (Appeals) Act 1993, newspaper articles labelled them as scroungers and benefit fraudsters. After the passage of the Asylum and Immigration Act 1996 and the subsequent legal challenges that obliged local authorities to support asylum-seekers, media discourses focused around cost to local people. The health service and education have emerged as local focus of anti-asylum sentiment. After September 11 and the London bombings of July 2005, the asylum-seeker emerged as a potential terrorist and a threat to national security.

While most anti-asylum stories are featured in the national tabloid and local print media, some of the quality broadsheets have also run hostile news items. Slightly different discourses have been used – that asylum means mass immigration and greater cultural diversity. Such diversity has been presented as a threat to national cohesion and 'British' values (Goodhart, 2004). Cultural difference is also presented as a metaphor for 'race' in other articles and used to justify restrictions on immigration.

It is easy to apportion blame for growing hostility towards asylum-seekers solely on the print media, but to do so would be inaccurate. Politicians and interest groups perceive asylum-seekers as unable to meet labour market requirements, as well as a threat to the State's control. They then mobilise the media to articulate their concerns about the legitimacy of asylum-seekers, afterwards using the rise in racial tension as a means of justifying further restrictive asylum policy (Statham, 2003). There is evidence to suggest that political party officials, as well as central and local government press officers, brief the press, feeding them hostile stories about asylum-seekers, particularly while bills are passing through Parliament.

Despite the overall trend of hostile media coverage, refugee advocacy groups have had some successes in placing sympathetic stories in the press. Statham's research indicates that during the period 1990–9 some 21.4 per cent of all claims-making featured within national news stories on asylum could be sourced to these organisations (Statham, 2003).

Four oppositional discourses on asylum have dominated material placed by refugee groups, namely:

- Humanitarian discourses: refugees are helpless and traumatised and need our support (see for example, Refugee Council, 2005a).
- Economic asset discourse: refugees are well-qualified individuals with valuable skills.
- Cultural enrichment discourses: refugee artists and musicians enrich our culture.
- Hard-facts discourses, with a focus on rational arguments and analysing statistical data on asylum (see for example, Refugee Council, 2005b).

An examination of the implications of these discourses is important. Foucault has been foremost in developing critical discourse analysis as a tool that throws light on the power relations involved in the production of text. For Foucault, discourses are sets of rules that establish knowledge or 'regimes of truths' about a subject or object, in this case the refugee or migration. Power is exercised through the struggles that are involved in producing dominant discourses or 'truths' about refugees. These truths in turn are the basis for the further manifestation of power (Fairclough, 1989, 1995; Foucault, 1972)

Western European states' hostility to refugees has meant that refugee advocacy groups have mobilised humanitarian discourses, mostly the discourse of trauma, in order to argue for asylum-seekers to be granted sanctuary. Additionally, the language of trauma has been invoked as an argument for greater healthcare and welfare resources. (Conversely, discourses of trauma are largely absent from documents produced by refugee community organisations. In researching this book the annual reports of 20 refugee community organisations were examined. Two mentioned mental health issues: suicide of young Ethiopians and the effects of the use of *qat*, a leaf chewed for its amphetamine-like qualities, among Somalis. Refugees generally do not define themselves as traumatised, despite the very real need for sympathy and public monies.) Pity – the outcome of humanitarian discourses – compounds the idea that refugees are different from us. They are different from us because they are traumatised and dysfunctional. Humanitarian discourses also contradict the economic asset discourse with its stress on refugees' skills and their ability to function in the job market. Harrell-Bond (1986) has also argued that humanitarian discourses also preclude governance, non-governmental organisations (NGO) and individuals from posing more difficult political questions about refugees. This is an issue examined in Chapter 7, where the way that teachers talk about refugees is analysed.

Cultural enrichment discourses predominate during Refugee Week, an annual event which aims to celebrate refugees' presence in the UK. Many of the events organised during Refugee Week comprise performances of music and dance. Hewitt's study of racialised attitudes among young people in South London suggests that such cultural enrichment discourses may increase hostility to migrants (Hewitt, 1996). He argues that events such as Refugee Week and 'international evenings' make no attempt to represent the culture of the white working-class English. This group then feels excluded, possessing no culture and thus not valued by the institutions of the State. The process of resentment and hostility begins.

Refugees – from a Small Issue to an Important Cause was an action research project that indicates the limits of hard-facts discourses. Commissioned by the Refugee Council and carried out by an advertising agency, it identified strategies that could be adopted by refugee agencies to generate sympathy towards refugees. A series of focus group interviews with people who did not have strong views on immigration highlighted the lack of contact with refugees and the majority community. Refugees were not part of everyday life, as they were 'hidden away' in hostels. As none of the interviewees had social contact with refugees it was easy for media stereotypes to take hold. Although many interviewees expressed superficial sympathy towards refugees, this was not coupled with identification. Refugees' backgrounds and plights were considered to be 'other-worldy'. The research stressed that the use of statistics and hard facts had limited use in challenging popular stereotypes of refugees; rather, refugee agencies should stress that refugees are ordinary people in extraordinary circumstances, by drawing on personal testimony and asking, 'how would you feel if …' questions. As one interviewee said: 'Instead of making it a charitable thing – oh look at the poor refugees – it makes you think about refugees as people like you.'

'Race' and race equality policy

Conceptualisations of 'race' and racism are also central to arguments advanced in this book. But the history of the construction and reproduction of the terms 'race', 'racialisation' and hence 'anti-racism', is long and often bitterly contested. It is, therefore, worth outlining some of the debates about the use of these terms.

The notion of race entered academic and public discourse in the early 19th century. Evolutionary biology, Mendelian genetics and biological anthropology, all new scientific disciplines, led a number of writers to suggest that humanity comprised a number of distinct types or sub-species: Caucasian, Negroid and Mongoloid. This type of racial classification was the hegemonic construction of race as European powers colonised much of Africa and Asia. It was widely believed that the success of European nations was due to the biological qualities inherent in the white 'race'. Such theories were refuted by the middle of the 20th century, as academia established that there were no distinct 'races'. Academic, and later policy, text began to use the more neutral term 'ethnic group' to denote a group that shared common cultural and geographical origins. This terminology is used in this book in this context; I also use racism and racialisation as terms to denote the differential treatment of ethnic groups. The racialised treatment of particular groups may be institutional or individual.

However, older phenotypic notions of 'race' have survived in the popular imagination, as well as among some policy makers. My school atlas, published in 1975, contained a map dividing humanity into four races and numerous sub-groups. Ten years later, the Swann Report still thought it necessary to include a substantial chapter refuting pseudo-scientific theories that the 'black race' was genetically and thus educationally inferior (Committee of Inquiry into the Education of Children from Ethnic Minority Groups, 1985). The British National Party continues to promulgate ideas of distinct races, racial separation and repatriation of those who are not white. And many teachers whom I met during my research considered that there were distinct races – black, white and Asian. Chapter 7 argues that within local authorities support for migrant children, including refugees, is often framed in terms of essentialist and reified notions of race.

Chapter 7 also examines some of the changes in 'race' relations policy during the past 35 years. These policy changes run alongside equally major changes in academic conceptualisations of 'race' and racisms. By the 1960s, the UK had experienced extensive immigration from the Caribbean, the Indian subcontinent, and a number of European countries. The new immigrants, most of whom had full citizenship rights, tended to experience marked labour market and housing segregation. Some of their social interactions with the white community were highly racialised and unpleasant. At this time, some of the first writing on race came from a Marxist tradition. Noting labour market segregation, Sivanandan, and Castles and Kosack argued that migrant workers fulfilled a specific socio-economic function found in all capitalist societies, namely to fill badly paid jobs and form a reserve army of labour (Castles and Kosack, 1973; Sivanandan, 1976). Notions of racial difference were a means of dividing the working class. For Sivanandan, black political resistance was one means of challenging capitalism. Rejecting Marxism and embracing Weberian notions of social stratification, Rex was also a key influence on later educational policy, with studies that examined the racialised educational, housing and employment experiences of Britain's ethnic minorities (see, for example, Rex, 1973; Rex and Tomlinson, 1979). Such analyses, however, had little influence on policy until the 1980s, when Rex and Sivanandan, among others, were influential critics of multicultural education policies.

Initially more influential in terms of public policy were new 'culturalist' studies of migrant and minority communities, which examined their cultural and linguistic forms (see, for example, Ballard and Driver, 1977). Central to many of these studies was the argument that individual cultural forms and language use may result in the unequal social position of minority communities. Factors such as the absence of male role models in Caribbean communities, or the so-called 'culture clash' between home and school, were factors that were blamed for inequality. Many of these early cultural and linguistic studies received intense and hostile criticism; some did adopt discourses of deficit – that the problem lay with the individual and community. But the antagonistic nature of the criticism highlighted a major issue within studies of 'race' and racism – little research had been ecological in its approach. Most studies have either taken a macro or institutional perspective. Studies that integrate an examination of individual, home, community, institutions and wider society are few.

A number of the early 'culturalist' studies influenced the development of multicultural social policies. Replacing the assimilative hegemony, multicultural education had its heyday in the late 1970s and early 1980s. Multiculturalism did not possess coherent ideology, but generally within education its policies aimed to promote linguistic and cultural diversity. There were two distinct goals:

- to improve provision for children from ethnic minority groups by boosting their self-esteem and ensuring the maintenance of their home languages
- to prepare children from the majority community for life in a multi-ethnic society.

Schools began to use bilingual resources and to celebrate non–Christian as well as Christian festivals. School textbooks were reviewed for their portrayal of minority cultures, and examinations were developed in languages such as Cantonese, Urdu and Punjabi.

But by the mid-1980s, multicultural education policies had been replaced by a new dominant discourse, that of anti-racism. While the Right saw multiculturalism as a threat to national cohesion, multicultural education had attracted growing criticism from activists and academics associated with the Left (see, for example, Sivanandan, 1982). They saw the multicultural project as emphasising cultural differences, and thus as a means of 'divide and rule'. More crucially, multicultural education was criticised as being a liberal response to the deep-rooted problem of racism and thus inequitable power relations within British society. A growing anti-racist movement, dominated by academia, activists and a number of local authority staff called for minority groups to unify as British blacks and fight racism. Some schools and local authorities began to develop policies that aimed to confront racism and promote equality of opportunity.

Throughout the late 1980s and early 1990s central government challenged anti-racist policies, prompted by lobbying from the New Right, which was adept at using the media to castigate educational and other public sector initiatives (Klein, 1993). The Education Reform Act 1988 also weakened the anti-racist education movement. It diminished the power of local authorities, institutions that had previously driven much anti-racist practice. In schools, implementing the National Curriculum made huge demands on teachers' time and energy. In such a climate, anti-racist education was no longer a priority.

Dominant constructions of race and anti-racism had also attracted academic criticism. Like previous multicultural policies, it was argued that anti-racism invoked essentialist and reified notions of race. Racism was constructed as a unified phenomenon and there was a failure to acknowledge the range of different racisms in the UK. The experiences of groups such as Cypriots, the Irish, Gypsy Roma and Travellers as well as Polish and Vietnamese refugees were often ignored in anti-racist policy text (Anthias and Yuval-Davies, 1992; Hickman and Walter, 1995; Rattansi, 1992). Academia turned its attention to the role of identity in challenging or sustaining racialised inequalities. Mac an Ghaill (1999) identifies two schools of analysis: materialism and differentialism. Materialist studies stress that factors such as labour market or educational inequality that impart one's identity in turn may influence political behaviour and other collective engagement.

Stuart Hall has been foremost in developing differentialist accounts of identity formation. He stresses that there are many components of identity, which is always in the process of being formed and reformed. He also theorises the notion of the 'other' in person identity – we define ourselves by what we are not, as well as what we are (Hall, 1991). Hall's work has been extended by studies of diasporic and transnational identities as well as examinations of syncretic and hybrid cultural forms, which are discussed in Chapter 10 in relation to young Somalis (Cohen, 1997; Griffiths, 2002). However, studies of ethnic identities do not translate into public with some academics suggesting that studies of identities and new ethnicities shift attention away from racial, class and gender inequalities in the UK. Multiple identity appears to be a poorly understood concept within schools, and as stated above, teachers and children still largely construct ethnicity in terms of colour.

In the policy world, the publication of the Macpherson Inquiry into the racist murder of Stephen Lawrence generated a revival of genuine debate in the media and in government about the racialised life experiences of the UK's ethnic minority populations (Macpherson, 1999). This report was followed by the passage of the Race Relations (Amendment) Act 2000. During 1999 and 2000 some government policy text recognised the inequalities and racisms experienced by many minority ethnic communities. But since late 2001, there has been a further discursive shift and terms such as racism and race equality have been replaced by a new agenda – that of social cohesion and integration. Debates about social cohesion are examined in later chapters where I argue that government should reject its present construction of integration, with its assimilative associations of 'them' becoming like 'us'. Refugee children's progress is partly dependent on their maintaining their own cultural forms and cultural space.

Educational change

The period 1987–2004 has also seen major changes in education and welfare policy in England, and to a lesser extent Wales, Scotland and Northern Ireland. Between 1945 and the mid-1980s both Labour and Conservative parties shared the same basic commitment to full employment, the welfare state and the co-existence of the public and private sector within the British economy. Education policy and its implementation involved a generally harmonious partnership between central government, local authorities, schools, teachers and academia. The mid-1980s saw the ending of the post-war educational consensus. New Right educational discourses of this period assumed the weight of legislation with the passage of the Education Reform Act 1988 (for a discussion about this legislation see Ball, 1994; Benn and Chitty, 1997; Chitty, 1992; Gewirtz *et al.*, 1995; Gillborn and Youdell, 2000).

The Education Reform Act 1988 introduced a market in education where schools would compete against each other for pupils. It also lessened the powers of local authorities. Further legislative and policy changes in the 1990s introduced the publication of OFSTED's school inspection reports and the results of national test and GCSE results, thus making schools 'accountable' to parents. Throughout the 1990s the dominant mantra emanating from central government concerned the need to 'raise standards'.

In 1997 a Labour government came to power after 18 years of Conservative administration. Two Labour administrations have re-introduced some discussion about equality and inclusion, and funded programmes such as Sure Start, initially targeted at the most needy under-fives. But at the same time Labour administrations have embraced fully the neo-liberal reforms of the preceding Conservative governments. In England, school league tables remain and the private sector has a greater role in education than ever before. The rhetoric about raising standards persists and the all-important measures of this policy are national test and GCSE results published annually in school league tables. In secondary schools the proportions of children securing five or more GCSE passes at Grade A*–C has become the all-important measure of success or failure of schools and their teachers.

There *has* been a national increase in the proportions of children securing the required levels in national tests and five GCSE passes at Grade A*–C. Since 2000 there is also evidence of higher levels of achievement among some minority ethnic groups within schools. But at the same time there appear to be ever-widening inequalities between different ethnic groups and, within these groups, between different social classes (see, for example, Gillborn and Youdell, 2000). Researchers such as Gillborn *et al.* argue that the post-1988 educational reforms and the operation of the educational market ensure that some children will succeed and others fail. The educational 'underclass' remains and today many refugee children are a substantial part of it. Their long-term educational and economic prospects are uncertain. Until central government fully and coherently engages with debates about inequality and social class, this excluded group will remain as a disaffected group within our schools.

The research and the book

In writing *Refugee Children in the UK* I drew on my field notes from the Refugee Council, as well as three research projects. These studies comprised:

- doctoral research examining the educational progress of 32 Congolese, Somali, Sudanese, Turkish/Kurdish and Vietnamese children who attended secondary schools in different parts of the UK
- contract research undertaken for a local authority on the educational experiences of Congolese children in primary and secondary schools
- case study research undertaken in four UK secondary schools prior to writing a third edition of *Refugees: We Left Because We Had To*, a citizenship education resource for 11–18 year olds (Rutter, 2004b).

The methodologies that I used in both my doctoral study and the contract research were very similar. In the schools that I visited I collected quantitative data and key policy documents. I interviewed key teachers, in particular children's class teachers, as well as English as an additional language staff and special educational needs coordinators. I undertook classroom observation of refugee children followed by semi-structured interviews with them. Much educational research neglects observation, but I felt it was important to see children in real-life situations.

Refugee Children in the UK comprises four sections. Part One sets the scene, with Chapter 2 examining migration and refugees. This chapter focuses on how we define refugees and the implications for educationalists of such labelling. Chapter 3 examines theoretical and research perspectives on refugee children, detailing how research studies have been dominated by the trauma literature.

Part Two examines host country responses to refugee children. Chapter 4 analyses previous settlements of refugees, tracing the emergence of present policy. Chapter 5 discusses modern asylum legislation and how it impacts on children. Chapter 6 examines how young British people view debates about asylum and migration.

Chapter 7 analyses national education policy. It suggests that there has been major policy disengagement by central government. Chapter 8 analyses school interventions.

Part Three presents case studies of three communities. Chapters 9 and 10 examine the life experiences of Congolese and Somali refugee children. These two chapters argue that factors that limit or promote the integration and settlement of refuge children are multiple, complex and sometimes localised. Interventions to support Congolese and Somali children must build on ecological models of child development and respond to the particular factors that limit their progress.

While many refugee children are failing to make progress in our schools there are also grounds for optimism. There is growing evidence that some groups of refugee children are achieving. Chapter 11 looks at what can be learned from the experiences of southern Sudanese children.

Throughout the UK, there are many examples of local interventions which have promoted refugee children's educational progress and well-being.

Almost all of these successful interventions are targeted at particular groups of refugee children rather than refugee pupils in general. These successful interventions view the child holistically, working to meet their psycho-social and learning needs. The work of these projects, as well as the resilience and success of some refugee children, ensures that we have the beginnings of a new vision for refugee children.

The final part of the book, Chapter 12, presents my conclusions and outlines these new visions. The chapter argues that policy makers need to disaggregate labels such as 'refugee child', giving greater focus to factors affecting particular children or groups of children. Policy makers and practitioners, too, need to move away from disempowering trauma discourses, the discourses of inaction, giving greater focus to the long-term promotion of children's integration and resilience. Most importantly, the final chapter argues that if refugee children are to make progress, inequalities associated with social class, migration and ethnicity must be tackled by holistic government interventions. In the early 21st century, the arrival of new immigrants in UK schools is inevitable and unstoppable. Faced with this reality, we need new educational visions, based on justice, equality and the notion of global citizenship.

WHO ARE REFUGEE CHILDREN?

Refugee Children in the UK has been written about a specific group of children – refugees. In the UK until recently, most children described as refugees had gone through the asylum determination process. But there is growing evidence that forced migrants are using other means to enter and remain in the UK. This, and the blurred boundary between forced and voluntary migration make refugee children a difficult group to define and count. This chapter examines some of the issues raised by attempts to define and enumerate refugee children.

The word 'refugee' was introduced into the English language by Huguenots who sought sanctuary in the UK in the late 17th century and is derived from the French *se refugier* – to seek shelter. When the Huguenots arrived, the status of being a refugee had no basis in law. There was no immigration control and travellers could enter and leave England as they pleased. The term refugee was an internal socio-political construction, specific to the UK and based on the obligation articulated by the government to give sanctuary to those fleeing danger in Catholic France.

The UK's first modern immigration law was the Aliens Act 1905, passed at the time when Eastern European Jews were arriving in the UK, another group that most historical accounts term as refugees. As the 20th century progressed, further immigration controls were enacted as government deemed it necessary to control borders. But it was not until 1951 that the term refugee became a legal construct with the UK's accession to the 1951 UN Convention Relating to the Status of Refugees. Passed in the aftermath of the mass displacements of the Second World War, the 1951 Convention and its 1967 Protocol define a refugee as someone who has fled a country of origin, or is unable to return to it 'owing to a well-founded fear of being persecuted for reasons of race, religion, nationality, membership of a particular group or political opinion' (from the 1951 UN Convention Relating to the Status of Refugees).

In legal terms being a refugee is a condition afforded by the competent legal authority in the state of sanctuary. The UK has acceded to both the Convention and the Protocol and they were incorporated into British immigration law in 1993. These legal instruments enshrine the rights of asylum-seekers and refugees, preventing them from being returned to countries where they fear persecution. Other international laws can be invoked to protect asylum-seekers and refugees, for example, Article 22 of the 1989 UN Convention on the Rights of the Child seeks to ensure that asylum-seeking and refugee children receive protection and assistance.[2]

The UN High Commissioner for Refugees (UNHCR) is the organisation responsible for ensuring that the humanitarian principles outlined in the 1951 Convention and its 1967 Protocol are observed by contracting states. With its headquarters in Geneva, the UNHCR has offices in over 120 states. By summer 2004 the UNHCR was working with 17,093,000 asylum-seekers, refugees and other persons of concern. The latter category includes persons afforded refugee-like humanitarian status (*de facto* refugees), persons granted temporary protection in host countries, recently returned refugees still needing support, some internally displaced persons (IDP) and some recently returned IDPs (UNHCR, 2005).

The US Committee for Refugees estimated that by the end of 2003 there were around 11.9 million asylum-seekers, refugees and those living in refugee-like situations outside their home country (USCR, 2004). It should be noted that refugee and IDP statistics are open to considerable debate. Where access to refugees is limited, perhaps because of armed conflict or because they are dispersed in large cities, many refugees may not be enumerated.

Applying for political asylum

In the UK, families of most children described as refugees have usually sought to regularise their immigration status by applying for political asylum. The asylum determination process is managed by the Immigration and Nationality Directorate (IND) of the Home Office.

An application for asylum can be made at the port of entry, or 'in-country' after an asylum-seeker has passed through UK immigration control. Those who make in-country applications include asylum-seekers who entered the UK legally, but perhaps did not know what to do when they first arrived or were anxious about applying for asylum at an airport. People who have entered the UK clandestinely, or remained after their leave to remain has expired, may also apply for asylum 'in-country'. In a family group, one or both adults usually apply for asylum, although very occasionally children within families apply in their own right (see Figures 2.1 and 2.2).

Those who apply at the port of entry are usually given an initial screening

---

[2] The UK has acceded to the Convention on the Rights of the Child with reservations, namely that children subject to immigration control, including asylum-seeking children are excluded from rights that the Convention enshrines.

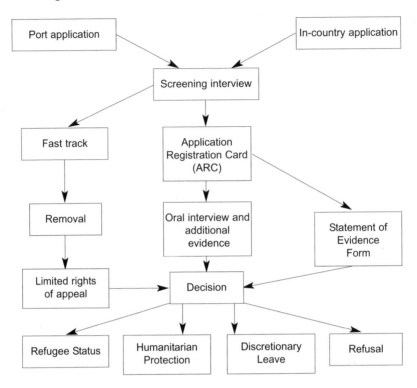

Figure 2.1 The asylum application process in the UK.
Source: Rutter (2003a)

interview by an immigration officer. During this interview, asylum-seekers (apart from very young children) are fingerprinted. The screening interview aims to establish whether an asylum-seeker has a legitimate claim to asylum or not. In future this interview will also establish in which 'stream' the asylum applicant's case will be placed (see Figure 2.2). Presently, those judged to have no legitimate claim, deemed 'a clearly unfounded application', enter a fast-track procedure and can be detained, usually in a designated Removal Centre. Asylum-seekers from a country that the Home Office judges to be safe may enter the fast-track procedure, as may those who have passed through a safe third country prior to arrival in the UK and could reasonably be expected to claim asylum there.

After the initial screening interview asylum-seekers are given an Application Registration Card (ARC) as an identity document. Oral interviews and the Statement of Evidence Form are presently used to collect evidence of persecution. Asylum-seekers have very tight deadlines in which to return written evidence to support an application, for example, the Statement of Evidence Form has to be returned to the Home Office within 10 working days of the initial screening interview. Failure to return the form within the deadline can result in an asylum application being refused.

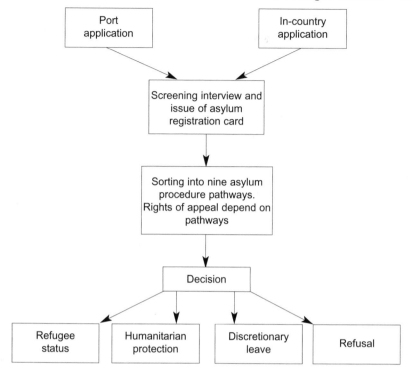

Figure 2.2 Probable future asylum application process

After giving evidence to the Integrated Casework Directorate of the IND – either in the Statement of Evidence Form, or in oral interview or both – an asylum-seeker then waits for a decision on the case. This may be rapid, perhaps within a month or so of arrival. Other asylum-seekers wait many months or years. But a decision will eventually be made. Where an asylum-seeker has dependants, the decision given to the principal applicant also applies to dependants.

If an asylum-seeker is judged to have 'a well-founded fear of being perse-cuted', he or she will be granted full refugee status. But there is no inter-nationally accepted definition of what constitutes a well-founded fear of persecution, as the interpretation of the UN Convention varies between countries. In order to try to overcome this subjectivity, the UNHCR outlines the interpretation of the UN Convention and Protocol in the *Handbook on Procedure and Criteria for Determining Refugee Status* (1992). This, country profiles (human rights briefings produced by the IND), Immigration Rules[3],

---

[3] Immigration Rules are statutory instruments that decide, in practice, whether and how a person can enter or stay in the UK. The Immigration Act 1971 gave the Home Secretary the power to make and change Immigration Rules without needing to amend legislation. Changes are simply presented to Parliament – which may or may not debate them. Parliament cannot amend Immigration Rules but can only accept or reject them.

the IND Handbook and Immigration Policy Instructions are meant to aid senior immigration officers' decisions. To be granted refugee status in the UK a person has to show with 'serious possibility' or 'reasonable likelihood' that he or she is likely to suffer persecution in the home country. There must be threats to life or freedom, or an accumulation of discriminations and dangers that amount to persecution. Someone granted refugee status must be endangered individually, though the reason for this may be membership of a particular group. People are not normally given refugee status if they are fleeing a generally unstable or dangerous condition, for example if there is a civil war in their home country.

When a person is granted refugee status s/he receives a UN Refugee Document. Those with refugee status are also granted other entitlements, such as the right to work. Recently the right of a person with Convention refugee status to remain in the UK indefinitely has been curtailed. Today, those with refugee status receive five years' right of residency, revocable at any time.

The Home Office has another immigration status that throughout the 1980s and 1990s was granted to a much larger proportion of asylum-seekers who were allowed to remain in the UK: Exceptional Leave to Remain (ELR). It was outside the provisions of the Immigration Rules and was granted at the discretion of the Home Secretary for 'humane and administrative reasons'. It did not afford the same rights as refugee status and was a form of temporary protection, renewed at intervals, usually of one year and then three years. After four years of ELR, indefinite leave to remain in the UK could be granted. Although rare, there were cases of extensions to ELR being refused.

People who were escaping civil war, and for whom return would be dangerous, were often granted ELR. Increasingly ELR was awarded to persons who in the early 1980s would have been granted refugee status. This was an EU-wide trend, with other governments also awarding temporary protection to increasing numbers of asylum-seekers (Danish Refugee Council and ECRE, 2003). Critics of this policy believe that the use of temporary protection is being used as a deterrent. It increases the power of the State, giving it the right to expel a person whose residency has expired, thus denying permanent protection.

In early 2002 the Home Secretary announced the replacement of ELR. From 1 April 2003, some asylum-seekers would receive decisions of Humanitarian Protection or Discretionary Leave. Humanitarian Protection is defined in the Immigration Rules. It is granted to asylum-seekers who have been refused refugee status, and who, if removed, would face in their country of return serious risk to life arising from the death penalty, unlawful killing, torture, or inhuman or degrading treatment. Those who receive Humanitarian Protection are usually granted it for a period of three years, although shorter periods can be granted. They have full rights to benefits and employment, but no automatic right to family reunion.

The Home Office also grants some people Discretionary Leave. This is granted by the Home Secretary outside the provisions of the Immigration Rules, to:

- those refused asylum, but who cannot be returned to their home country or a safe third country
- unaccompanied children who have been refused asylum or Humanitarian Protection, who cannot be legally returned until they are 18
- other cases where individual circumstances are so compelling that it is considered appropriate to let that person stay, for example a person with a life-threatening illness.

The period of Discretionary Leave granted by the Home Secretary varies. Those with Discretionary Leave are barred from applying for Indefinite Leave to Remain for a significant period of time, at present until at least six years of Discretionary Leave has expired.

Table 2.1 Asylum applications and decisions 1988–2004

Year	Applications	Refugee status (%)	ELR (%)	Refusal (%)
1988	3,998	23	58	19
1989	11,640	32	55	13
1990	26,205	23	60	17
1991	44,840	10	44	46
1992	24,605	6	80	14
1993	22,370	9	64	27
1994	32,830	5	21	74
1995	43,965	5	19	76
1996	29,640	6	14	80
1997	32,500	13	11	76
1998	46,015	17	12	71
1999	71,160	42	12	46
2000	80,315	10	12	78
2001	71,700	9	17	74
2002	85,865	10	24	66
2003	49,370	6	11*	83
2004	33,930	3	8**	88
2005	25,720	7	10	83

* Figures for 2003 include those granted ELR, Humanitarian Protection and Discretionary Leave. *Source*: Home Office. Figures exclude dependants.
** In 2004 no applicants were granted Humanitarian Protection when an initial decision was made, while 8 per cent of decisions were that of Discretionary Leave or ELR.

As Table 2.1 indicates, the majority of asylum-seekers have their cases refused in the UK. Reasons for refusal include:

- failure to attend an interview, provide additional evidence to support an asylum application, or failure to submit the Statement of Evidence Form
- a weak or badly prepared asylum application, or a case that is judged to lack credibility, with the Home Office not believing the story
- internal flight options – asylum-seekers who could have fled to another part of their own country where they would have been safe.

As a result of the high proportions of refusals and the success of many asylum-seekers at appeal, human rights and refugee organisations have raised concerns about the quality of the asylum decision-making process, citing a 'culture of disbelief' held by many immigration officers, as well as a routine and mechanistic approach to discounting an asylum-seeker's account of persecution (Amnesty International, 2004). That one in five asylum appeals results in the initial asylum decision being overturned is testimony to the quality of initial asylum decisions. Among asylum appellants from Somalia, around 43 per cent won their appeals in 2003 (Home Office, 2004a).

Throughout the asylum process, good quality legal representation is essential. Unfortunately, good immigration lawyers are in short supply, especially outside Greater London. Asylum-seekers may end up being represented by inexperienced lawyers and advisers or those who have no interest or commitment to asylum-seekers. Other asylum-seekers may have no legal representation at all (Amnesty International, 2004).

Other forced migrants in the UK

Asylum-seekers, those granted refugee status and forms of temporary protection such as ELR, Humanitarian Protection and Discretionary Leave, and those in the asylum appeals process or awaiting removal from the UK are the target groups of refugee advocacy groups such as the Refugee Council (Refugee Council, 1995). Two further target groups of the Refugee Council are:

- those granted refugee status overseas and admitted to the UK as part of a settlement programme – Programme Refugees such as the Chileans and Vietnamese, as well as those arriving on the new Refugee Resettlement Programmes[4]
- those fleeing persecution or armed conflict overseas and granted temporary protection while overseas such as Bosnians (1992–5) and Kosovars evacuated on the 1999 Humanitarian Evacuation Programme.

The implication of refugee advocacy groups and much refugee educational literature is that refugee children are a clearly demarcated group. But consider the cases of the children below:

'Emiliano'[5] is 12 years old and was previously internally displaced in Colombia. He arrived in the UK with his uncle and aunt in 2002, entering with a visitor's visa. Emiliano has remained in the UK, overstaying his visa.

'Vijay' is a Sri Lankan Tamil from Colombo. He arrived in the UK in 1987 with his parents and siblings. The family secured Exceptional Leave to Remain. Today they are quite open about the fictitious 'atrocity story'

---

[4] About 50 Liberian refugees were admitted to the UK from various West African countries in 2004, the first arrivals on the Refugee Resettlement Programme.
[5] The case studies were collected during the author's doctoral research.

told the Home Office to secure their right of residency in the UK, and admit that the conflict had not touched their lives substantially.

'Richard' is 12 years old and from Jamaica. He lived with his grand-mother in Kingston, in a part of the city experiencing much crime and gang-related violence to which Richard was exposed. His grandmother was also unlawfully detained by the Jamaican police. Richard's mother is a British citizen and he has now joined her, although he is finding it difficult to settle. Richard frequently experiences nightmares and intru-sive thoughts as a result of his previous experiences.

'Joseph' is from Sierra Leone. He is 14 years old and witnessed the vio-lence of the rebel invasion of Freetown in 1999. His mother was raped and then killed at this time. He and his father arrived in the UK as clandestine entrants not long after this and are living with relatives. Joseph's father was so traumatised and shamed by the rape of his wife that he was unable to discuss his experiences with anyone for a long period of time. He did not apply for asylum and has continued to live as an irregular migrant since then. He has supported himself and Joseph through illegal work in food processing and cleaning.

'Zizi' is the daughter of a Zimbabwean nurse. Her family is Ndebele and from Bulawayo. Zizi's mother has secured a work permit and is working as a nurse in London.

'Anna' is a Czech Roma. She and her family sought asylum in the UK. On 1 May 2004 Anna ceased to be an asylum-seeker when the Czech Republic joined the European Union.

Many, although not all of these children have experiences of forced migra-tion. They include a British citizen, an EU national, a work permit holder and a visa overstayer. The parents of 'Vijay' used the asylum system to gain entry to the UK; arguably he could not be termed a forced migrant, although he would be counted in national statistics on refugees. The testimony and case histories indicate that refugee children are not a clearly demarcated group, even in a narrow legal and bureaucratic sense.

The case studies raise questions about how institutions identify 'refugee' children. Where migratory patterns are complex, how do refugee children differ from other groups of migrant children? An examination of migration theory as it applies to refugees throws light on these questions.

Migration and refugees

Forced migrants are a part of a larger migratory movement, comprising many millions of people each year. However, public discourses about migration in the UK have constructed the international migrant as being an asylum-seeker. (Very rarely does the British press feature stories about overseas students or work permit holders.) But many more people enter the UK to work or study than to seek asylum. In 2002, Home Office immigration statistics suggested that around 369,000 overseas students entered the UK, compared with 85,865 asylum applicants (Home Office, 2003a, 2003b). Other groups who entered in that year comprised work permit holders and dependents (120,000), working holidaymakers (41,700) and spouses/fiancés (30,300).

Like most sociological concepts, there is no clear-cut definition of what constitutes migration or who are migrants. The UK Government, in its International Passenger Survey defines a migrant as 'a person who has resided abroad for a year or more and who states on arrival the intention to stay in the UK for a year or more' (cited in Dobson *et al.*, 2001).

The Home Office publishes annual migration statistics. However, statistics rely on precise definitions of different groups of migrants. It is easy to become trapped by policy definitions and consequently most migration theorists adopt a looser definition of migration. The Migration Research Unit, University College London, suggests migration is a sub-category of a wider concept of human mobility that also embraces commuting (Clarke *et al.*, 2003).

Until the 1970s most migration research focused on labour migration (for an overview of earlier migration research see Castles and Miller, 1998; Faist, 2000). Analysis of migration focused on *micro-factors* and systems or *macrofactors* and systems. Micro-level analyses of migration examined household decision making, suggesting that migration resulted in judgements made about securing survival, wealth, status, comfort, love or the minimisation of risk. Macro-level analyses suggest that migration is caused by socio-spatial differences such as wage differentials and the availability of employment and land. More recently, some researchers have tried to integrate these micro-level and macro-level analyses of migration, with meso-level and systematic studies. For example, Boyd and Koser suggest that social networks facilitate migration, with macro-level information about employment conditions and safety circulating among social networks, thus influencing household decision making (Boyd, 1989; Koser, 1997).

Since the 1970s researchers have distinguished between forced and voluntary migration. The International Association for the Study of Forced Migration defines forced migration as:

> a general term that refers to the movements of refugees and internally displaced people (people displaced by conflicts) as well as people displaced by natural or environmental disasters, chemical or nuclear disasters, famine, or development projects.
>
> (from IASFM website www.iasfm.org)

Early researchers of forced migration portrayed forced migrants as largely distinct from voluntary migrants. Among these researchers was Kunz, who formulated a kinetic model of refugee movement, incorporating both micro- and macro-factors that push and pull a forced migratory flow (Kunz, 1973, 1981). Kunz's model assumes that the distinction between forced and voluntary migration is intrinsic to the migrant and relatively demarcated. Later researchers have questioned this boundary. Among them are nominalists who would consider the boundary between forced and voluntary migrants to be *nominated* by governance and agencies of assistance, for example in the way that immigration status is determined, or the way that assistance is granted by agencies such as UNHCR (Richmond, 1993; Zetter, 1991). Foremost among nominalists is Richmond who suggests that the dichotomy between voluntary and forced migration be replaced by a continuum between proactive and reactive migration (Richmond, 1993). He based his model on structuration theory – the notion that individuals are social actors, have agency and that their behaviour is not solely determined by forces they neither comprehend nor control (Giddens, 1984). Richmond constructed a multivariate model of migration. His variables are threefold:

- proactive and reactive migration
- push and pull factors
- enabling circumstances (for example, social networks) and structural constraints (for example, immigration controls and immigration labels).

Richmond's migration system also incorporates positive and negative feedback. However, its fault lies in the assumption that forced migrants lack agency while voluntary migrants possess it. This is not always the case: a forced migrant fleeing persecution may manifest a great deal of agency in reaching the country of final asylum.

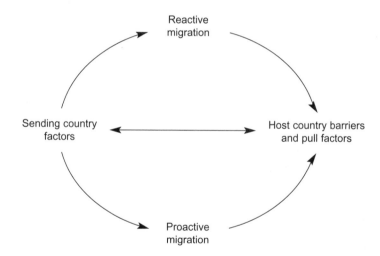

Figure 2.3 Reactive and proactive migration, adapted from Richmond (1993)

Richmond was among the first migration theorist to acknowledge the blurred boundary between forced and voluntary migration. His work has been augmented by recent research on the asylum-migration nexus. Castles and Loughna (2002), among others, argue that in western Europe, the distinction between asylum-seekers and other groups of migrants has become increasingly blurred:

Although some people entering western countries are clearly refugees while others are clearly economic migrants, there have always been people who could not be easily categorised. Often migrants respond to migration rules and policies of receiving states in deciding on their mode of migration. From the migrants' perception such rules and policies can be seen as opportunity structures, rather than absolute definitions.

Castles and Loughna argue that the asylum–migration nexus has three different components:

- *Treating refugees as migrant workers* Many migrant workers who moved to France and Germany in the 1960s and 1970s were escaping authoritarian regimes in Spain, Portugal, Greece and Turkey. Today, Zimbabweans with experiences of forced migration are choosing to seek admission to the UK with work permits, rather than endure the lengthy and uncertain asylum process. Zimbabweans are being admitted because the UK needs their labour, not because they need protection.
- *Migrants with mixed motivations claiming asylum* Until the mid-1980s, Tamils fleeing worsening conflict in Sri Lanka sought entry first as Commonwealth immigrants and later as overseas students. After the mid-1980s, entry as an overseas student became increasingly expensive and difficult. For some Tamils, claiming asylum became the only legal route to enter western Europe (McDowell, 1996). This does not imply that some of the claims were not genuine. But people who had previously been admitted as workers and students now had to claim asylum.
- *Asylum seekers moving as irregular migrants*[6] Since the late 1980s EU member states have enacted legislation changes that are designed to keep refugees out, including the introduction of visa requirements and carrier sanctions. The would-be asylum-seeker has little choice but to use the services of a people trafficker or smuggler and enter Europe as an irregular migrant. That asylum-seekers have been prevented from working legally since 2002 is an incentive for them to remain in a state of irregularity.[7] Although there is little national research on irregular migrants, local studies do indicate an increase in this condition.

While acknowledging the mixed motives for the migration of many of those who seek entry to western Europe, Castles and Loughna argue that the 'push' factors within countries of origin are very similar. Their research suggests that indicators of conflict are far more significant than indicators of underdevelopment as a cause of migration.

Despite the sympathetic conclusions of Castles and Loughna, refugee agencies have been extremely reluctant to acknowledge the asylum–migration nexus. Indeed any discussion of this issue is heavily policed. Obviously, in the face of an unsympathetic government, refugee agencies have to argue that their clients' motives are 'genuine'. But their oppositional construction

---

[6] Irregular immigrants include clandestine entrants who remain as such, visa overstayers, and those who violate their visa requirements, perhaps by working more than permitted.
[7] At the time of writing in 2005 there has only been one prosecution under the Asylum and Immigration Act 1996 for employing those without the right to work.

of the refugee as being the saintly, persecuted and grateful activist has implications for practitioners, such as teachers, who are often perplexed by refugee families whose decision to migrate may be complex and involve economic factors.

In a number of local authorities, too, educational support systems for new arrivals from overseas are entirely built around the structures of the National Asylum Support Service (NASS). Children who arrive as a result of NASS dispersal receive a well-planned induction and language support service. Children who are forced migrants, but arrive using other migratory pathways receive little or no support.

Labelling refugee children

Zetter (1991) has developed nominalism into labelling theory, suggesting that the 'refugee' is a bureaucratic identity assigned by outsiders. He undertook extensive fieldwork among post-1974 refugees living in a large housing complex in southern Cyprus. The label of refugee was used as a basis to allocate housing. Initially the Cypriot refugees were grateful for this label and the subsequent intervention; later some began to resent their labelling. Zetter's work concludes that labelling refugees is a process that involves disaggregating existing identities, stereotyping a group, then forming a new bureaucratic category, usually with little participation of the refugee population. Labelling usually involves unequal power relations between the labeller and the labelled. Zetter's labelling theory has parallels with some of the writings of Werbner (1997) who suggests that some minority ethnic categorisation is 'imagined' by the State as a means of controlling populations and allocating resources.

In the early 1990s, a number of local authorities resisted labelling refugee children, declaring that their needs were no different from other groups of minority ethnic groups. (Two local authorities resolutely refused to give estimates of numbers of refugee children, stating that they would only collect demographic data on children from minority ethnic communities, as there was no difference, except in the eyes of those employed by refugee organisations.) Since then the pendulum has swung in the other direction. Many local authorities have increasingly assigned labels to refugee children, and ensured that only children with a particular immigration label such as NASS-supported asylum-seekers are afforded support.

The demographic challenge

The blurred distinction between voluntary and forced migrants presents many challenges to policy makers in education, healthcare and social care. Welfare monies are limited and policy decisions have to be taken in order to allocate finite resources. Most local government-targeted finance requires a local authority to present a population estimate of client groups.

But how can refugee children be counted? It may not be conducive to a child's welfare to ask intrusive questions about immigration status, and, as discussed above, children who are forced migrants are not a clearly demarcated group. In the UK there is also a lack of demographic data about refugee populations, both nationally and locally (Stewart, 2004). Nor are there any credible demographic data on irregular immigrants, among which population are those who have experienced forced migration (Duevell, 1998).

Refugee population data that are available include Home Office Asylum Statistics and NASS Statistics. The NASS collects basic data on asylum seekers supported by this service. Home Office asylum statistics are published quarterly and include (i) numbers of asylum applications, broken down per country of origin; (ii) outcomes of asylum cases and appeals, broken down per country of origin; (iii) numbers of unaccompanied children, broken down per country of origin; and (iv) data regarding detention and removals. However, Home Office statistics do not include any local data on asylum-seekers' places of residence. There are also no published data on the numbers of accompanied children who apply for asylum as a dependant of a principal asylum applicant.

Census data can be used to estimate refugee populations. The 2001 Census included a question on country of birth, information which can provide some estimation of some populations of refugees, where asylum is the main means of entry to the UK. However, census data are collected at ten-year intervals and therefore lack immediacy. They also have limited use where populations comprise both forced and voluntary migrants. Finally, there is always under-enumeration among migrants, inner-city populations, those who may lack fluency in English, and among populations where higher proportions of adults lack functional literacy.

Other sources of population data are available. Many refugee organisations collect data on their clients, sometimes used to estimate population numbers but which may often over-estimate the size of their client population.

In England, the Department for Education and Skills (DfES) is increasing its data collection by allocating each school student in England a number called the Unique Pupil Reference Number. This number aids an annual pupil census termed the Pupil Level Annual School Census (PLASC). Data on pupil numbers, their ethnicity and home language are collated by the local authority and eventually by the DfES. Unfortunately DfES guidance on ethnicity categories means the PLASC presently cannot collect much useful data on the numbers of refugee pupils or on their achievement. The DfES has elected to use broad categories: White UK (WTUK), White Other (WOTW), Black Caribbean (BCRB), Indian (AIND), Pakistani (APKN) and so on. Local authorities, however, can break down these broad groups further, using extended categories. The London Borough of Lewisham, for example, has decided to include Somali as a sub-category of Black African, and to include Tamil as a sub-category of Asian Other. Indeed, some local authorities use the annual pupil census to collect their own very detailed data on ethnicity, home language and achievement (DfES, 2005). However, unless all local authorities refine the DfES ethnicity categories, it may be difficult to collect data about refugee groups.

The above-mentioned lack of precision has led some local authorities to conduct annual refugee surveys, which can be conducted in two different ways:

- by asking children or parents/carers about their immigration status, and if they are asylum-seekers, have refugee status or have leave to remain
- by using a process of triangulation and basing an estimate on a range of different data such as local authority language surveys and National Asylum Support Service (NASS) data and teacher information.

Schools rarely ask pupils about their immigration status. While this may be the most accurate way of approaching a refugee survey, asking such a direct question may arouse fear and suspicion. An alternative is to look at information collected in language surveys carried out at the same time as the PLASC, and to supplement this with other information known about the child. A child who speaks Krio or Somali, for example is highly likely to be a refugee and to have experienced forced migration. Class teachers may also know about the prior experiences of a child.

There are difficulties in calculating refugee numbers for some linguistic groups. For example, children who speak Arabic, French or Turkish may or may not be refugees. Here supplementary data are needed, such as teacher information, the country of birth, whether the family is supported by NASS, data from refugee community organisations, census data on countries of birth, and information about other languages spoken by the family. For example a French-speaking child who also speaks Lingala is likely to be a refugee from the Democratic Republic of Congo.

A better implementation of the Pupil Level Annual School Census, using more detailed ethnicity categories, would secure the most up-to-date information about the numbers of children from particular countries. This in turn could be used to estimate the numbers of children who may be forced migrants – if such data are really needed. At present, with a bewildering array of different statistics, local authorities and refugee agencies can only make estimates.

What demographic data indicates

Almost all local authorities in the UK have resident refugee populations, small or large. Since 1989, asylum migration, asylum-initiated chain migration, and labour migration have caused considerable localised ethnic change in many parts of the UK, most particularly in Greater London. Not all this demographic change has the air of permanency as some communities have settled and then moved on. For example, Somalis were a dominant group among refugees settled in the London Borough of Greenwich in the early 1990s, but today many have moved out of the area. The Czech and Slovak Roma communities in Dover and Margate have largely left, many of them removed from the UK.

The indistinct boundary between refugee and non-refugee means that collecting demographic data on refugee children is very challenging. It requires a bureaucratic decision about who should be defined as a refugee during the gathering of statistics, a process fraught with contradictions. But statistics may be needed to secure funding and also illustrate important trends, discussed below.

Total numbers

The 2001 Census data suggest that about 57,000 school-age children with likely experiences of forced migration were living in the UK in 2001[8]. Their main countries of origin were Somalia (largest community), Sri Lanka (second largest), Turkey (third), Zimbabwe (fourth), Iraq (fifth), Afghanistan (sixth) and Iran (seventh).

An analysis of language and refugees undertaken in the period 1994–2003 suggests larger populations, as shown in Table 2.2. This is because it was largely based on language and refugee survey data. Language surveys have a lesser possibility of under-enumeration, as their numbers represent actual pupils. Additionally, language surveys do not distinguish country of birth, for example counting Somali children born in the UK as Somali refugees.

Table 2.2 Population estimates of refugee children in UK

Date	Refugee children in Greater London	UK Total
Dec 1993	20,127	–
Dec 1995	28,075	–
Dec 1997	39,765	–
Dec 1998	47,138	–
Dec 2001	62,666	82,000
Dec 2003	64,734	72,500–98,900

Source: Refugee Council (1994, 1996, 1998c, 1999a, 2001), Rutter, (2003b).

Local authority distribution

In 2003 the local authority with the largest population of refugee children was the London Borough of Newham, with 7128 refugee children, followed by Haringey (second) and the City of Manchester (third). The London Borough of Haringey has the highest proportion of refugees in the UK, with 19.4 per cent of the school role being refugees. A large proportion of Haringey's housing stock is privately rented accommodation, and in London many local authorities with the largest refugee populations are usually those with large amounts of such housing.

Local authorities with more than 2000 asylum-seeking and refugee children in schools are Barnet, Brent, Camden, Ealing, Enfield, Hackney, Haringey, Hounslow, Islington, Lewisham, Newham, Redbridge, Waltham Forest, Westminster, Manchester, Glasgow and Birmingham. The number of local

---

[8] 5–16 year olds.

authorities educating more than 500 refugee children in their schools increased between 1994 and 2003. In 1994, 19 local authorities were educating more than 500 refugee children in schools. Apart from Manchester and Cardiff, both cities with Somali communities, all these local authorities were in Greater London. By 2003, some 39 local authorities were educating more than 500 children. Local authorities outside Greater London with more than 500 refugee children in their schools include Birmingham, Cardiff, Coventry, Glasgow, Leicester, Liverpool, Manchester, Newcastle, Nottingham and Sheffield.

While most local authorities have seen an increase in the numbers of refugee children in their schools, a number of London local authorities have seen recent decreases, caused by decreased use of temporary and hostel accommodation for asylum-seekers, as well as other secondary migration.

Greater dispersal throughout the UK

Since 1997, the proportions of refugee children resident in Greater London has fallen, from 85 per cent in 1994, to 65 per cent today. This has been caused by: the arrival of asylum-seekers who entered the UK clandestinely and were often left by their smugglers along major trunk roads or in port towns; the dispersal of asylum-seekers out of London since 1996, particularly since the introduction of the National Asylum Support Service (NASS) housing dispersal in 2000. Today almost all asylum-seekers who need accommodation are housed outside Greater London and Kent.

Despite the NASS dispersal system, some asylum-seekers are remaining in Greater London in greater numbers than might be expected, including many Sri Lankan Tamils and Turkish Kurds.

Secondary migration

This term is usually used to describe the in-country movement of international migrants, from an initial residence to another area of settlement. Robinson was the first to analyse this population movement, with his study of the secondary migration of Vietnamese from their first permanent homes throughout the UK, to housing in London, Manchester and Birmingham, suggesting that Vietnamese secondary migration was caused by greater employment opportunities in cities and the desire to live near compatriots (Robinson and Hale, 1989).

Demographic data on refugee children in schools indicate substantial and complex secondary migration. This is often caused by the temporary nature of their housing. There is also evidence of community consolidation within cities, involving some degree of refugee agency, with particular groups moving to specific areas to be near compatriots, for example the secondary migration of Congolese from all parts of London into the London Borough of Haringey.

Housing and educational segregation

The schools demographic data, as well as other research, show considerable housing segregation among some refugee communities, caused by the availability of particular forms of accommodation, restricted employment opportunities, cultural pulls, primary chain migration and secondary migration within the UK.[9] Examples of such housing concentration include Turkish and Kurdish 'heartlands' of Islington, Hackney, Haringey and Enfield, and the northern Somali community in Tower Hamlets, Newham and Redbridge. But demographic data from schools and the research literature establish a diversity of housing segregation experiences among refugee communities. Thus, Turkish Kurds appeared to be a highly segregated community, while Iraqi Kurds were much less geographically segregated in the period 1989–99. That the Iraqi community comprised higher proportions of graduates than did the Turkish community meant that Iraqi Kurds were able to secure better jobs. Wider employment opportunities and the ability to buy housing resulted in a less segregated community.

Housing segregation means that the refugee populations in some local authorities and schools may be dominated by a particular national group. However, educational segregation, which is often more marked than housing segregation, can have other causes, explored in Chapters 7 and 8. (Refugee children tend to be very over-represented, in schools that are judged to be 'underachieving' or 'unpopular', by sectors of the population that experience less housing mobility.) In the UK, local authorities appear to fall into two groups: those where one, two or three national groups form the majority refugee population, and local authorities where there is no dominant group. For example, in 1999, Somalis and Iranians were the dominant group in the London Borough of Barnet, while there is no dominant group in Croydon.

A dominant group within a school or local authority may mean that educational policy responses focus on a particular community. More subtly, a dominant national group within a local authority or school may mean that educationalists frame their personal construction of refugee children in terms of the dominant group. Their ways of seeing refugee children may be consciously or unconsciously influenced by the dominant group.

Conclusions

So what conclusions can be drawn from trying to define refugee children? First, it is important to realise that refugee children are not a clearly demarcated group and that there are no clear distinctions between refugees and non-refugees, between voluntary and forced migrants, or the proactive and reactive migrants of Richmond's system. Demarcation is often imposed by the

---

[9] There is some research on refugee settlement patterns in the UK, although more literature on minority ethnic communities (see Peach, 1998; Phillips, 1998; Robinson and Hale, 1989; Robinson *et al.*, 2003).

State, as a legal status such as Convention refugee status, or a bureaucratic status, for example a group in receipt of the European Refugee Fund.

Policy interventions targeted at children who are forced migrants should not exclude a group purely on the basis of immigration status.[10] Children who are irregular migrants, or the children of work-permit holders or overseas students may well have experiences of forced migration and have the same needs in the UK as asylum-seekers.

Being a refugee is a bureaucratic identity. Much research and policy text about refugee education assume that the condition of being a refugee is a major determinant of children's educational progress (see, for example, Reakes and Powell, 2005). As Chapters 9, 10 and 11 argue, it is often pre-migratory experiences specific to particular countries or groups that determine educational progress, rather than 'refugeeness'. Policy makers and practitioners need to be critical of labels attached to children and understand the implications of labelling a child as a refugee. Such labels can influence how schools and local authorities view refugee children.

Finally, refugee populations are very heterogeneous and those working with refugee children need to acknowledge this. Welfare, healthcare and educational responses need to flexible and not of the 'one size fits all' type.

---

[10] Some statutory funds do stipulate that those supported have a particular immigration status, including the European Refugee Fund.

THEORETICAL AND
RESEARCH PERSPECTIVES
ON REFUGEE CHILDREN

This chapter examines theoretical and research literature about refugee children, looking at factors that influence their educational experiences. It draws on two different sources: research on refugee children and literature on the education of children from minority ethnic communities.

Until the 1980s there was very little research about refugee children. The Vietnam War changed this, and generated an extensive body of North American literature, dominated by studies of Central American and South East Asian refugees. Today, most published research about refugee children still comes from North America.

Research on refugee children can mostly be grouped into four types of study:

- texts on trauma and interventions to support children who are defined as having traumatic prior experiences
- a later body of psychological writing on refugee children's resilience and vulnerability and interventions based on promoting resilience
- a multidisciplinary literature on refugee children's identity and adaptation, drawing from ethnographic studies as well as psychological assessment
- research on refugee children's social worlds, including their experiences of educational and welfare services.

Trauma

By far the largest body of research about refugee children examines their experiences of trauma and psychological adaptation after such 'traumatic events'.

A psychological trauma or traumatic stressor might be defined as 'an overwhelming event, resulting in helplessness in the face of intolerable danger, anxiety and instinctual arousal' (Eth and Pynoos, 1985). Until the late 19th century, trauma was understood as a physical reaction to injury, but as the psychiatric and psychotherapeutic professions began to emerge, the notion of trauma was extended to include the psychological sequalae of distressing events (Young, 1995). Shell-shock was a diagnosis given to ex-combatants who were unable to function after experiencing the trench warfare of the First World War. 'Concentration camp survivor syndrome' was a later diagnosis attached to some of those who had survived the Nazi Holocaust. During the 1970s, epidemiological and psychometric studies, mostly conducted in the USA,[11] generated a new condition: post-traumatic stress disorder (PTSD). This condition was given full recognition in the *Diagnostic and Statistical Manual – Version Three (DSM-III)* of the American Psychiatric Association (American Psychiatric Association, 1980). It is diagnosed if a patient exhibits a range of symptoms, defined as:

- symptoms of intrusion, such as nightmares, flashbacks and intrusive thoughts
- symptoms of constriction and avoidance, such as efforts to avoid places or activities that are reminiscent of the trauma
- symptoms of increased arousal such as poor concentration or insomnia (American Psychiatric Association, 1994; Bracken, 1998).

There is some evidence that suggests that younger children diagnosed with PTSD manifest a different range of symptoms from adults. They may be less likely to experience visual flashbacks and more likely to repetitively re-enact in their play the original violent event (Hamblen, 1998). There is extensive and contested debate about the causal factors of PTSD, with some researchers suggesting the condition is caused by the incomplete processing of 'traumatic memory'.

Academic writing about refugee children is dominated by literature about trauma and PTSD, indeed there is much more writing about this than areas such as refugee law. This trauma literature has three different foci:

- analyses of exposure to potentially traumatic experiences (see for example, Kinzie *et al.*, 1986; McCallin and Fozzard, 1990; Maksoud, 1992)
- examination of the psychological sequalae of experiences defined as being traumatic
- discussions of interventions for refugee children who manifest PTSD or other mental illness.

Maksoud's (1992) research highlights the varied exposure of children to conflict and deconstructs the notion that traumatic experiences are universal among displaced populations. Older children, boys and children from poorer families were more likely to have experienced multiple traumatic events in her study of children displaced by the Lebanese conflict; a richer family was more likely to have the resources to send their children to a safer part of the

---

[11] Some of these studies were conducted among servicemen newly returned from the Vietnam War.

country. Both Kinzie and Maksoud include persistent and long-term economic deprivation as being a potentially traumatic experience.

A second body of literature examines the psychological sequelae of experiences defined as being traumatic (see, for example, Arroyo, 1985; Chimienti *et al.*, 1989; Espino, 1991; Fazel and Stein, 2000; Hodes, 2000; Liebkind, 1993). This research largely relies on self-assessment questionnaires and/or tests to determine children's psychological functioning – tests usually conducted in clinical settings. For example, Liebkind (1993) used two self-reporting symptom assessments with young Vietnamese: the Hopkins Symptom Checklist 25 and the Vietnamese Depression Scale. The latter was developed to acknowledge cultural differences in symptom expression. Clinical notes and observation of children's function in social settings are rarely used as a means of triangulation.

Most of the research concludes that the greater the exposure to violence, the greater the likelihood that a child will be diagnosed with PTSD (Espino, 1991). The majority of research seeks evidence of PTSD by which to judge the psychological sequelae of war. Childhood depression and anxiety are hardly discussed, suggesting PTSD to be the sole consequence of exposure to armed conflict or persecution. This is despite evidence that high proportions of patients with PTSD manifest other psychological disorders, most often depression and anxiety (Hamblen, 1998).

Much research on the psychological sequelae of war and persecution concludes that refugee children manifest high levels of mental illness, meaning that their ability to function in normal social settings is severely and adversely affected (Fazel and Stein, 2002; Hodes, 2000). Hodes suggests that 40 per cent of refugee children in the UK manifest psychiatric disorder. Another study, conducted among unaccompanied refugee children in public care in London, concluded that 23 per cent of the sampled group manifested 'severe psychological distress' (Hodes, 2000; Hollins *et al.*, 2003). Both research studies were undertaken through questionnaires delivered in clinics. None of the children were observed in social settings such as schools or their homes. There was no control group in either study and it is not clear whether a larger or smaller proportion of non-refugee children in their schools' care manifested severe psychological distress. This is an important consideration in the UK where refugees usually reside in areas of high deprivation. Chapter 8 suggests that in many schools attended by refugee children, it is the non-refugee population who manifest greatest psycho-social dysfunction.

There are a small number of studies that suggest that refugee children *do not* experience increased long-term psychiatric morbidity compared with other urban child populations (Allodi, 1989; Munroe-Blum *et al.*, 1989; Rousseau and Drapeau, 2003). Munroe-Blum *et al.* looked at the strength of association between child immigrant status and child psychiatric disorder, poor school performance and use of mental health and social services. The cohort studied included many refugees (Munroe-Blum *et al.*, 1989: 510–519). It concluded that immigrant children in Ontario, Canada, were not at increased risk of psychiatric disorder or poor school performance. The authors attributed this partly to the selective nature of migration – it is the most innovative and resourceful families that are the first migrants. Rousseau and Drapeau interviewed 57 young Cambodian refugees, then conducted a follow-up interview after four years. Data were compared with a control group of 45 young people born in Québec. Rousseau and Drapeau noted the large discrepancy between intense psychiatric symptoms at the first interview and the good social adjustment of this group after four years. The authors suggest that the young Cambodians exhibit a high degree of resilience, enabling them to 'recover'.

Some research on the psychological sequelae of war and persecution also examines children's social and cognitive development – important issues for teachers. Freire (1990) suggests that the poor mental health of newly arrived refugees may impede English language acquisition in Canada. Melzak and van der Veer, both psychotherapists working with refugee populations, note 'uneven development' among their clients. Development that may be obstructed in an adolescent may include the development of personal identity, the integration of sexual impulses, overcoming egocentric reasoning, and moral development (Melzak and Warner, 1992; van der Veer, 1992: 131). Van der Veer concludes that children who have grown up in the midst of extreme violence may show arrested moral development that can only lead to a continuation of violence in that society.

A third body of literature examines interventions for refugee children who manifest PTSD or other mental illness. Within the general child population there is a range of treatments for children who have experienced potentially traumatic events, or who have been diagnosed with PTSD. A range of agencies may be involved in the treatment of refugee children with PTSD, including child psychiatrists, clinical psychologists and sometimes educational psychologists. Drug treatment, most usually antidepressants and minor tranquillisers, are administered to adults with PTSD in the UK, but rarely to children. Crisis intervention or critical incident debriefing are used in some UK schools after events such as the violent or unexpected death of a pupil (Dyregov, 1991; Yule, 1998). Obviously, this type of intervention is not used with refugee children in the UK, due to the lack of immediacy of the traumatic event. Cognitive and behavioural therapies are used with refugee children in the UK, as well as individual psychotherapy, group psychotherapy, art and play therapy (Richman, 1998a; van der Veer, 1992). However, an omission from the literature is any attempt to evaluate different types of treatment and support.

Challenging the hegemony of trauma

Research literature about the traumatic experience of refugee children has had a major impact on how they are viewed by their teachers. Many policy texts about these children assume an almost universal prior experience of a traumatic event. Among most educational, social welfare and healthcare professionals there is a general acceptance that PTSD is a condition to which refugees seem particularly vulnerable. The term 'trauma' has entered practitioner discourse and is widely used when talking about refugee children. Refugee advocacy groups are complicit in this process; such organisations have had to mobilize discourses of trauma in order to argue for asylum-seekers to be granted sanctuary. Additionally, the language of trauma has been invoked to argue for greater healthcare and welfare resources.[12]

Increasingly, however, psychological treatments for PTSD, as well as the construction of PTSD itself, have become contested (see, for example, Bracken, 1998; Chatty and Hundt, 2004; Richman, 1998b; Summerfield, 1998, 2000; Young, 1995). Much of the writing that attempts to deconstruct PTSD has been produced by clinicians, but critiques of PTSD sometimes enter practitioner discourse, probably because they play into populist criticisms of psychiatry.

The concerns about PTSD are numerous. Loughrey (1997) suggests that PTSD is a construct of psychiatry and clinical psychology, and asserts that there is no evidence of increased PTSD symptomology after the Second World War or at the height of the Troubles in Northern Ireland. Summerfield (1998, 2000) discounts the assumption that PTSD arises from a failure to process traumatic memories, disputing that traumatic memory exists in isolation from social memory. Boyden and de Berry (2004) criticise PTSD because it ascribes passivity to children living in refugee camps or war zones and neglects children's own agency, even in difficult circumstances. Other writers present critiques of psychological and psychotherapeutic interventions, questioning the relevance of western psychotherapy to non-western societies, in particular its emphasis on the individual and individual insights (Bracken, 1998; White and Marsella, 1982).

Most critiques of PTSD are opinions rather than empirical research. Polarised (and sometimes acrimonious) debates about PTSD pose questions to an educational practitioner. Many teachers recount stories of refugee children who are clearly distressed and whose ability to function socially at school and to learn is minimal.[13] Ethnographic research, as well as psychological research, indicates that some individuals do experience considerable distress after a violent event to the extent that they are unable to function. Discussions about the reification of PTSD seem abstract when faced with a distressed child. However, the hegemony of the trauma discourse raises important issues. Later chapters examine the experiences of Congolese, Somali and Sudanese children, showing their varied pre-migration and post-migration experiences. But as a consequence of the language of trauma entering the vernacular, refugee children's background and needs are framed by educatonalists largely in terms of trauma. An understanding of pre-exile experiences, other than the 'trauma', is neglected. The post-exile experiences of

---

[12] It is notable that refugee community organisations' own reports seldom refer to trauma. An analysis of 20 annual reports from refugee community organisations held at the Refugee Council Archive, University of East London, only came across eight references to mental health needs. Refugees seldom perceive themselves as a group that is very prone to mental illness.
[13] My fieldnotes made at the Refugee Council include observations of five very distressed children.

refugees in the UK, which may include material deprivation, loss of social status, and racist attack, are deemed less significant. In exile, refugee children are constructed in an homogeneous manner – and labelled as universally traumatised. Refugee children's problems in schools are viewed as mental health problems that require a medicalised response, most usually provided by the health service. At the same time the refugee may have other complex educational and social needs, which cannot be met by the health service alone.

Resilience and vulnerability

As a result of critiques of PTSD, in particular its sidelining of the social worlds of refugees, some recent psychological literature on refugee children has suggested new frameworks for understanding their adaptation: those of psycho-social need and resilience.

The term 'psycho-social' defines the interaction between the internal, the psychological and the external, social worlds of a person. Psycho-social interventions attempt to meet the social needs of a vulnerable person at the same time as meeting internal and medical needs. Thus, in the UK, advocacy and advice on issues such as housing would be provided at the same time as medication and psychotherapy.

The concept of resilience draws on Michael Rutter's work with physically and sexually abused children and the observation that some children survive abuse without manifesting severe psychological distress while others do not (Rutter, 1985). Rutter and others outline protective factors (sometimes called mediating factors) and resilience on one hand, and risk factors (adverse factors) and vulnerability in children's lives. Protective factors are attributes or conditions that make it more likely that children will achieve some degree of resilience as an outcome and less likely that a child will manifest distress severe enough to render them dysfunctional. Risk factors are attributes or conditions that make it less likely that children will achieve some degree of resilience (Elbedour et al., 1993). Masten et al. (1991) provide another definition of resilience as 'the process of, capacity for or outcome of successful adaptation despite challenging or threatening circumstances'.

Notions of resilience draw on ecological models of children's development outlined in Chapter 1, where children are influenced by the settings in which they live (see Bronfenbrenner, 1992; Brooks-Gunn, 2001). Ron Baker, a social worker and himself a child refugee, wrote much about ecological aspects of refugee adaptation. He formulated the concept of a 'relationship web' shown in Figure 3.1 – a well-adjusted person is centred by a series of relationships. What exile does is to strip refugees of their anchors at the centre of the web. Baker (1983) suggests that those who provide social care for refugees should help them reconstruct the links in the web. Thus schools can help children establish new friendships and re-establish language links.

For refugees, risk and protective factors can be divided into:

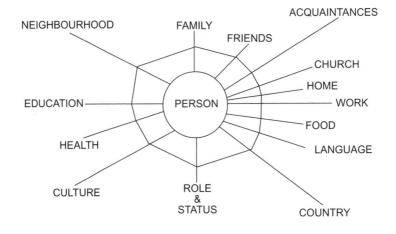

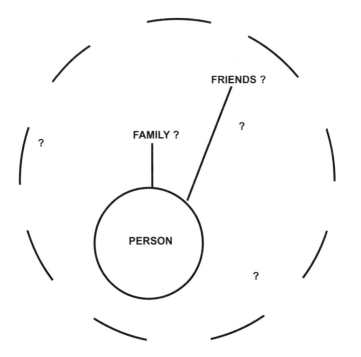

Figure 3.1 Baker's Relationship Web
Sources: Baker (1983) and Rutter and Jones (1998).

1. those related to personal characteristics and the personal world of the child
2. those particular to the home country and flight, such as repeated exposure to stressors
3. those due to the immediate milieu in exile, such as quality of parenting, or secure housing
4. those which are part of the external environment, including school, for example academic progress (Baker, 1983; Elbedour *et al.*, 1993: 805–819).

While there is much generic research about children and resilience, there are few studies that have examined refugee children as a specific group (Witmer and Culver, 2001). Most writing about resilience is practitioner text; protective factors described in these documents are listed below (Bolloten and Spafford, 1998; Melzak, 1997).

Protective factors drawn from practitioner text about refugee children

- having parents who can give their children full attention and good quality childcare
- having an extended family network
- having access to other people, particularly from their own community, who can give friendship and support
- having some understanding about the reasons for exile
- being able to integrate their experiences into their belief system
- age at the time of flight and arrival in a new country – not being under five or an adolescent
- having access to permanent housing, a permanent immigration status, and enjoying a reasonable standard of living in a new country
- being able to maintain some links with their homeland
- remembering good things about life in the home country
- being happy in a new school, making friends and being able to achieve at school
- feeling optimistic about the future and about making progress
- having good self-esteem
- being able to talk about stressful events and thus gain mastery over them
- being able to ask for help when things go wrong
- having a hobby or interest to pursue.

Almost all academic studies of forced migration and resilience focus on the home milieu, particularly on parents as children's prime carers. Although conducted before 'resilience' was conceptualised, Freud and Burlingham's British study of child evacuees during the Second World War concluded that separation from parents was more stressful than exposure to bombing (Freud and Burlingham, 1943). A study of Cambodian refugee adolescents living in refugee camps in Thailand concluded that those with the best mental health were those with intact families (Kinzie *et al.*, 1986). UK research on refugee children highlights the high proportions of refugee children who experience changes in care arrangements, such as the absence or death of a parent (Richman, 1995). Massoud and Dowling's research concluded that refugee children who were not coping in London schools experienced greater family upheaval, including changes of carer (Massoud and Dowling, 1997). Levels of parental education may be a protective factor: in a study of Vietnamese refugees in the USA less-educated Vietnamese parents from rural areas had greater difficulty in managing transition to urban America (Rumbaut, 1991: 58). Intergenerational conflict has also been examined as a possible risk factor (Liebkind, 1993).

Despite the paucity of the literature, the concept of resilience is very relevant for educationalists, a key question for schools, which makes some refugee children resilient and others not. From this, schools and educational support workers can consider interventions to minimise vulnerability and maximise resilience. Indeed many interventions to support refugee children in less economically developed countries use resilience as their conceptual framework and focus on rebuilding refugee children's social support systems. Such interventions might focus on supporting refugee parents as primary carers for very young children and ensuring children had access to schooling (for a discussion of such projects see Tolfree, 1996). But while the concept of resilience is given backing by some educational professionals working with refugee children in the UK, this is often tokenistic. As discussed in Chapter 7 many of those working with refugee children feel they have little power to help children become more resilient.

Studies of refugee children's identity, acculturation and adaptation

A third body of literature on refugees concerns their identity, adaptation and acculturation in countries of exile. This comprises psychological as well as sociological research. It is an important area of study, as identity and acculturation may influence the process of integration. Aspects of refugee children's identity and adaptation may also impede or facilitate their educational progress.

Acculturation refers to the changes that occur when two or more cultures come into contact. Studies of acculturation draw from ethnography, but also from an extensive sociological literature on secondary socialisation (Chapters 4 and 11 discuss the notion of 'habitus' among Vietnamese, Tamil and Sudanese children).

One of the most widely cited models of acculturation is that of Berry's intercultural strategies given in Figure 3.2 (Berry, 2001; Berry et al., 1987). Berry's model has been developed by Bourhis who considers cases where individuals have negative attitudes towards their own as well as the 'host' or majority culture. Bourhis suggests that 'anomia' (extreme and damaging non-conformist behaviour) or individualisation are the outcomes of rejection of home and majority culture (Bourhis et al., 1997). Berry and Bourhis's models attempt to conceptualise integration, at present a policy concern of the UK Government, and discussed in later chapters. But both models are rather static. They do not take into account wide variations in identity and cultural norms with refugee and majority communities, variations documented in

	Strategies of minority group		Strategies of majority society	
	Maintenance of own culture	*Loss of own culture*	*Maintenance of minority cultures*	*Loss of minority cultures*
Contact with majority society	+ Integration	Assimilation	Multiculturalism	Melting pot
	– Separation	Marginalisation	Segregation	Exclusion

Figure 3.2 Varieties of intercultural strategies in immigration groups and in the receiving societies
Source: Berry (2001 as cited in Hamilton and Moore, 2004).

ethnographic studies such as Griffiths' study of Somali and Kurdish refugees in London (Griffiths, 2002).

Neither do Berry or Bourhis account for shifting and multiple identities – refugee children who are able to move between the cultural norms of school and those of home with ease. There is rather an inconclusive debate about shifting identity among refugee children. Some literature suggests that children do negotiate the cultural differences between home and school without difficulty (for a discussion see Eriksen, 2002). Other writing indicates that living in a bicultural world presents a major problem for a child, citing much intergenerational conflict (see, for example Community of Congolese Students in UK, 2002; Kahin, 1997; Lambeth, Southwark and Lewisham Health Action Zone, 2000).

Other models of acculturation acknowledge change over time. Such writing generally falls into two groups:

- Staged approaches to the study of refugee acculturation and identity
- non-staged conceptualisations of identity: segmented assimilation theory and multiple and shifting identities.

Staged approaches to the study of refugee identity stress the processual nature of refugee adaptation and place great emphasis on temporal dimensions of exile (Griffiths, 2002). Vasquez and Arayo (1989) outline the stages through which Chilean refugees in France pass, from initial trauma, loss, rejection of the host society and idealisation of home through to a stage of transculturation. Baskauskas's study of Lithuanian refugees in the USA offers another staged approach to the study of refugee identity and adaptation with stages comprising:

- *Initial conservatism* soon after arrival in the host country, traditional cultural norms reactivated as a safeguard against the new and unfamiliar
- *Bereavement* a process of working through loss of home
- *Innovation* recovering from the loss of the old, and moving forward, to a new hybrid identity (Baskauskas, 1980).

Harrell-Bond and Al-Rasheed advance a further staged model with their concept of 'liminality' – a threshold and dislocated state where refugees' social structures and identities break down (Al-Rasheed, 1993; Eastmond, 1993; Harrell-Bond and Voutira, 1992). Refugees go through three stages:

- physical segregation as refugees in a new host country
- the stage of liminality where old forms of social stratification and cultural norms break down:
- reincorporation – either into the home country, as a juxtaposed community or into a new hybrid identity.

> In the limbo/liminality phase, social structures tend to dissolve or collapse. Above all, the old meanings attached to structures, institutions, values and norms cease to be meaningful. What emerges in liminality is a society which is unstructured, and relatively undifferentiated communities.
>
> (Al-Rasheed, 1993: 91–92)

However, all processual studies of identity assume a more or less linear pathway towards eventual incorporation into the host society or return – in short, a story with a happy ending.

Non-linear models of adaptation

Segmented assimilation theory is a challenge to the staged model of adaptation. Drawing on fieldwork in the United States, Portes and Zhou (1993) suggest that the children of immigrants as well as children who migrated to the United States at a very young age (the 1.5 generation) may follow one of three assimilation trajectories. First, some immigrant children enjoy educational success at the same time as assimilating into the cultural forms of middle-class, white America. Second, a group of children experience downward social mobility. They do not succeed at school, because they assimilate into the cultural forms of the 'underclass'. Third, the children of immigrants may enjoy educational and economic success at the same time as maintaining the social networks and cultural forms of their minority community (Portes and Rumbaut, 2001; Portes and Zhou, 1993; Rumbaut and Portes, 2001).

Much of the above-cited research has involved the analysis of educational achievement data in relation to parental and child values. *The Children of Immigrants Longitudinal Survey* followed 5262 children who came to the United States before they were 12, or who were born in the United States to immigrant parents. The children came from 77 different national groups and were resident in San Diego, Miami or Fort Lauderdale. The study showed differential patterns of achievement among the national groups. Children of Chinese and Vietnamese origins did best, while black Caribbean migrants performed least well at school. Despite the differential patterns of achievement, children of immigrants manifest lower school drop-out rates than their peers (Portes and Rumbaut, 2001; Rumbaut and Portes, 2001). Portes and Rumbaut explain differential patterns of achievement as being caused by the maintenance or loss of immigrant values that emphasise hard work and educational achievement.

Much research on segmented assimilation examines the experiences of Vietnamese refugees (see, for example, Caplan *et al.*, 1991; Rumbaut and Portes, 2001; Zhou and Bankston, 1998). Caplan *et al.*, in a US study, showed that Vietnamese children, although attending schools in poor urban areas, scored better than their school peers and the national average in both mathematics and spelling tests (Caplan *et al.*, 1991: 5–13). The study links high educational achievement to values, rather than to family income, social class or to maternal education and concludes that high achieving children were more likely to come from:

- families that viewed the past as important in children's lives and had strong respect for their culture
- families where there was little inter-generational disagreement about key cultural values, and where children' cultural values and acculturative change were similar to their parents
- families where there was gender equality, in particular in spousal decision making, parental involvement in school-related matters and participation in the labour force (Caplan *et al.*, 1991: 101)
- families where there was high parental involvement in education, including reading to children and encouraging homework and the need to do well at school.
- families who felt they had control over their lives and that the actions that they took, including hard work at school, would build for their future (Caplan *et al.*, 1991: 90–101).

Segmented assimilation theory stresses the preservation of immigrant values as the means of achieving economic advancement in the United States. As Rumbaut states below, loss of such values – neglecting homework, eating junk food and hanging out with the wrong kids – results in permanent disaster:

> We believe, however, that the finding that educational achievement improves for younger refugees and over time in the United States cannot be projected indefinitely. Rather, we predict this effect will soon plateau and then begin to diminish if and when the younger family members become more inculcated with the values prevailing among American youth which (according to national poll data) emphasize self-fulfillment and gratification over self-sacrifice and hard work – a process of 'becoming American' that may ironically prove counter-productive for educational attainment.
>
> (Rumbaut, 1991: 88)

Importantly, segmented assimilation theory challenges the assumption, prevalent in UK policy text, that successful economic integration can only be achieved by abandoning the culture of the home country. With its emphasis on personal and family values, segmented assimilation theory is now the dominant American explanation for the differential educational performance of immigrant communities. But it has attracted critics (for a discussion, see Alba and Farley, 2002; Boyd, 2003; Waldinger and Feliciano, 2003). The conceptualisation of an 'underclass' as a discrete, permanent and easily defined group has been challenged. Boyd suggests that segmented assimilation theory may not be applicable to states such as Canada, which do not have a poor, over-racialised and spatially segregated population of African-Americans into which new immigrants may be assimilated, presumably to their peril.

The gendered assumptions behind segmented assimilation theory have been questioned. Indeed, there is a troubling undercurrent of antipathy towards African-American males in many of its proponents. Portes, Rumbaut and Zhou continually write of the 'adversarial culture' of US-born minorities (Portes and Rumbaut, 2001; Portes and Zhou, 1993). Their work also suggests a dislike of youth sub-cultures. From the perspective of those concerned with refugee education in the UK, the works of Portes, Rumbaut and Zhou have three weaknesses. First, their work does not account for children who are happy straddling the cultures of home and of school. These were the majority of the Congolese, Somali and Sudanese children whose life histories are examined later in this book. Second, downward social mobility of the second and '1.5 generation' is assumed to be a real and permanent condition. But the Children of Immigrants Longitudinal Survey only examined change over a five-year period and there are no longitudinal studies of individual child migrants and refugees in the UK. And does migration from a lower middle-class neighbourhood in Kinshasa to local authority housing in London comprise downward social mobility? For those in unskilled jobs, wages may be low in London, but healthcare and education are free of charge and running water and electricity are constant. Finally, in its emphasis on social capital and the values of immigrant communities, segmented assimilation theory appears too narrow in its explanations for differential educational progress. Most pre-migration factors other than parental social class receive no consideration in such research. The role of schools, pedagogies and social interventions are also not examined. While values and dispositions – habitus – do matter, research and explanations for lack of educational progress among migrant groups need to be more ecological in their analyses.

Globalised identities

Other non-staged approaches to the study of ethnic identity have developed in the context of accounts of globalisation which has brought about:

- erosion of national identity and its replacement with cultural homogeneity in some instances
- strengthening of national or ethnic identity in other instances, as a way of resisting globalisation
- greater juxtaposition of different cultures in the same neighbourhood
- syncretisation and the development of new identities of hybridity to replace old national identities in other instances.

The globalised subject is an individual with multiple, shifting identities, perhaps with sometimes contradictory components, a person whose identity is socially, spatially and historically defined (Cohen, 1997; Hall, 1991, 1992). Central to much writing about identity and globalisation are the concepts of diaspora, transnationalism and home. Diasporic and transnational identities have been increasingly examined by researching refugees (Cohen, 1997; Griffiths, 2002). Home can mean the space in which a person lives, the nation, the region, the town or village of origin, the place where parents lived. It can be a non-material concept, such as a collection of memories or the place where one feels one belongs (for a discussion about the significance of home for refugees see Al-Ali and Koser, 2003). Narratives of home feature in many refugee children's testimonies (see Gezim, Jasmine and Saliha's stories in Rutter, 2004b). As later chapters argue, narratives of home influence older children's career choices and the decision to engage in school, put down roots and make friends.

Cultural syncretisation and the emergence of new ethnic identities are also features of migration and transnational communities. There is research on the development of new identities among young refugees in UK schools. Griffiths writes about the renewal of Kurdish identity among Kurds from Turkey now resident in London. In Turkey the use of the Kurdish language was banned until 1992, as were political parties that called for Kurdish autonomy or independence. Griffiths cites cases of young Kurds manifesting pride in learning Kurdish for the first time, or being involved in Kurdish political organisations. Research, as well as practitioner text, has also described the association of black African refugees with African–Caribbean cultural forms (Griffiths, 2002: 118–120; Kahin, 1997). In many cases it appears to be a survival strategy, motivated by a desire to be accepted by the 'lads'.[14] Neither Griffiths nor Kahin discuss the gendered nature of this syncretisation: there is little evidence that this is a strategy adopted by girls.

Refugee children's social worlds

Compared with studies of trauma and identity, research on refugee children's social worlds comprises a much smaller body of literature. Most writing concerns refugee children's experiences of support services within less economically developed countries.

During the past five years international NGOs, as well as UNHCR, have acknowledged that too few refugee children have access to education. Greater recognition has been afforded to the importance in emergency situations of establishing schooling earlier rather than later (Retamal and Aedo-Richmond, 1998). School gives structure and normality to children's lives and is recognised as a factor that provides psychological protection (Boyden and Ryder, 1996; Crisp, 2002). For teenagers, particularly boys, the opportunity to go to school can take the pressure away from being a child soldier. Education can be used to deliver supplementary feeding as well as health and welfare messages important to refugees' survival. There is a growing body of research and

---

[14] My field notes also refer to shifts in class identity among other young male refugees, again young men adapting white working-class 'laddish' cultural forms, as a strategy to gain acceptance.

practice literature examining education in the emergency situations of refugee camps. However the educational needs of dispersed urban refugees in cities such as Cairo, Khartoum and Nairobi is neglected (Harrell-Bond, 2002).

In less economically developed countries the safe return of refugees is considered to be an ideal endpoint of the refugee 'cycle'. Where refugees' home countries have experienced armed conflict, there is an acknowledgement that return has to be linked with reconstruction. Research literature examines educational issues within the return and reconstruction process, for example, children returning after a long period of exile may need to learn the official and academic languages of their home country.

Writing on education for return and reconstruction also examines peace education pedagogies (Bush and Saltarelli, 2000; Sommers, 2002). Sommers is among the policy makers who acknowledge that if return is to be a stable process, schools have to incorporate conflict resolution into the curriculum, for both returnees and host population.

However, research about educational issues relating to return is conspicuously absent from academic and policy text from European countries; indeed research on children's return seems taboo. Among refugee educationalists there is the assumption that return is never in the child's best interests. Yet children do return, voluntarily or involuntarily, and in most cases they have little preparation for this process.

Developed country literature

The paucity of developed country literature about education for return also reflects the broader lack of research about refugee children's education. Most developed country literature on refugee education is practitioner text (see, for example, Bolloten and Spafford, 1998; Lodge, 1998; Rutter, 1994).

In the UK, concerns about refugee children's educational achievement and progression have been articulated since the mid-1990s, particularly in relation to Somalis. However, there has been little educational research among refugee child populations in the UK until recently. In the past five years a number of studies have indicated underachievement among Congolese, Somali, and Turkish and Kurdish refugee children (Jones and Ali, 2000; Mehmet, 2000; Enneli et al., 2005; Rutter, 2004a). In 2005, DfES research showed that in 2003, 22 per cent of Somali and 30 per cent of Turkish-speaking children secured five grade A*–Cs at GCSE, compared with an average of 51 per cent for all children in England (DfES, 2005)

There is some research that analyses how refugee children experience the education system. McDonald (1995) provides an account of 14–19-year-old refugees' experiences. Delays in accessing education, poor initial assessment of need, discontinuity of provision and low teacher expectations emerged as dominant themes. Some of these themes also emerged in a peer research project supported by Save the Children. Young refugees from the Horn of Africa were trained as social researchers. Bullying emerged as a theme in many of their interviews (see Chapter 6 and Save the Children, 1997).

Research on how refugee children experience schooling also highlights differences in teaching strategies between the home country and country of exile (McDonald, 1995; Park, 2000; Timm *et al.*, 1998). Children's difficulties with group work, inquiry-based learning and open-ended questions are documented. Poor communication between home and school also emerges in educational research about refugee children (Arshad *et al.*, 1999; Bell, 1993; Humpage, 1999; Jupp and Luckey, 1990; Vincent and Warren, 1998). Humpage's study of Somali refugees in New Zealand secondary schools highlighted poor parent–school communication and cultural dissonance between home and school, including children's career aspirations (drawn from the home) being discounted as unrealisitic by their teachers. Rousseau *et al.* (1996) highlight the mismatch between parents' perceptions of their children's difficulties and those of their teachers.

However, the notion that home–school liaison is problematic for schools and refugee parents is contested, as is the assumption that refugee parents lack agency in their choice of schools and relationships with teachers. Vincent and Warren undertook ethnographic research in four case-study primary schools in London and Birmingham, looking at relationships between the home and school. Crucially, they concluded that refugee parents were no more nor less likely to experience difficulties in securing good links with their children's school than other groups of parents (Vincent and Warren, 1998). Their finding supports other research undertaken in the UK: recent research commissioned by the Department for Education and Skills reports that greater proportions of parents from minority ethnic communities are satisfied with their involvement in their children's education than are white parents (Desforges, 2003).

Linguistic issues are another area identified in practitioner literature about refugee education: the need to acquire fluency in the language of the home country and the need to maintain the home language or languages. Research undertaken by the Home Office suggests that about 70 per cent of adult refugees arrive in the UK and report that they speak little or no English (Carey-Wood *et al.*, 1995). While there is an extensive literature on language acquisition among migrant and minority communities resident in more economically developed nations, there is much less research on language issues specific to refugees. Integrity of prior education appears to influence refugees' language acquisition, with refugee children who have a complete prior education making best progress in their learning of a new language (Caplan *et al.*, 1991; Humpage, 1999; Westermeyer and Her, 1996).

Social welfare

There are a number of studies about the impact of social conditions on the education of refugee children. Most of them conclude that poverty and bad housing impact on children's educational progression as well as their resilience. Power *et al.* (1998) examine problems faced by asylum-seeking families living in temporary accommodation (see also Chapter 5). Dobson's research on pupil mobility notes the high proportions of asylum-seeking and refugee pupils among those groups experiencing frequent moves of school (Dobson and Pooley, 2004; Dobson *et al.*, 2000).

There is considerable research on the inadequate levels of support given by British social services departments to unaccompanied refugee children. Services for them range from adequate to poor, with many placed in hostels without access to named social workers (Munoz, 1999; Stanley, 2002; Williamson, 2000). Difficulties in enrolling in school and college and frequent moves of school and college are educational issues highlighted by Munoz, Stanley and Williamson. McDonald (1995) highlights the lack of access to on-going support and careers advice as an issue affecting unaccompanied children. All of these factors impact on unaccompanied refugee children's educational progress. However, many local authorities construct unaccompanied refugee children as being an educational success. This is because social workers and other local authority staff are comparing their educational achievements with other groups of looked-after children.

There are also major gaps in the research literature. Despite increased collection of quantitative data on educational achievement, there is much missing, particularly that which might inform those concerned about the education of refugee children. The lack of analysis of local quantitative data is a major gap in knowledge. There is very little research on changes in gender roles and how this might affect refugee children's social worlds. Finally, there are no British longitudinal studies about refugee children's experiences of education.

Literature on social and educational issues affecting children from minority ethnic communities

In addition to research that specifies refugee children, there is a considerable body of literature that examines the educational experiences of children from minority ethnic communities. Although not specifically about refugees, much of this research highlights issues that also affect refugee groups. British literature largely focuses on interactions within the school and examines two issues: children's language acquisition and children's racialised experiences of schooling. However, little of the British literature about minority ethnic children gives mention to the specific experiences of refugees. The reasons for this are complex. Some researchers and policy makers have resisted seeing refugee children as having needs which may be different from those of other minority ethnic children. The Department for Education and Skills has also perpetuated a racial essentialism. Its own demographic data do not classify white European and white other children as ethnic minority populations. In many local authorities, Turkish, Kurdish and Albanian refugee children are not considered to be from minority ethnic groups. These positions have afforded refugees invisibility within much research about minority ethnic children.

Language acquisition and development

Research and theorising of children's acquisition of a new language has received extensive coverage in a large number of texts (see, for example, Baker, 1996; Cummins, 1981b; Hamilton and Moore, 2004). Such literature has examined factors that promote or inhibit the acquisition of a new language. One of the best-known socio-linguists is Jim Cummins, whose work includes analysis of the social context of language learning. He suggests that children must understand the social context of their learning in a second language if they are to make progress. Context is enhanced through providing visual cues, using body language and relating learning to children's previous experiences (Cummins, 1981b, 1996). Despite this, Chapter 8 describes how much teaching in secondary schools is abstract, lacks visual cues and does not provide the context to help newly arrived refugee children learn effectively. Other theoretical models have examined the cognitive links between the first and second languages (Cummins, 1977; Toukomaa and Skutnabb-Kangas, 1977). The relationship between first-language and English-language use for Congolese children is further examined in Chapter 9.

Racialised school experiences

Another body of literature on children from minority ethnic communities examines their racialised experiences of schooling. In the UK this research dates back to the late 1960s, when community activists, as well as academics, began to express concerns about the schooling of children from minority ethnic groups, in particular African–Caribbean students. The literature comprises analysis of quantitative and qualitative data.

Quantitative data from schools paint a complex picture about the education of minority ethnic children in the UK. Some local authorities have collected data on examination success among different ethnic groups since the mid-1960s and the DfES has collected and analysed national data since 1997.[15,16] National data that have been available since 1997 in England include:

- numbers of pupils from minority ethnic communities per local authority
- numbers of pupils for whom English is an additional language per local authority
- permanent exclusions from school per local authority broken down by broad ethnic categories
- EAL students entitled to free school meals

---

[15] The DfES analysis uses broad ethnicity categories: White British, White European, White Other, Black Caribbean, Black African, Black Other, Indian, Pakistani, Bangladeshi, Asian Other. LEAs also have power to introduce sub-categories according to local conditions.

[16] There has been significantly less collection of data in Scotland and Wales.

- pupils' absences and truancy from schools, broken down by broad ethnic categories
- pupil performance at 7, 11, 14 and 16 broken down according to broad ethnic categories
- youth cohort studies at 17, 19 and 21 which show participation in full-time education, vocational education and work broken down by broad ethnic group.

Local data mostly comprise language surveys listing pupils' home languages and levels of competence in English. However, language survey data remain under-analysed and are rarely examined in reference to other factors, such as test and GCSEs results. As discussed in Chapters 9 and 10, there is evidence that in a number of local authorities, decisions have been taken to ignore data on the underachievement of particular refugee groups such as the Congolese and Somalis.

National and local data show that students of Chinese and Indian origin secure better test and GCSE results than all other groups in England. Across the UK, African–Caribbean, Bangladeshi, Pakistani, Turkish-speaking, Somali and Traveller/Gypsy/Roma children achieved less well than their white peers (DfES, 2005). However, there are considerable local differences and there are local authorities where Black British, Bangladeshi and Pakistani pupils are the highest achieving. (Data also indicate that there are considerable localised differences in the achievement of some refugee groups – in two London local authorities Somali pupils outperformed their white peers in 2004, although Somalis are one of the lowest achieving groups nationally.)

Girls from most, but not all, ethnic groups outperform boys and among all ethnic groups social class affects school achievement: children whose parents are employed in non-manual jobs enjoy greater success in tests and examinations than children of those in manual employment or without work (Bhattacharya *et al.*, 2003; Gillborn and Mirza, 1998).

Research studies on underachievement have attributed it to many different factors. Among Bangladeshi pupils, entering the school system with limited fluency in English appears to disadvantage younger pupils. There are also recent concerns about the development of academic literacy among children with English as an additional language, suggesting that a lack of support to more advanced learners of English limits their achievement (OFSTED, 2003c). Low teacher expectations of minority ethnic pupils is another factor identified in a number of studies as contributing to underachievement (Gillborn, 1995; Mac an Ghaill, 1988). Anti-education, working-class male sub-culture – 'laddishness' – has also been blamed for the underachievement of black and white males (Archer and Francis, 2003; Sewell, 1997).

Deprivation and higher rates of unemployment among minority ethnic communities appear to have educational consequences for students from these communities. Research also highlights bullying of a racist nature as being a frequent experience of children from minority ethnic communities, leading to disengagement with education (Cline *et al.*, 2002; Troyna and Hatcher, 1992).

Data from England indicate that Black Caribbean, Black African and Black

Other students are over-represented among pupils permanently excluded from schools. Most analysis on school exclusions uses the Department for Education and Skills's broad categories of ethnicity, so, within the group 'Black African' it is impossible to calculate if Somalis are excluded more than other groups. Schools and local authorities rarely analyse data on temporary exclusions; there may be other groups of pupils who are disproportionally affected by the use of temporary exclusions within schools (Osler *et al.*, 2002). Many explanations have been advanced to account for the over-representation of black and minority ethnic students among those excluded from school. Studies have indicated high levels of conflict between teachers and African–Caribbean students in primary and secondary schools, and the perception among black pupils that school disciplinary systems treat them unfairly and in a different manner from their white peers. This can lead to student disaffection and cultures of resistance to education, as well as the disproportionate use of exclusion as a punishment (Gillborn, 1995; Mac an Ghaill, 1988; Osler *et al.*, 2002; Sewell, 1997). Teachers' constructions of some black male pupils as being dangerous and a threat to order is another factor identified in research about school exclusion (Sewell, 1997). Ethnic minority students also tend to be over-represented in schools where all pupil behaviour is poor.

Black and Asian students are more likely to be enrolled in further education at 17, 19 and 21 than their white peers. (The annual Department for Education and Skills Youth Cohort Study indicated that 90 per cent of black and Asian 17 year olds were in further education in 2003.) White 17 year olds are five times more likely to be in full-time work than students from minority ethnic communities. While the higher participation in further education is positive, it may also reflect difficulties experienced by some minority ethnic communities in finding work.

Within schools, there is much quantitative and qualitative information about setting and streaming. Indeed, there is concern about the often discriminatory nature of setting and streaming practices within secondary schools. The Commission for Racial Equality (CRE) undertook a formal investigation into this practice in 1992 and concluded that setting did indeed discriminate against black students (Commission for Racial Equality, 1992). More recently, Gillborn and Youdell undertook a study of the impact of judging schools by the proportions of pupils who have gained five grade A*–C at GCSE. They suggest that the 'A to C economy' affects decisions made about support to individual pupils with some pupils being judged as 'without hope' and unlikely to secure the required five A*–C grades. (No-hopers received little additional education support to enable them to lift their grades.) Gillborn and Youdell note that disproportionate numbers of black students were deemed 'without hope' (Gillborn and Youdell, 2000: 133–164). This issue is discussed further in Chapter 8.

There is also a growing body of research on what might comprise successful multi-ethnic schools (Bourne and Blair, 1998; OFSTED, 2002; Runnymede Trust, 1993). Much of Bourne and Blair's study examines parental involvement and home–school liaison. (Many other researchers, writing about majority and minority communities have suggested that strong parental involvement in their children's schooling is one of the most important factors promoting children's progress). Bourne and Blair suggest that 'successful' multi-ethnic schools make parents aware of the nature and purpose of parental involvement and address language and cultural barriers. They cite home visits at the start of Year 7 as being good practice (Bourne and Blair, 1998). Their research is of significance to those working with refugee children.

PART TWO:
UK RESPONSES TO
REFUGEE CHILDREN

4

LEARNING FROM HISTORY: RESPONSES TO REFUGEES 1900–89

The arrival of international migrants in the UK is no new occurrence. This chapter looks at what can be learned from the settlement of previous groups of refugees, in particular, in relation to educational and welfare policy.

The first group of refugees who were recipients of State-funded education in the UK were Eastern European Jews who had migrated from the Russian Empire, Austro-Hungary and Romania. Immigration statistics at this time were unreliable, but estimates suggest that about 500,000 Jews spent at least two years in the UK, although the number that settled permanently was much smaller (Gartner, 1960). Amid the poverty of the East End, many newly arrived Jewish families sought to educate their children. While some boys received religious education in *cheder* (rooms attached to a synagogue) and *yeshivot* (religious seminaries), most children attended London School Board elementary schools in the East End or the Jews' Free School (JFS), then also located in east London. By 1900, there were 4250 pupils in this school (Black, 1998:1).

The outbreak of the First World War prevented Jewish emigrants from crossing war-torn Europe. But in 1914 and 1915 over 250,000 Belgian refugees arrived in the UK, forming one of the biggest migratory movements in British history. It is also a migration that has been erased from national consciousness. The Belgian refugees included at least 33,000 children between ages 5 and 14 (de Jastrzebski, 1916 as cited in Myers, 2001: 155; Kushner and Knox, 1999: 48).

The Belgians were fleeing the advancing German army and were portrayed as brave heroes in the popular press – the plucky little Belgian resisting the mighty German – all this at a time of growing anti-alienism (Kushner and Knox, 1999: 52). Resentment of the refugees was rare. Local Belgian Refugee Committees were founded by concerned members of the public with over 2500 such committees in 1916. The involvement of the public in supporting refugees has not been matched since then.

Initially an NGO – the War Refugees Committee – assisted the Belgian refugees. But by late 1914, government took responsibility for them, with the Local Government Board (LGB) being the lead department. This was a milestone: it was the first time that government had taken policy responsibility for the settlement of refugees. The LGB organised the dispersal of the Belgians to reception camps where they stayed until more permanent housing was found (Cahalan, 1982: 71–83; Holmes, 1988: 100; Myers, 2001: 145). Most Belgian children were sent straight to local schools. Myers argues that this decision was informed by two important factors. First, it was assumed that that the refugee children would be in the UK for a short period of time, thus British education would not affect their long-term prospects. Second, the initial popularity of the Belgians meant that they were welcomed in schools as a visible means of supporting the war effort (Myers, 2001: 155–156). At school the Belgian children were simply absorbed into mainstream classes (there was no space for separate provision). School Inspectors record:

> Our inspectors say that all over the country these children are finding their way into the elementary schools in a very normal and easy manner . . . The Belgian children seem very happy at school, through sometimes they do not like leaving their compatriots.
> (Local Government Board, 1916)

The period 1915–18 was marked by a real involvement of central government in refugee education. But by 1916 the Belgians had started to return home – the 1921 Census recorded less than 10,000 Belgian nationals settled in the UK.

The 1930s

Soon after the First World War, new immigration legislation was passed: the Aliens Restriction Act 1919 and the Aliens Order 1920. Together they gave almost unlimited powers to the Home Secretary to exclude at the port of entry anyone deemed 'undesirable'. (The Aliens Order 1920, with a few minor amendments, was annually renewed until finally replaced by the Immigration Act 1971.)

The 1930s saw the arrival of refugees fleeing Nazi-occupied Europe, as well as nearly 4000 unaccompanied Basque children. The former attracted hostility while the Basque refugee children enjoyed the popularity of the Belgians. They were endearing as children and the labour movement was in favour of the evacuation, as the children had fled the onslaught of fascist forces.

The Spanish Civil War began on 17 July 1936 and by August 1936 the Basque cities of Irun and San Sebastian were under siege. In the UK, diverse interest groups – both religious and political – formed the National Joint Committee for Spanish Relief – a rather fractious network. In February 1937, this group discussed the possibility of bringing Basque children to the UK, and formed a sub-group called the Basque Children's Committee. After the bombing of Guernica, the Home Office agreed to the evacuation, providing certain conditions were met. There was to be no cost to the Treasury and the children had to be housed in private institutions, rather than foster homes. Basque children were not to attend state schools (Legarreta, 1984).

Leah Manning, a Labour MP and educationalist, travelled to the Basque region to arrange for the evacuation. Within two weeks over 20,000 children had been signed up for 4000 places. Some 3889 children, 219 teachers and aides and 15 Basque priests eventually disembarked in Southampton on 23 May 1937. Legarreta (1984) provides a detailed account of their reception facilities. A tentèd reception camp was set up at Stonham, near Southampton. There was little by way of an organised educational programme, later judged to be a major mistake. There were strong class and political differences among the children. Older boys were identified as a problem group soon after their arrival.

The Basque Children's Committee then formed local groups to start the work of moving children to more permanent 'colonies'. The main organisations that ran the colonies were the Salvation Army, the Roman Catholic Church, the Quakers and trade unions. The conditions in many of the colonies were grim, and noted for the strong discipline, lack of love and terrible food. In Clapton, London, one boy noted:

> When we arrived at Clapton they served us a stew of sorts, nothing identifiable. We all sat there unable to eat it. Reproaches such as, 'We'll see if you eat it or not,' and 'How many British children would love to eat this food,' followed. The same food reappeared at lunch and dinner; again no-one ate. A hunger strike!
>
> (Legarreta, 1984: 60)

In most of the Catholic boys' colonies, Basque priests provided children's education, while in the girls' colonies this was organised by the evacuated female teachers. There remains long-standing criticism of the quality of education provided for Basque refugee children. The Basque Children's Committee deliberately decided not to make national policy on education; instead decisions about children's education were *ad hoc* and depended on the colony in which they lived. Central government also disengaged – by refusing Basque children access to state education. The net effect of this educational shortcoming was that most of the Basque children who remained in the UK ended up in manual jobs. (In September 1939, of the 3889 children brought to the UK, eight had died, 2726 had been repatriated and 1155 remained in the UK.) Legarreta notes:

> They particularly resented the fact that, by and large, their education was neglected in England. Many found this to be a lifelong handicap. Most, having come to England without having completed primary school, were given only occasional English lessons and some religious instruction for the three years they lived in colonies. Those sent to English Catholic boarding schools received a normal British education, but these children were usually the first to be repatriated. Relatively few of those who stayed on went on to secondary level, even fewer to the technical colleges. Only about thirty went to the university, using funds from the Juan Luis Vives trust, administered by the Spanish Republican Government in Exile. Of

those given university scholarships, more than half attended for only one year.

(Legarreta, 1984: 255)

Legarreta's research is the only empirical study of Basque children. She draws many conclusions relating to children's psychological adaptation. Positive attachments to the home culture was a protective factor for these children, especially the maintenance of Euskera and Spanish, as was the political ideology held by some children, which helped them make sense of their changed circumstances. Legarreta noted that older children, particularly boys, had more difficulty in adjusting to life as a refugee. That Basque refugee children felt their welcome in the UK, was also a protective factor and many children felt sensitive to changes in the host country's policy towards Spain. Legarreta also suggests some good practice still relevant today:

- The presence of older male Basque mentors was very important particularly for boys.
- Siblings must not be separated in child care arrangements (today unaccompanied refugee children in the UK are still being separated from siblings).
- Educational opportunities must be available at the earliest opportunity for refugee children to provide a sense on normality and progress.

At the same time as the Basque exodus, refugees from Nazi-occupied Europe were also fleeing to the UK. An estimated 56,000 refugees from Germany, Austria and Czechoslovakia arrived between 1933 and 1939, among them 9354 unaccompanied refugee children arriving as part of the *Kindertransporte*, as well as smaller numbers of unaccompanied children on other child rescue schemes. The educational arrangements made for children accompanied by their families was very different from the arrangements made for unaccompanied children. Most accompanied children entered mainstream schools in the UK, with comparatively large numbers securing places at independent schools, through the availability of scholarships.

The *Kindertransporte* rescue was organised by the Refugee Children's Movement (RCM) (Kushner and Knox, 1999: 154). As with the Basque evacuation, local committees were formed, often with the same membership as the Basque committees. These groups organised support, housing children with foster families or in hostels. While some children were able to attend mainstream schools (both state and independent) the lack of education for older children is a theme in many papers written about the *Kindertransporte*. Some vocational education was organised for them, often by Zionists who supported the idea of young Jews learning a skill before emigration to Palestine. But many older children were sent to work, despite educational success in their home country. John Grenville, later a Professor of History at Birmingham University, had his entrance to grammar school blocked by the Cambridge Refugee Committee which threatened to withdraw their support for him and his siblings. Instead, at 16 he became a gardener. One of Grenville's brothers had his education ended at 13 and was forced to work in a Sheffield foundry (Kushner and Knox, 1999: 156–157). The tendency to direct refugees into manual work was determined at a local level by groups supporting the children. It was a time of labour shortage and workers were needed to help the war effort. Young refugees, it was thought, could work to pay back the hospitality they had received in the UK.

1945: the Poles

The Poles are the largest refugee group to have settled in the UK. Most arrived between 1946 and 1951 and policy responses to them were determined by acute shortage of workers in mining, agriculture, manufacturing and the new service industries.

Very few of the 163,000 Poles who were resident in Britain in 1952 came directly to the UK. They arrived in different migratory waves described below (Sword, 1989: 22–24, 72–74, 135–138):

- the exodus of September 1939, who left after the German invasion of Poland, of whom 60 per cent were Jewish (Marrus, 1985: 195).
- the escape of Poles attached to the Polish Government in Exile, based in France until 1940.
- General Anders's army and dependent civilians. In September 1939, Poland was partitioned, 1.8 million Poles found themselves under Soviet rule and were soon deported eastwards to Siberia (Marrus, 1985: 245–246, 250). In 1941, after the Nazi invasion of the Soviet Union, the Polish Government in Exile was allowed to recruit a Polish army. Led by General Wladislaw Anders, about 220,000 Poles left in the Soviet Union on foot and made for Iran. The army comprised 180,000 soldiers and 40,000 civilians, including 20,000 children. After Tehran, they walked to Baghdad, Jerusalem and then to Cairo. Here the soldiers were organised into the Polish Second Corps who fought with the Allies in Italy. The civilians were dispersed to camps around the British Empire. After VE Day in 1945, some Polish combatants returned to Poland while others remained in refugee camps in Italy. The latter were then brought to the UK to work in key industries. They were later joined by Polish civilians, mostly unaccompanied children, often malnourished from their time in refugee camps (Sword, 1989: 245).
- Displaced Poles who found themselves in refugee camps in the British sector of post-war Germany.
- European Volunteer Workers. Some 14,000 Poles arrived in the UK between 1946 and 1949 as part of the European Volunteer Worker Scheme (EVWS). This scheme provided a controlled supply of workers drawn from displaced persons' camps in Europe (Kay and Miles, 1988; Sword, 1989: 73).
- 'Westwarders' 1945–47, comprising about 1500 persons who fled from the turmoil of post-war Poland.

As well as comprising different migratory movements, class and ethnicity formed points of difference. Jews constituted about 12 per cent of the population of pre-war Poland (Landau, 1992: 316). Of those who survived the Holocaust some 90 per cent left Poland as refugees. Yet most of the refugee literature that documents 'Polish' refugees scarcely mentions Jews, or other minorities such as Ukrainians, Germans or Lithuanians. There were also major political fractures within the Polish community. Sometimes these were based on pre-war political allegiances, but more often they related to the perceived notions of home. Supporters of Anders intended to remain as a nation in exile, whereas supporters of Stansislaw Mikolajczyk[17] wished to encourage a return to Poland, and to work for political change in the home country. Poles also framed their relationship with the UK in different ways. They may have seen themselves as refugees awaiting return to the homeland, permanent exiles or members of a minority ethnic community. Political differences (the Anders–Mikolajczak split) and the relationship with the country of exile impacted on the planning of education for Polish children.

Policy responses to the Poles

In early 1940, soon after the Nazi invasion of Poland, the British government gave diplomatic recognition to the Polish Government in Exile, then headed by General Sikorski. As well as coordinating Polish combatants, the Government in Exile had an education department which ran Polish schools and a Polish university. In February 1945 the Allied powers met in Yalta and agreed to recognise a Polish provisional government of national unity. The British government was then presented with a dilemma. Poles had fought bravely for the Allied cause and many of them were now living on British soil. But the continued existence of a (largely anti-Soviet) Polish Government in Exile was a political embarrassment for the newly elected Labour government which, pre-1949, saw itself as an 'honest broker' between East and West.

The solution to this problem was dictated by the demands of the post-war labour market. In July 1945, the Polish Government in Exile was derecognised. Poles would be allowed to stay in the UK, but would be billeted to work in key industries. The responsibility for supporting Poles in the UK was passed from the Government in Exile to the Interim Treasury Committee (ITC). This comprised civil servants and Polish nominees who oversaw the organisation of the Polish Resettlement Corps (to billet Polish workers to key industries) and other functions such as Polish education. The ITC was wound up in 1947 just before the implementation of the Polish Resettlement Act 1947. This Act was not immigration legislation but rather a legal framework for the settlement of Polish refugees, moving responsibility for Polish affairs from the ITC to various government departments.

Polish education

Polish refugee children were the only 20th-century refugee group who received an education separate from the British mainstream. Between 1940

---

[17] Mikolajczk succeeded Sikorski as Premier of the Polish Government in Exile. He returned to Poland in 1945, although he was forced into exile again in 1947.

and the mid-1950s about 50 per cent of Polish children received some or all of their education in separate Polish schools.

In 1940 the policy of the Polish Government in Exile was to encourage Polish children to go to British schools (Ministry of Education, 1956). But the size of the Polish community soon increased as refugees arrived via France. The Government in Exile then opened Polish medium primary schools, then in 1941, two secondary boarding schools.

In 1945 the British government, through the ITC, gained responsibility for Polish education. Under its administration the numbers of Polish schools initially increased, prompted by the notion, supported by Mikolajczyk, that many families would return to Poland and thus needed to speak Polish. But by 1947, the British government was aware that most Poles had not returned. So the aims of education changed – children should be educated for a future in the UK. The Polish Resettlement Act 1947 gave responsibility for the education of Poles to the Ministry of Education (or the Secretary of State for Scotland). The Ministry of Education then delegated management of Polish schools to the Committee for the Education of Poles in the UK, a policy community comprising both Polish and British educationalists.

The Committee for the Education of Poles in the UK was bequeathed six nursery schools, eight primary schools, four grammar schools, three vocational schools, a Polish University of 1189 students and the Polish School of Medicine. One of its immediate challenges was to improve the English language proficiency of children attending Polish schools. So in 1947, the medium of education changed from Polish to English, apart from classes in the Polish language, literature, history and religious education. This was not a decision that was taken easily and there was a great deal of dissent within the Committee for the Education of Poles in the UK, as well as the wider Polish community.

By 1952, many unaccompanied child refugees had completed their secondary education. Many parents were also of the opinion that even if their children had attended Polish primary schools, British secondary schools offered greater opportunities. There was much less demand for places in Polish schools. By 1954 only two Polish secondary schools remained. At government request, the work of the Committee ended in September 1954. The two remaining Polish schools were transferred to local authority control. One educational legacy of this period is the Polish supplementary school movement, comprising seven Polish supplementary schools in Greater London mostly organised by Polish parishes (Refugee Council, 1991a).

1956: the Hungarians: from State responsibility to charitable care

The earlier settlement of Basque, Jewish and Polish refugees was criticised for not being well coordinated by government. Supposedly as a response to this lack of coordination, the British Council for Aid to Refugees (BCAR) was formed in 1950, at the request of the Foreign and Commonwealth Office (BCAR, 1980). (There may have been other motives: direct involvement with settlement of anti-communist refugees from Eastern Europe may have been embarrassing to the Labour Government.[18]) In 1981 BCAR merged with a small campaigning organisation to form the British Refugee Council.[19]

The founding of BCAR was a key policy shift: responsibility for the settlement of refugees was handed from central government to an NGO. However, NGOs have little control over central and local government policy in the field of housing, benefits, health and education. That responsibility for settling refugees falls on NGOs may lead to less coordination of services, rather than better coordination.

The arrivals of Hungarian refugees saw BCAR expand in size. The Hungarian Uprising of October and November 1956 caused 200,000 people to flee (Fischer, 1996). In mid-November 1956 the Home Office invited two agencies to implement the settlement of a quota of Hungarian refugees. A maximum of 3500 refugees were to be supported by the National Coal Board – and sent to work in coal mines – the remainder by BCAR. Some 21,451 Hungarian programme refugees entered the UK via camps in Austria, including 400 unaccompanied refugee children (de Kisshazy, 1979).

Hungarian children of school age attended mainstream schools where they received little or no additional help in their learning of English. (EAL teachers as a professional group did not exist until the 1970s.) There is little documentation about Hungarian children's education. This may have demographic causes: the low proportions of younger children in the group. It may also be a construct of a refugee child as being unproblematic. De Kisshazy (1981) notes, 'The most rapid knowledge of English was acquired by school-aged children who picked it up, almost automatically, at the state schools they attended'.

Similarly, Czech children were considered an unproblematic group. BCAR (1980) estimated that about 5000 Czech refugees settled in the UK following invasion of Czechoslovakia by the armies of the Warsaw Pact countries in August 1968. They were not initially recognised as refugees, either by UNHCR or by the British Government. The Home Office took the lead in coordinating their settlement granting them visas and permission to work –effectively treating them as guest workers. Those who had additional social needs were supported by BCAR. Of its caseload, some 4.5 per cent of cases brought children's educational problems and BCAR concluded, 'In most cases, schooling of children has presented no problems' (BCAR, 1969). This contrasts with the Czechoslovak experience in Australia. Thirteen years after arrival around 20 per cent of the 5–14 age group did not speak English well (Gigler, 1983). That Australia recruited manual workers from countries of first asylum to settle as refugees may partly account for this – perhaps a group who might be less able to support their children's learning.

---

[18] Interview with Nancy Rice-Davies, 8.2.94.
[19] The British Refugee Council became the Refugee Council in 1991.

1972: Ugandan Asians in Britain

On 4 August 1972, Idi Amin, then President of Uganda, decreed that Uganda's Asian community had 90 days to leave the country. Despite popular resistance, the British Government accepted for settlement some 28,000 Ugandan Asians who held British travel documents and 400 stateless households. There was a policy change with central government taking a direct role in formulating and implementing settlement policy for the Ugandan Asian 'refugees'. The Government founded the Uganda Resettlement Board which reported to the Home Office. BCAR had very little involvement with the Ugandan Asians, only assisting with family reunion (BCAR, 1973, 1974).

The Ugandan Asians arrived at a time of changing educational policy, with assimilative policies changing to those deemed as 'multicultural education'. Although lacking in a coherent agenda, advocates of multicultural education sought to improve provision for children from ethnic minority groups by ensuring the maintenance of their home languages and cultures. Multicultural education also aimed to prepare children from the majority community for life in a multi-ethnic society. The Swann Report marks a point when multicultural education policies had maximum impact, and describes many practices in of this era (Committee of Inquiry into the Education of Children from Ethnic Minority Groups (Swann Report), 1985).

The Ugandan Asians were the first refugee group to receive English as an additional language (EAL) support funded through Section 11 of the Local Government Act 1966 (see Chapter 7). Section 11 funded language centres, attended by children prior to entering mainstream schooling. Here children were taught English using a pedagogy based on the teaching of modern languages in schools. But withdrawal meant that children missed important parts of the curriculum, and also the opportunity to converse with their English-speaking peers. (For an overview of the debate on withdrawal, see Jaine, 2000.)

Withdrawal began to be discouraged on linguistic grounds in the early 1980s, then in 1985–86 the Commission for Racial Equality (CRE) conducted a formal investigation into the English language support offered to children in Calderdale, a local authority in Yorkshire. Here children who were newly arrived from the Indian subcontinent were required to take an English test. Those who did not pass were placed in a separate language class or language centre where they spent months or even years following a narrower curriculum. The CRE referred its findings (the Calderdale Judgement) to the Secretary of State for Education, who agreed that separate provision was discriminatory and thus unlawful under the Race Relations Act 1976 (CRE, 1986). Following the Calderdale Judgement, language units were closed. Some local authorities actively discouraged all withdrawal, including small group teaching in schools. But the debate about separate teaching and withdrawal resurfaced in the late 1990s, as Chapter 7 describes.

Conditions experienced by Ugandan Asians were examined one year after their arrival by Community Relations Councils.[20] Housing was cited as the most acute problem faced by the refugees. Four of 59 Community Relations Councils reported problems in children's access to education, mostly concerning older children who faced difficulties finding school places (Community Relations Commission, 1974). Twenty-five years later the children of Ugandan Asian refugees are enjoying considerable educational success (Gillborn and Mirza, 1998: 14).

1974: Cypriots in Britain

Less educationally successful than the Ugandan Asians were the Cypriots, of whom an estimated 10,000 fled to the UK in 1974 and 1975 following the partition of Cyprus. The 1974 arrivals joined a larger Cypriot community that had largely migrated to work in the UK. Greek Cypriots outnumber Turkish Cypriots in Cyprus, but the Greek and Turkish Cypriots communities in the UK are approximately the same size because the poorer Turkish community migrated in proportionately larger numbers. London is the centre of settlement (Taylor, 1988).

Concerns about Cypriot children's educational achievement were raised as early as 1968, with an analysis published by the Inner London Education Authority (ILEA) showing underachievement among both Greek and Turkish Cypriot children (ILEA, 1969). The Swann Report highlighted underachievement among the Cypriot community, with Turkish Cypriot children doing less well than their Greek peers. It attributed this to limited fluency in English, poor home–school links, parental illiteracy, low teacher expectations, and a tendency among Cypriot pupils to misbehave in the freer atmosphere of British schools. The higher educational achievements of Greek Cypriot children were attributed to higher levels of parental education among the wealthier Greek Cypriot community (Committee of Inquiry into the Education of Children from Ethnic Minority Groups (Swann Report), 1985).

Twenty years on, Turkish Cypriot children are still securing lower results in national tests and GCSEs than their white peers, although Greek Cypriot pupils now secure similar results (Enneli *et al.*, 2005). As with many other ethnic groups, there is a marked gender gap, with Turkish girls securing better results than boys (Mehmet, 2001). Community activists attribute underachievement to many of the factors identified in the Swann Report, although acknowledging that parental illiteracy is no longer a problem (Dedezade, 1994; Mehmet, 2001). (Most Turkish Cypriot children at school today have parents who themselves have been through British schools.)

---

[20] These were small non-governmental organisations first set up in the 1960s. They aimed to promote better 'race' relations.

Chileans, Vietnamese and Tamils

Three further refugee groups who arrived in the period 1970–80 were the Chileans, Vietnamese and Tamils. The Chileans and Vietnamese were programme refugees who were admitted to the UK as part of a government quota.

In September 1973 the socialist government of Salvador Allende was toppled in a coup. During the next 15 years, 9 per cent of the population of Chile fled as refugees (International Catholic Migration Institute figures cited in Kay, 1987). In 1974, around 3000 Chileans were admitted to the UK as part of a government programme subcontracted to BCAR and the World University Service (World University Service, 1974). Children's educational issues were not identified as a major area of concern by these organisations. However, the Chileans were the first refugee group in the UK among whom there was research on gender issues. Kay's research draws important conclusions, namely that there is a bias towards men as informants on refugee issues. In most societies children's issues are seen as a woman's responsibility and any needs analysis which depends on men being key informants may, therefore, not pick up on refugee children's needs (Kay, 1987).

Between 1978 and 1988 the British government admitted about 24,500 Vietnamese who arrived in the UK as part of three settlement programmes (the First Vietnamese Settlement Programme 1979–82, a second group of resettlement schemes that ran from 1983–88 and the Third Vietnamese Resettlement Programme of 1988–92). All three Vietnamese programmes comprised high proportions of children – an estimated 35–45 per cent (Jones, 1982). About 80 per cent of those admitted to the UK were northerners. They comprised about 25 per cent ethnic Vietnamese (or *Kinhs*) and 75 per cent ethnic Chinese (*Hoas*) (Lam and Martin, 1994; Refugee Council, 1991b: 1).

Almost all of the Vietnamese were housed in reception centres on arrival before being moved into permanent housing. Children attended local schools. Some local authorities made school-based support teachers available to help children learn English while others did not. At a local authority level, support for the Vietnamese children was often organised in isolation from support for other children who had limited fluency in English. Funding arrangements for EAL support institutionalised this split. EAL support for the Vietnamese was not funded by Section 11 of the Local Government Act 1966, as the Vietnamese had not come from a Commonwealth country. Instead it came out of local authorities' 'no area pool' funds (replaced in 1988 by Section 210 funding of the Education Reform Act 1988).

Evaluations of the three Vietnamese programmes highlight the lack of central and local government involvement in the settlement of the refugees. Both government and the NGOs that ran the reception centres were also criticised for focusing on the short-term needs of the refugees, and not involving themselves with their long-term requirements. The term 'front-end loading' was used to describe this approach, with almost all financial resources put into reception, rather than long-term support (Refugee Council, 1991b).

Vietnamese children

Three government studies of the Vietnamese highlight high adult unemployment and lack of adult proficiency in English, but make no mention of children's needs (Commission for Racial Equality, 1983: Duke and Marshall, 1995; Jones, 1982). Indeed, UK research on the adaptation of Vietnamese refugee children is sparse, although the Vietnamese arrived at a time of growing concern about the education of children from ethnic minority communities. That the Vietnamese were stereotyped as being hard-working, rather than a social problem, may have generated less government funding for research.

Much more research on Vietnamese children has been conducted in North America, with analyses of children's responses to persecution, flight and dislocation, as well as their long-term adaptation (see Chapter 3). A number of studies have analysed Vietnamese children's educational progress at school (see for example, Caplan *et al.*, 1991; Rumbaut and Portes, 2001; Zhou and Bankston, 1998). These studies, by proponent of segmented assimilation theory, suggest that high levels of social capital and the maintenance of 'Asian' cultural values are predictors of academic success. Today, educational achievement data from Lambeth and Southwark, two London local authorities at the heart of the Vietnamese community in the UK, indicate that Vietnamese and Chinese children are consistently outperforming all other ethnic groups (Lambeth, London Borough of, 1998; Southwark, London Borough of, 2002). Around 47 per cent of Vietnamese pupils in Southwark gained 5 Grade A*–C grades at GCSE in 2001, compared with 34 per cent of white pupils.

London local authority data show significant differences between girls' and boys' achievement at 14 and 16 years, with Vietnamese and Chinese girls securing far better test and examination results (an average gap of 23 per cent). This gender gap may be caused by the 'laddish' behaviour of adolescent Vietnamese and Chinese boys and their unwillingness to be identified as 'boffins' (Archer and Francis, 2003). Archer and Francis's research about Chinese pupils' educational experiences in London mirrors much US research on Vietnamese and Chinese educational achievements (see Caplan *et al.*, 1991; Rumbaut and Portes, 2001; Zhou and Bankston, 1998). However, their analysis draws on Bourdieu's notions of embodied cultural capital, rather than the notion of segmented assimilation. Bourdieu modifies Marxist notions of class and capital.[21] He suggests that class differences can be distinguished by the possession of different forms of capital in different amounts:

- economic capital
- social capital, comprising resources based on social networks
- cultural capital

---

[21] There is very little writing about social class and refugees. However, Van Hear (2003) links the ability to migrate to the possession of social and economic capital.

- symbolic capital – the value that is attached to economic, social and cultural capital (Bourdieu, 1986; Bourdieu and Passeron, 1977).

Bourdieu further distinguishes different forms of cultural capital. It can exist in an objectified state, as objects such as books, paintings and musical instruments. Cultural capital may exist in an institutionalised state – in the form of academic qualifications. It may also exist in an embodied state – within the dispositions of the individual. The commitment to self-improvement through education is a form of embodied cultural capital which Bourdieu terms 'habitus' – a socially acquired and embodied system of dispositions that cause one to act in a certain way and are determined by the way a person is socialised by family, peers and wider society (Bourdieu, 1986). Archer and Francis (2003) describe the values of many Chinese children and propensity for hard work as 'diasporic habitus' – and suggest that this accounts for high levels of achievement, even in inner-city schools.

Tamil children

There is also growing evidence to suggest that Sri Lankan Tamil children are another refugee group experiencing educational success in the UK. The first Tamils to settle in the UK were not asylum-seekers, but educated labour migrants, many of whom arrived in the 1960s. South-west London became the hub of this first community. The first large-scale movement of Tamil asylum-seekers to the UK began in 1983. Between 1984 and 2004 there were 49,545 asylum applications from Sri Lanka, the vast majority of whom were Tamils (Home Office, 2004a, 2005a; Refugee Council, 1998a).

Most Tamil refugees in the UK are from the Jaffna peninsula and the northern islands. Most Sri Lankan Tamils are Hindu, although a minority are Christian, mostly Roman Catholic. Tamil society is class- and caste-stratified. Dominant economically and socially are *brahmins* (priests), *vellalars* (traditionally landowners) and *karaiyars*, (traditionally traders and deep-sea fishermen) (McDowell, 1996). Artisan castes and 'untouchable castes' generally enjoy lower incomes and lower social status.

Caste identity affects social interactions in Sri Lanka, and in rural areas to a much greater extent. Class and caste identity, too, has affected migration pathways as well as settlement patterns in the UK (McDowell, 1996). The early migrants and the first asylum-seekers were largely middle-class *vellalars* and *karaiyars* from the Jaffna peninsula, the northern islands and from Colombo. As the 1980s progressed the economic and class profile of the Tamil asylum-seekers changed, with asylum-seekers from poorer families arriving in the UK (Steen, 1993). Such migration patterns have implications for educationalists. McDowell notes that as the 1980s progressed, the level of prior educational attainment of Tamils entering Switzerland fell. He suggests that while the original 'pioneer migrants' were well-educated, the process of chain migration ensured that as time progressed more women and the less well-educated arrived in Switzerland (see Table 4.1). This is not a phenomenon solely restricted to Tamils, as noted in later chapters about Congolese and Somali refugees.

Table 4.1 Educational experiences of Tamil refugees in Switzerland and UK

Educational experience	Switzerland 1983–91 (%)	London 1997 (%)
Less than 3 years formal education	5	17.5
Completed primary education	35	20
Completed secondary education	42	37.5
Some/all of undergraduate programme	18	12.5
No reply	10	–

Sources: Haringey, London Borough of (1997) Survey of Swiss Federal Office for Refugees' Asylum Archives as cited in McDowell (1996).

In the UK, the same caste and peer networks that facilitated migration are often used to find work, much of which is in the retail sector, in off-licences, small grocers and petrol stations. Such employment is usually badly paid and involves long hours at work. These jobs offer little opportunity for promotion and prevent many adult Tamils from studying. Children and adults are often vocal in their belief that such work compromises integration into UK society:

> My mum says I should never work in a shop. You have to work at night and you can get robbed. She said find a job where you only have to work in the day, like in an office.
>
> (14-year-old boy, south-east London)

Setting up one's own business – usually a small grocer's shop – is a progression route for some young male Tamils who use caste and peer networks to raise capital. But this goal is only for those who possess permanent rights of residency in the UK. For those without this certainty, earning money is the pre-eminent activity – so as to return to Sri Lanka with cash if removed from the UK.

There are many foci of Tamil community life in London. These include temples and churches, restaurants and bars, cultural organisations and events such as Heroes Day. Of all recently arrived refugee communities, Tamils probably have the best organised community school structure. As well as teaching Tamil, most of the community schools have sports and cultural programmes. Research indicates that a far higher proportion of Tamils attend community schools than other large refugee communities in the UK. In one survey around 64 per cent of a sample of Tamil children of secondary school age attended community schools (Tamil Information Centre, 1998). The same survey also showed how children maintained their fluency in Tamil:

- Around 59 per cent of children spoke Tamil with other family members, less than many other refugee communities, reflecting that English is usually the second language of educated Sri Lankan Tamils.
- Around 60 per cent of Tamil children regularly listened to Tamil radio broadcasts and 73 per cent listened to Tamil cinema music.
- Children were also exposed to the Tamil language by attending cultural events, temples and churches, socialising within the Tamil community and writing to relatives (Tamil Information Centre, 1998).

It is likely that almost all Tamil children growing up in London have access to written Tamil and at least half can read or write the language. That the Tamil community is one of the largest refugee communities in the UK and is concentrated in London means that language maintenance through community schools, radio and publications is feasible for most families. Perhaps a smaller or more dispersed community might be less able to maintain the home language.

Like the Vietnamese, speaking Tamil and attending a community school may also promote the maintenance of Tamil values and habitus orientated towards educational achievement. As with the Vietnamese, there are probable cognitive advantages to being a 'balanced bilingual' and having fluency in English and Tamil (Cummins, 1977; Toukomaa and Skutnab-Kangas, 1977). Tamil music and dance encouraged by community schools may have their own intrinsic cognitive benefits. Attending a community school and having fluency in Tamil may also afford psycho-social benefits, promoting psychological resilience and a positive sense of ethnic identity.

Learning from history

The lessons of history are of relevance to those working with refugee communities today. Yet there is a real lack of transmission of knowledge about the settlement of refugees from one migratory movement to another. Better ways of promoting reflexivity and institutional learning need to be developed.

So what conclusions can be drawn from an examination of previous settlements of refugees? Apart from Belgian and Polish children, the 20th century is characterised by the disengagement by central government from the formulation of education policy on refugee children. No explicit national policy directives on refugee education were published by central government between 1954 and 2001. Central government involvement and cross-departmental government coordination of refugee policy was particularly weak after 1954.

The divide between refugee education and education for minority ethnic children has its roots in recent history. By the late 1960s, government Section 11 monies had secured funding for educational support for children from Commonwealth counties (usually, the sons and daughters of labour migrants). But most refugee children were theoretically excluded from this support by virtue of not being from the Commonwealth. One of the legacies of Section 11 of the Local Government Act 1966 was to institutionalise a split between refugee education and the education of children from minority ethnic communities.

Notions of permanence and home have changed. Belgian, Second World War and Polish refugee children were largely constructed as a group of children whose status in the UK was temporary. This was used to justify educational responses. For Belgian children it was acceptable for them to go to mainstream schools because they were only going to be in the UK for a short period and would not be 'damaged' by English-medium education. For Basque and Polish children the intended temporary nature of their stay was used as a justification for separate education. But since the 1950s educationalists have assumed that almost all refugee children will stay UK. Today, any discussion that refugee children may just be temporary residents in the UK is almost taboo in refugee issue networks. Children's future outside the UK is hardly discussed. This may be an oppositional position, used as a means of challenging Home Office policy on the removal of asylum-seekers. But does the suppression of debate on refugee children's future and their notions of home serve them well?

History contains examples of educational success among refugee communities, as well as examples of communities whose children fail to make progress. Factors that contribute to progress are complex and multi-factorial.

A final conclusion relates to one of the central arguments of this book – refugee children's labelling as universally traumatised. As the historical evidence shows this is a recent phenomenon. There was much less articulation of refugee children being a 'problem' before the 1980s. That they *are* a problem may be a conclusion drawn from research evidence and arguably, the post-1980 dominance of 'trauma research'. The problematisation of refugee children may also be a recent social construct of a refugee support bureaucracy.

MODERN ASYLUM POLICY AND ITS IMPACT ON CHILDREN

Since 1989, throughout western Europe there has been increased international migration at levels unsurpassed since 1945–65. Migration, in particular asylum migration, has become a public discourse, an integral part of national debates on 'race' and belonging, as well as a political problem to which politicians have to be seen to respond. Since 1989 more immigration legislation has passed through the UK Parliament than at any other time during history. This chapter examines asylum and settlement legislation and policy, focusing on its impact on children.

Both asylum and settlement policies are operational statements of intent. Asylum policy comprises issues that relate to border control, the determination of asylum applications, the asylum appeals system and the removal of failed asylum applications. 'Settlement policy' is the term this book uses to describe housing, healthcare, and educational and other social welfare policy for asylum-seekers and refugees (Refugee Council, 1997b: 15). Asylum and settlement policy are not always discrete entities, for example Morris (1998) argues that restrictions on asylum-seekers' rights to social housing (and thus the requirement of housing officers to check immigration status) are a form of internal immigration control.

Policy implementation

Early studies of the policy process adopted linear models. Policy was generated and then implemented – policy was 'written' and then 'done'. Academic studies of this linear process comprised debates between 'top-down' writers and those advocating a 'bottom-up' approach (Hill, 1997; Hill and Hupe, 2002).

Top-down approaches to the policy process suggest that policy change starts with a government decision. This is then implemented by public and private sector agencies. The focus of the policy-making system is to achieve the Government's intended outcomes. Policy generation and implementation are seen as distinct activities, with the state generation of policies being relatively remote from their implementation. A major criticism of top-down models of the policy process is that the policy process is viewed from the perspective of decision makers in central government and neglects other actors.

Exponents of bottom-up approaches to the policy process place much greater emphasis on peripheral actors. Among them is Michael Lipsky with his analysis of frontline workers, such as teachers, whom he terms street-level bureaucrats (Lipsky, 1980). He argues that 'the decisions of street level bureaucrats, the routines they establish, and the devices they invent to cope with uncertainties and work pressures, effectively become the public policy they carry out' (Lipsky, 1980). Lipsky's work is examined in again in Chapter 8.

Since Lipsky published *Street Level Bureaucracy* there have been a number of attempts to sythesise top-down and bottom-up approaches and to develop circular, rather than linear models of the policy process. Bowe and Ball's Policy Trajectory Model, based on Foucauldian discourse analysis (see Chaper 1), is one circular model of the policy process (Bowe and Ball, 1992). They suggest that policy content is represented by text. The policy process takes place in three different arenas (see Figure 5.1).

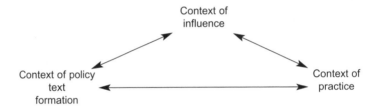

Figure 5.1 The Policy Trajectory Model
Source: Bowe and Ball (1992: 9).

The *context of influence* is where public policy is initiated. It is here that interested parties struggle, their behaviour determined by basic constitutional structures. Policy discourses are formulated within these elites and articulated in the second site – the *context of policy text production*. Policy texts can take different forms: legislation and documents such as Green Papers, but also informal texts such as press releases, speeches and the TV performances of ministers. Bowe and Ball suggest that while discourse within the context of influence may be dogmatic, policy texts are more usually phrased in the language of public good. Policy texts are then interpreted in the *context of practice* – the local authority, school, border control post and so on. Here text is received, interpreted and recreated. The process of interpreting text is again a matter of struggle, with actors exercising different amounts of power. While deviant or minority interpretations may be important, one or more view will eventually predominate as a 'truth'.

Another circular approach to the policy process is the advocacy coalition framework (Hill, 1997; Sabatier and Jenkins-Smith, 1993). This starts from the premise that the most useful way to analyse the policy process is not from the perspective of a particular government department, but rather a policy sub-system. Such a sub-system includes actors from a variety of organisations who are concerned with a particular issue. Many circular models of the policy process acknowledge that external discourses influence the content of government policy.

Both the policy trajectory model and the advocacy coalition framework stress the importance of networks within the policy process. Marsh and Rhodes (1992) suggest that there are two types of networks: policy communities and issue networks. Policy communities have a limited membership and a limited number of decision centres and are able to exercise power. Issue networks, such as the Steering Group on Refugee Education discussed in Chapter 7, have a less defined and often fluctuating membership, with members able to exercise less power.

Key actors in asylum and settlement policy

In a complex society such as the UK, policy formulation involves different actors with different quantities of power, operating in different arenas. For example, asylum policy is generated in the Home Office and the Cabinet Office. Pressure groups such as the Refugee Council or issue networks such as the Asylum Rights Campaign generate oppositional policy discourses

The Home Office has overall responsibility for immigration and asylum, with its Immigration and Nationality Directorate (IND) taking the lead. Within the IND, the Integrated Casework Division processes asylum applications, while the National Asylum Support Service (NASS) administers housing and sustenance for asylum-seekers. The Home Office also has lead responsibility for race relations.

Other government departments play a more peripheral role in asylum policy. The Department of Constitutional Affairs has ultimate responsibility for the Immigration Appellate. The Foreign and Commonwealth Office (FCO) contributes towards the human rights assessments that form the basis for judging asylum cases. It is also involved in the coordination of overseas aspects of refugee evacuation programmes. Both the FCO and the Department for International Development have been involved in international policy debates about migration. Since 1997, both the Cabinet Office and the Prime Minister's private office have assumed greater roles in formulating migration and asylum policy.

Central government departments are also involved in settlement policy. However, in England, central government coordination of settlement policy is weak. *Ad hoc* contacts between civil servants do occur. During the period since 1989 there have been three short-lived interdepartmental working groups on refugee issues. Two were facilitated by the Home Office and dealt with issues relating to the Bosnian and Kosovan evacuations. From 1987–96 the Department of Social Security facilitated the Refugee Employment and Training Working Group. Set up in 2001, the National Refugee Integration Forum (coordinated by the IND) was also meant to provide for greater coodination between government departments, local government and NGOs. The forum is divided into sub-groups, for example, on education and on healthcare. But central government has afforded the National Refugee Integration Forum little support and the civil servants that attend meetings are low in departmental hierarchies. At meetings of the education sub-group there have often been no representatives from the Department for Education.

Greater coordination on refugee settlement policy has been achieved in Scotland and Wales. Here responsibility for healthcare and education has been devolved to the Scottish Executive and the Welsh Assembly.[22] The Scottish Executive has a team responsible for asylum and refugee policy and has formulated a refugee integration plan for Scotland (Scottish Refugee Integration Forum, 2003). The smaller number of organisations responsible for settlement policy in Scotland – effectively the Scottish Executive and Glasgow City Council – have operated as a tight-knit policy community, although not always in agreement. The Scottish Executive has also sometimes espoused different views on immigration to the Home Office, most recently over managed migration policy.

Of non-departmental government bodies, the Commission for Racial Equality (CRE) should have greatest engagement with asylum and settlement policy. Legal duties laid down in the Race Relations Act 1976 and the Race Relations (Amendment) Act 2000 have a major impact on the well-being of refugees and the CRE is obliged to see that these duties are observed. However, it has made very few public statements on asylum and did not have any specific policy on refugee issues until 2004. Commentators have suggested that the CRE views asylum as being separate from the mainstream of race equality issues in the UK.

While the Home Office has determined asylum policy, it has been local statutory services that have driven forward settlement policy. Local authorities are responsible for housing about 40 per cent of asylum-seekers who are being supported by NASS. (The remainder are housed by private landlords and housing associations.) In order to promote better regional coordination of services for asylum-seekers, the UK has been divided into 12 regional asylum consortia, usually led by the regional local government associations and comprising members co-opted from local authorities, the police, health authorities and refugee agencies. Some asylum consortia have set up sub-groups looking at issues such as education.

In the UK, a large number of NGOs work with refugees. These comprise over 800 refugee community organisations working with specific groups and providing advice and welfare casework. In many areas there are also small refugee agencies that offer practical support to refugees in the locality. There are a number of national refugee organisations such as Refugee Action, the Scottish Refugee Council and the Refugee Council. The latter act as pressure groups, lobbying on asylum and settlement issues.

---

[22] The Scottish Parliament may pass educational legislation. In Wales, there is only partial devolvement of powers, as the Welsh Assembly may not pass primary legislation on education.

Modern asylum policy: the first restrictions

From the end of the Second World War until the late 1960s, European countries encouraged primary migration at a time of labour shortage. The British government encouraged the migration of nationals from its former colonies who were automatically granted citizenship until the passage of the Commonwealth Immigrants Act 1962. This was the first post-war restriction on primary immigration to the UK, passed at a time when there was no longer such a demand for labour, as well as popular agitation against immigration.

Over the next 20 years further legislative barriers made primary immigration more difficult, but in the UK asylum-seekers faced few restrictions until the late 1980s. Asylum numbers were small – between 3000–4000 persons a year. Since many asylum-seekers were white Eastern Europeans they were also afforded a degree of invisibility. Small numbers and racialised constructions of asylum-seekers as white Europeans meant that in the UK asylum was viewed as a largely separate issue from immigration.

But this was soon to change. By the mid-1980s asylum applications had substantially increased in Germany, reaching 121,315 applications in 1989 (European Council for Refugees and Exiles, 2004). Carrier sanctions were introduced, and the German constitution, which guaranteed a right of asylum, was amended. Emerging inter-governmental cooperation on asylum led the UK, too, to adopt carrier sanctions, with the passage of the Immigration Carriers' Liability Act 1987. In the same year the Government enacted changes to social security regulations, restricting the benefits paid to asylum-seekers to a level of 90 per cent of that granted to other claimants. But in 1987 asylum was not a public discourse.

The year 1989 marked a turning point, with the start of an asylum migration of Somalis, Turkish Kurds, Congolese and Angolans. Within government, asylum started to be viewed as a policy problem. Since 1989, government has moved towards a four-pronged approach in changing asylum policy:

- Erecting barriers that prevent asylum-seekers entering the UK, for example visa requirements, carrier sanctions and immigration checks at overseas airports.
- Processes to ensure the rapid determination and removal of asylum applicants judged to have unfounded cases.
- Restricting asylum-seekers social and economic citizenship rights, as a deterrent measure. Such deterrents include the use of detention, the restriction of welfare benefits, housing, work and education. This is an EU-wide trend, with constantly shifting boundaries between citizen, denizen[23] and outsider (Levy, 1999; Minderhoud, 1999; Morris, 2004).
- Tightening the criteria by which the Home Office judges an asylum application, so that in 2004 some 87 per cent of initial asylum applications resulted in refusal.

---

[23] Tomas Hammar (1990) describes denizenship as the halfway point between full citizenship and outsider.

Asylum and Immigration (Appeals) Act 1993

The first attempt at changing asylum legislation occurred in 1991, with the publication of the Asylum and Immigration (Appeals) Bill. Within the context of influence – senior Home Office civil servants and ministers – the policy drivers that led to this legislation included increases in UK asylum applications and fears of greater immigration from the 'East'. The identification of asylum as a major political issue in Germany also influenced debate within the context of influence, with German government pressing other European countries for joint action on asylum, through the Schengen Group and the then Steering Group on Asylum and Immigration. Ministers were also influenced by an increase in negative media coverage of asylum issues from the end of 1989.

The Bill failed to become law in 1992, but was presented to Parliament again and received Royal Assent in July 1993. The Asylum and Immigration (Appeals) Act 1993 amended housing entitlements for asylum-seekers, who lost their right to be accepted as 'homeless' and in need of social housing if they had any other accommodation, 'however temporary', Moreover, while an asylum case was being determined, no asylum-seeking household could be offered a secure social housing tenancy. Instead, they could only be offered temporary housing. One impact of this restriction on social housing was that Homeless Person's Units were required to inquire of a person's immigration status – a form of internal immigration control (Morris, 1998). This highlighted asylum-seekers as being 'different' from other users of local authority services.

After the passage of the Asylum and Immigration (Appeals) Act 1993, schools, local authorities and refugee NGOs noted increases in asylum-seeking children's mobility (Dobson et al., 2000; Power et al., 1998; Rutter, 2003b). Greater London OFSTED reports during the period 1993–96 cited pupil mobility in some schools with large numbers of asylum-seeking pupils as being 10 per cent in a year, and among the asylum-seeking pupils themselves as being 60–100 per cent (Rutter, 1999). Research on the effect of temporary housing on children has highlighted problems in securing school places, protracted periods out of school and difficulties in building social relationships within the school (Power et al., 1998). Continuity of care for children with healthcare or special educational needs is adversely affected. Other pupils, too, can be affected by high pupil mobility: teacher time is spent settling in new students and it is difficult to deliver a curriculum that has continuity in situations of high pupil mobility (Shelter, 1995: 31). There is also an administrative cost in enrolling new children. School funding formulae are also calculated on the basis of an annual pupil census and this assumes a largely static school population. Teaching staff can also be unwilling to invest time and effort into supporting a child if they know that child will be moved on at very short notice.

Since 1993 many refugee children have spent protracted periods without school places. Often the only schools that have places mid-term are the ones that are under-subscribed as a result of being less popular with the settled population. Consequently within a local authority there tends to be an inequitable distribution of refugee children, as well as homeless families. In London, every local authority has one or two such secondary schools where pupil mobility may comprise as much as 30 per cent in a year. (There are number of secondary schools in London where pupil mobility is much higher, sometimes in excess of 2000 per cent.) These high mobility schools are often establishments with existing problems and high staff turnover.

Two further policy changes were enacted at the same time as the Asylum and Immigration (Appeals) Act 1993. Immigration Rules were amended. (These are statutory instruments attached to immigration law that determine in practice how a person can enter or stay in the UK.) The changes widened the criteria for refusal of an asylum application, for example an asylum-seeker who could reasonably live in another part of their home country would be refused asylum in the UK (Rutter, 1994: 38). Consequently there was a large increase in the proportions of asylum-seekers refused asylum, from 27 per cent in 1993 to 74 per cent in 1994. But while refusals were high, few who were refused asylum were removed from the UK, suggesting that the tightening of the criteria for granting asylum was a symbolic deterrent.

Asylum and Immigration Act 1996

In October 1995, Peter Lilley, then Secretary of State for Social Security, announced that benefits would be removed from all asylum-seekers who had lodged their claims 'in country' rather than at the port of entry, as well as those appealing against a negative initial decision. This proposal was met by initial disbelief among refugee advocacy groups who immediately undertook a period of intense campaigning. Faith groups, the Labour movement and human rights activists were mobilised to voice their opposition. Although the campaign was unsuccessful, it involved many previously uncommitted organisations and activists.

At the Refugee Council, campaigning was combined with planning for the support of large numbers of destitute asylum-seekers. A day centre was opened and the organisation purchased large amounts of plastic sheeting. However, few asylum-seekers were rendered destitute. Within days of the removal of their benefits, a legal challenge was mounted and Courts reversed this policy. The Government did not accept the legal judgment and published the Asylum and Immigration Bill soon afterwards. This gained Royal Assent in July 1996, again removing benefits. It also further restricted the rights of asylum-seekers to social housing, barring them from being placed on a waiting list for social housing. The new legislation again attracted legal challenges, invoking the National Assistance Act 1948, the Children Act 1989, the Children Act (Scotland) 1995 and the Social Work (Scotland) Act 1968. These were successful and made local authorities responsible for supporting asylum-seekers who had been denied benefits.

In England and Wales families with children were supported by local authority social services departments under the provisions of the Children

Act 1989.[24] They were given a cash allowance and some form of temporary accommodation. But the 1996 Act had many negative effects on asylum-seeking children. First, it marked the point when significant numbers of asylum-seekers began to be housed outside Greater London, often in hostels or poor quality hotels in seaside towns.

Second, pupil mobility among asylum-seeking and refugee children increased very substantially after 1996. Third, the Asylum and Immigration Act 1996 magnified anti-asylum sentiments in the UK. Dispersal outside London was accompanied by such negative media coverage, in the local and national press, that the public could only feel concern about demonised newcomers (Fekete, 2001; ICAR, 2004a). Local authorities were not fully compensated by central government for the services they provided for destitute asylum-seekers. In order to meet statutory requirements to support asylum-seekers, social service departments were forced to make cuts from other parts of their budgets. Consequently asylum-seekers grew increasingly unpopular with some local authority officers and councillors. Some of the less scrupulous councils briefed the press. Headlines such as 'Influx of refugees costing thousands' (*Kettering Evening Telegraph*, 7 August 1998), 'Old folk's home to be hostel for refugees' (*Harrow Leader*, 16 July 1998) became commonplace.

The 1996 legislation also normalised the illiberal treatment of asylum-seekers. Local authorities sought to minimise the numbers of asylum-seekers for whom they were caring and many employed staff who would assess the local connections and neediness of asylum-seekers. The Refugee Council documented many instances of brutal treatment of asylum-seekers by local authorities. Cases included a family with small children who were forced to walk between Haringey and Ealing (a distance of 30 kilometres) while the two authorities disputed who was responsible for supporting them. The justification for such treatment was good governance – the need to spend local authority finances in a wise manner.

Immigration and Asylum Act 1999

The new Labour Government inherited an asylum support system that both local government and refugee advocacy groups regarded as chaotic. By 31 March 1998, Greater London social service departments were responsible for 20,421 asylum-seeking households without access to benefits (London Research Centre, 1999). A number of local authorities in Greater London and the south-east lobbied central government to repeal the Asylum and Immigration Act 1996. The Immigration and Asylum Act 1999 was the result. It

---

[24] In England and Wales, asylum-seekers without children were supported under the provisions of the National Assistance Act 1948. This obliged local authorities to provide warmth, shelter and sustenance, the latter usually in the form of vouchers redeemable at a single supermarket. Case law prevented local authorities from giving a cash allowance.

also had a response that continued negative media coverage, as well as the perception within government that asylum migration now challenged the State's control. More and more asylum-seekers were evading border control by arriving as clandestine entrants. Most crucially, their skills did not always match the current needs of the labour market.

However, debates within the context of influence were certainly not unified. There is evidence of different discourse communities, as well as conflict between them. In particular, there was a struggle between those who believed that the answer to the asylum 'problem' lay with building strong external border controls and those who believed that a fast and efficient asylum determination system was needed. The former understood that once asylum-seekers were here, it was very difficult to remove them. The latter believed that speedy processing of claims, plus removal of those whose claims were rejected, would resolve the perceived chaos.

Civil servants began working on a White Paper on immigration and asylum in spring 1998. It appeared that it would recommend a Home Office-administered benefits system, whereby asylum-seekers would be given a cash benefit by this government department rather than the Benefits Agency. The White Paper was discussed in Cabinet on 9 July 1998. Tony Blair allegedly opposed the cash benefit and told Jack Straw, then Home Secretary, to pursue a voucher system similar to that of a number of German states. Civil servants had less than three weeks to make substantial changes to the White Paper. This was eventually published on 28 July 1998 as *Fairer, Faster and Firmer: A Modern Approach to Asylum and Immigration* (Home Office, 1998). It proposed a cashless system for supporting asylum-seekers, with its stated aim:

> to ensure that genuine asylum seekers cannot be left destitute . . . to provide for asylum seekers separately from the main benefits system; and to minimise the incentive to economic migration, particularly by minimising cash payments to asylum seekers.
>
> (Home Office, 1998: para 8.17)

Following the White Paper, the Immigration and Asylum Bill was presented to Parliament in February 1999, receiving Royal Assent in November 1999. This legislation profoundly changed the way that asylum-seekers were housed and supported in the UK. It removed the right to income support from all asylum-seekers, as well as sustenance under the National Assistance Act 1948, the Children Act 1989 and the equivalents in Scotland. Asylum-seekers also lost their right to housing under homeless persons' provision. The Immigration and Asylum Act 1999 set up a new housing and sustenance scheme for asylum-seekers to be administered by the National Asylum Support Service (NASS), a new division within the Immigration and Nationality Directorate of the Home Office.

The passage of the 1999 Act left the refugee advocacy sector in a state of shock. Individual campaigners for refugees, many of whom had a long history of involvement with the Labour movement, were surprised that a Labour government should pass such a repressive measure. The Refugee Council – the organisation that viewed itself as the leading national voice for refugees – took a different line. It regarded the Immigration and Asylum Act 1999 as the legislation that would determine future support for asylum-seekers. The Refugee Council stood back from campaigning against the legislation. Instead, its role was to 'make the Act work for asylum-seekers'. Staff were informed that the Refugee Council had to be involved in the new support system, or else the organisation would be 'designated to obscurity'.[25] From summer 1999, the Refugee Council busied itself in defining its role in the new asylum support system. Its Deputy Chief Executive was seconded to the Home Office in autumn 1999, to be involved in the setting up of NASS. For once, the Refugee Council was part of the asylum context of influence.

To prepare for dispersal, the UK was divided into regional groupings termed 'asylum consortia'. Initially, these were not based on the boundaries of the Government's regional offices, although there was some later redrawing of boundaries. The consortia worked to encourage local authorities to offer empty local authority housing for use by asylum-seekers. At the same time, NASS commissioned housing from nine private-sector organisations, which in turn contacted local landlords to provide them with rented accommodation. On 1 December 2000, local authorities became responsible for all new asylum-seekers under the Interim Support Scheme for Asylum-Seekers. NASS came into operation on 4 April 2000 and by late summer 2000 was responsible for supporting all new asylum applicants in the UK.

Homeless asylum-seekers were housed in specially commissioned emergency accommodation when they first arrived in the UK. Here their meals were provided for them, along with packages of toiletries, in a system reminiscent of refugee camps. Asylum-seekers who needed housing and sustenance were assisted in their application to NASS by NGOs such as the Refugee Council, Migrant Helpline and the Refugee Arrivals Project. They had the option of applying to NASS for a 'support-only' package, or for support and accommodation. Until April 2002 support entailed a cash allowance of £10 per person per week, plus vouchers exchangeable at designated retail outlets. (NASS vouchers were abolished in April 2002 after a successful campaign and replaced by a cash allowance.)

From its outset, the asylum support system was beset with problems. NASS was unable to process applications for support and move asylum-seekers within its seven-day deadline. Consequently people remained in emergency accommodation for protracted periods – sometimes as long as six months. Some of the emergency accommodation was unsafe and dirty. Here asylum-seekers complained that they could not obtain food that their young children would consume (McLeish, 2002).

NASS vouchers did not reach asylum applicants. Asylum-seekers also faced problems in making purchases, for example, in Burnley, Lancashire, they faced a 14 kilometre walk to buy bread and milk, as local shops did not accept asylum vouchers.[26] Some of the housing offered by private sector landlords was of poor quality, something acknowledged even by the Home Office

---

[25] Quotes from Nick Hardwick, Chief Executive, Refugee Council at staff conference, July 1999.
[26] Documented by the Refugee Council in October 2000.

(Home Office Press Release, 25.3.04). Much of the accommodation offered by local authorities was previously empty council property, often on deprived outer-city estates. Local authorities renovated and furnished these properties, a move interpreted by excluded local populations as favourable treatment for asylum-seekers. This, and negative campaigns in the local media increased local racial tensions. Many asylum-seekers requested to be moved as a result of racially aggravated attacks.

The independence of non-governmental organisations such as the Refugee Council was also compromised by its involvement with NASS. Refugee Council staff were obliged to turn away asylum-seekers who requested rehousing after racial harassment. Inevitably, the Refugee Council's potential to lead pro-asylum campaigns was weakened by its links with NASS.

The NASS system had a major effect on children's education and well-being. The long wait in emergency accommodation meant that some children missed long periods of schooling. Housing quality for those opting for 'support only' and living with family and friends is an issue of concern – it is inevitably of a temporary nature and overcrowded. On 31 December 2004 around 51 per cent of asylum-seekers supported by NASS were in receipt of subsistence-only support. While proportionally more households with children opt to be housed, about one third of families decline NASS housing and dispersal, largely remaining in Greater London or Manchester. There is evidence that housing mobility among asylum-seeking children living in Greater London increased after 2000, as families who opted for 'support only' move between different types of accommodation when hospitality is exhausted (Association of London Government, 2005). There has also an impact on the hosting household, whose living space and scarce household income is shared among more people.

Although voucher support was replaced by cash support on 8 April 2002, adult asylum-seekers are still supported at levels 30 per cent below income support. An account of the poverty faced by many asylum-seekers is given in *Poverty and Asylum in the UK* which describes many of them experiencing hunger on a regular basis (Refugee Council and Oxfam, 2002). School uniform, a requirement by most primary and secondary schools, is outside the budget of families supported by NASS. Yet school uniform grants are discretionary and some local authorities do not award them at all. Inevitably the NASS system has increased parental stress – research on psychological vulnerability in refugee children has concluded that one of the most important factors is the presence and quality of parenting (see Chapter 3). Any policy intervention that places greater stress on refugee parents – isolation, stress or extreme poverty – may render a child less likely to cope.

Racism and the new social cohesion agenda

Spring 1999 saw the publication of the Macpherson Inquiry into the racist murder of Stephen Lawrence, a black south-London teenager. The inquiry was convened by the Home Secretary in response to widespread anger at the bungled police investigation. In the months after the inquiry there was some genuine debate in the media and in Government about the racialised life experiences of Britain's ethnic minority populations. However, this debate was restricted to Britain's minority citizens – descendants of migrants from the New Commonwealth and Pakistan. While the national tabloid press ran stories that were supportive of the Lawrence family, they also continued to demonise asylum-seekers. The Home Secretary visited mosques at the same time as presenting asylum migration as undesirable. For a while, the Home Office appeared to be saying that some minority populations were deserving and others not.

The Macpherson Report made over 150 recommendations, most of which were targeted at the police. It led to the passage of the Race Relations Amendment Act 2000 which required local authorities, schools, and other public bodies to publish race equality policies, in order to outlaw unlawful discrimination, promote equality of opportunity and ensure good race relations. Public bodies were also obliged to conduct race equality impact assessments before enacting major policy changes. Both requirements offer opportunities to support refugees. There is evidence to show that many local authorities took their statutory duties seriously and attempted to provide leadership on race equality. However, few schools responded. Some simply did not fulfil their legal obligation to draft a race equality policy. Other schools stated that their existing equality policies were sufficient. Of the case study schools featured in Chapter 8, only one reviewed its race equality policy at this time.

During 1999 and 2000 some government policy text recognised the inequalities and racisms experienced by ethnic minority groups. But since late 2001, there has been a further discursive shift. Terms such as race equality have been replaced by new agendas – social cohesion and integration.

Social cohesion and social solidarity were concepts first discussed by Durkheim and Toennies, (1893/1933) in relation to the interdependence of people in newly industrialised cities in Europe. In the early 1990s moral panic about urban decay fuelled research into social cohesion in North America, where conceptualisations of social cohesion were also influenced by communitarianism (Vertovec, 1999). Social cohesion is a process and an outcome and at its core lies a sense of belonging to a locality. Griffiths *et al.*, in a study of refugee community organisations argue that social cohesion comprises three components. Firstly, it may comprise inclusion in the labour market and other dominant types of social activity. Secondly, social cohesion may comprise membership of collective bodies – social capital. Thirdly, it may comprise shared values and cultural norms (Griffiths *et al.*, 2005: 211–215).

In the UK, notions of social cohesion influenced the urban regeneration policies of the 1997–2001 Labour Government. The Office of the Deputy Prime Minister set up the Neighbourhood Renewal Unit which funded a number of regeneration programmes such as New Deal for Communities. During the period 1997–2001 there was also a greater acknowledgement in government policy text that in order to secure greater social cohesion, Government interventions would have to ensure less economic disadvantage. But since 2001, social cohesion has taken on new and sometimes contradictory meanings. In some government text, social cohesion is used as a euphemism for race equality and good race relations (Home Office, 2005b). In other texts, migration, ethnic diversity, and 'multiculturalism' are presented as threats to social cohesion – because migrants and minorities are not 'integrated' (Government Office for London, 2003).

This discursive and policy shift was caused by growing moral panic about the Islamic fundamentalism after the September 11 bombings. The panic grew after the Oldham and Bradford disturbances and the publication of the Cantle and Ousely reports into these events (Home Office, 2001). Both reports identified the housing, educational and employment segregation of communities of Pakistani origin within a number of British cities. Suddenly Muslims – no longer British Pakistani and British Bangladeshis – became a problem community who did not 'integrate'. British policy makers were also influenced by discourses within European governments, where some migrant and refugee communities were presented as 'unassimilable cultural minorities' (Lutz et al., 1995). Previously taboo in the UK, because of its association with cultural racism, it suddenly became acceptable to present the cultural forms of minority groups as problematic. Most targeted were Muslims, who the media and many politicians homogenised, and whose alleged views on gender and marriage were presented as a barrier to integration.

Elements within the police and the Home Office expressed concern about the racial harassment meted out to asylum-seekers in new areas of dispersal as a threat to social cohesion. The policy agenda was also influenced by the views and life experiences of David Blunkett, Home Secretary from 2001–04, and a man influenced by American responsive communtarianism.[27] The above factors prompted the Home Office to assume the policy lead on social cohesion. Its Community Cohesion Unit defines social cohesion as a process that aims to:

> build a common vision and a sense of belonging for all communities, value diversity of background and circumstances, and develop strong positive relationships between people of different backgrounds in workplaces, schools and neighbourhoods.
>
> (Home Office website, March 2005)

The Home Office omits equality from its definition of social cohesion, although the Office of the Deputy Prime Minister retains this commitment. The conflation of social cohesion with 'race' policy has led to other axes of inequality being neglected within the Home Office, yet disparities of income also prevent social cohesion. That Government uses social cohesion as a euphemism for 'race' policy, too, has led some practitioners within local authorities to believe that race equality is no longer a government priority.

---

[27] Communitarianism has emerged as a critique of liberalism. It is rather a diverse assortment of ideas, with the common notion that the individual does not have a direct and unmediated relationship with the State (Frazer, 1999). Communitarianism writers such as Etzioni (1996) stress the achievement of social order, the promotion of common values of community. In the UK, communitarianism has had an influence on the development of citizenship education.

Alongside social cohesion, Labour administrations have re-introduced two further policy terms: integration and citizenship. The Home Office defines integration as a process that helps migrants to:

> achieve their full potential as members of British society; contribute fully to the community and access public services to which they are entitled.
>
> (Home Office, 2004b)

Integration is a contested term, but, within the UK, a commonly accepted definition suggests the removal of barriers that stop participation in mainstream society (Refugee Council, 1997b). Ager and Strang, in research commissioned by the Home Office, suggest that refugee integration comprises:

> outcomes, within employment and education which are equivalent to those in the majority society; social connections, within the refugee community and to members of other communities; and sufficient linguistic competence and cultural knowledge, sufficient sense of security and stability to engage in society in a manner consistent with shared notions of nationhood and citizenship.
>
> (Ager and Strang, 2004)

The same research suggests some indicators of refugee integration. For children, these include the proportions of a refugee population who secure five grade A*–Cs at GCSE. For adults, indicators of integration include average annual earnings compared with the majority community (Ager and Strang, 2004). Indeed, all recent British policy papers on integration make strong connections between economic advancement and cultural integration – suggesting that you cannot progress economically without a considerable degree of cultural assimilation into the mainstream. This is a view challenged by a number of academics, including those advocating segmented assimilation theory (see Portes and Zhou, 1993). It is also a view challenged in Chapter 11 which examines the educational experiences of southern Sudanese children.

The Nationality, Immigration and Asylum Act 2002 provided the legal basis for a citizenship and English language test, to be taken by applicants for British citizenship. The Act also outlines a citizenship ceremony involving an oath of allegiance to Queen and country. Government is presently funding a pilot integration project: the Sunrise Programme (Home Office, 2004b). Every person granted refugee status or leave to remain is allocated a caseworker who helps formulate a Personal Integration Plan, during a 28-day period immediately after status is granted. That such tight time limits have been imposed is indicative of a lack understanding of the integration process. Most refugees tell of the long-term nature of securing a sense of belonging to locality and nation.

Refugee agencies have embraced the new discourses of social cohesion, integration and citizenship, and critiques are few and far between. Government text attaches blame on the migrant, and policy initiatives focus on the migrant rather than the host community. There is a failure to acknowledge that integration is a two-way process and that the hostile views of the majority community prevent the migrant from developing a sense of belonging. Over the past 15 years curtailments of citizenship rights have also reduced the ability of migrants to develop attachments to community and nation state. Permanency of immigration status and permanency of housing tenure help develop a sense of belonging, but both have been restricted.

2001 and 2002

Asylum issues continued to grab the headlines throughout much of 2001. Pressure from Prime Ministerial advisers resulted in another White Paper on immigration and asylum: *Secure Borders, Safe Havens: Integration with Diversity in Modern Britain* (Home Office, 2002). As well as proposing many of the measures that were eventually implemented in the Nationality, Immigration and Asylum Act 2002, the White Paper was the first public articulation of a managed migration programme.

From 2000 onwards, the Labour Government began to listen to some migration experts and business leaders who argued for managed and documented migration pathways into Europe (Schuster, 2003). *Secure Borders, Safe Havens* put the case for giving the potential 'bogus' asylum-seekers legal ways of entering the UK. Not all civil servants were in favour of managed migration; the notion that once immigrants gained entry to the UK they would be here for good was still a dominant policy discourse among some Home Office civil servants.

Legislation followed soon after *Secure Borders, Save Havens,* introducing further changes to the asylum support system, as well as removing asylum-seekers' rights to appeal. The Nationality, Immigration and Asylum Act 2002 gave a legal basis for accommodation centres, where, in future, some asylum-seekers would be housed and supported. Within sites holding about 800 persons, asylum-seekers would receive full board, healthcare and education. Despite being expensive to build and maintain, the Home Office was clear in its justification of the new accommodation centres as a means of preventing asylum-seekers from working illegally (Home Office, 2002). Accommodation centres were also meant to ease the removal of failed asylum applicants – by preventing them from putting down roots in local communities. Sections 36, 37 and 38 of the Nationality, Immigration and Asylum Act 2002 outlined the provision for the separate education of asylum-seeking children who were resident in the new centres.[28]

The new legislation also gave the Home Secretary the power to withhold NASS support from some asylum-seekers, such as those who cannot provide a clear and coherent account of how they came to the UK. It changed detention, appeals and removals procedures. The 2002 Act also gave a legal basis for funding refugee resettlement programmes,[29] whereby persons of concern to

---

[28] Plans to build the centres were quietly shelved in 2005 with Government arguing that falling asylum applications no longer made them a priority.

[29] Three programmes are in operation: the Gateway Protection Programme, the Mandate Refugee Programme and the Ten or More Plan.

UNHCR would be identified by them and brought to the UK. This aspect of the legislation was another example of concessions to the refugee advocacy movement (who receive funds for participating in the Gateway Protection Programme). At the time of writing a mere 150 programme refugees have been settled in the UK.[30] Only two local authorities – Sheffield and Bolton – have offered housing for the refugees, with many local authorities declining to offer accommodation.

The campaign against the 2002 legislation was flawed in its approach. Opposition was led by the trade union movement, faith groups and children's charities, the latter under the umbrella of the Refugee Children's Consortium. The public campaign largely focused on the separate education of children within accommodation centres. Terms like 'educational apartheid' were used in lobbying text (Association of Teachers and Lecturers, 2002). Other issues such as the curtailment of rights of appeal proceeded with almost no discussion. Arguably, the latter change has a far more detrimental effect on children's welfare than their separate education within accommodation centres. But the nature of the campaign highlights how difficult it is to mobilise against much asylum legislation. Concerned activists and many civil society organisations find it difficult to grasp changes in asylum legislation and policy, especially those at EU level. The campaigning that exists tends to focus on easy-to-understand issues such as asylum vouchers and the separate education of asylum-seeking children. More damaging and illiberal changes proceed without debate.

The 'anything goes as long as it reduces asylum numbers' period

By the end of 2002 the Home Office identified eight potential sites for its proposed accommodation centres. Planning applications for accommodation centres proved to be a focal point for anti-asylum campaigns (ICAR, 2004b). Another focus for anti-asylum sentiments was the publication of quarterly asylum statistics. This event became a racialised ritual. The Home Office published these data and the tabloid media responded with articles on the growing asylum crisis. But in focusing on 'the crisis in numbers' the Government constructs an image of hordes of people seeking to enter to UK.

Throughout 2001 Home Office ministers articulated the need to cut asylum numbers – but privately suggesting that they expected numbers to increase by an annual 10 per cent. But in 2002, after reported pressure from the private office of Tony Blair, David Blunkett suggested that the Director-General of the Immigration and Nationality Directorate be given a 'free rein do whatever he likes to cut asylum numbers'.[31] This 'free rein' included ensuring that as many asylum-seekers as possible were rejected on initial application, even if the reasons for rejection were spurious and later overturned on appeal:

---

[30] The refugees who have arrived are from Liberia, Sierra Leone and Eastern Congo.

[31] Off-the-record interview, senior civil servant Home Office, 2003.

Blunkett wants as many people as possible to be rejected. He wants people to think that the asylum system is not worth bothering about. He doesn't care if people enter illegally, as long as they don't apply for asylum.[32]

In July 2002, all asylum-seekers lost the right to work, a policy that appeared to contradict the increased allocation of work permits. The same Home Office source stated:

Blunkett and Blair don't really care if it [the removal of the right to work] forces more people to work illegally . . . They want the asylum system to be like the workhouse, so miserable that no-one will bother to apply.[33]

In January 2003 the Government enacted Section 55 of the Nationality, Immigration and Asylum Act 2002, rendering asylum applicants who failed to lodge an application within a three-day period ineligible for NASS support. Hundreds of people were left destitute and more were obliged to work illegally (Greater London Authority, 2004). After an extensive campaign, the Courts reversed this decision in June 2004 under Article 3 of the European Convention on Human Rights (Court of Appeal SSHD vs. Limbeuela 21/5/04). Then in February 2003, in response to further hostile media coverage, Tony Blair committed his Government to halve asylum applications by Autumn 2003. The move was made without consultation with the Home Office, reportedly leaving David Blunkett, then Home Secretary 'incandescent with rage' (Pollard, 2004). At the same time Blair's private office leaked copies of *New Visions for Refugees*, a Cabinet Office paper that proposed Regional Protection Areas and Transit Processing Centres. The former would comprise zones of protection and be located near the origins of an asylum exodus. Transit Processing Centres would be located on the fringes of Europe and provide for the extra-territorial processing of European asylum claims (Noll, 2003).

In April 2003, the Home Secretary ended the granting of Exceptional Leave to Remain (ELR), a form of temporary protection that was granted to many asylum-seekers. Some civil servants had argued that ELR was a pull factor for asylum-seekers. It was replaced by the new statuses of Humanitarian Protection or Discretionary Leave.

Two further restrictions on asylum-seekers' citizenship rights were made in Spring 2004 when the Government introduced a limit to the amount of legal aid that could be claimed for an initial asylum application. From this time, legal aid costs were limited to five hours' work, unless special permission was granted from the Legal Services Commission. Lawyers formed the Campaign Against Legal Aid Cuts, arguing that the five-hour limit was insufficient for a complex asylum application (Refugee Council, 2005c). A number stopped undertaking asylum cases, including Bindmans and Wesley Gryk, two

---

[32] ibid.
[33] ibid.

renowned London firms. In the same month, the right to free non-emergency secondary healthcare was removed from 'failed' asylum-seekers. This move, too, followed hostile newspaper articles, such as reports about the higher prevalence of HIV among migrants from sub-Saharan Africa ('HIV soars by 20%, migrants blamed for increase', *Sun* 25.11.03). Later in 2004, the Department of Health published a proposal to prevent 'overseas visitors' from obtaining free primary healthcare, including immunisations (Department of Health, 2004).

Refugee advocacy groups collected many accounts of the application the above changes in health policy, including that of a mother and a four-year-old child, both HIV positive, who were refused anti-retroviral treatment. Today, the removal of healthcare rights has become a *normalised* bureaucratic practice in a country that views itself as a liberal democracy. Ministers, civil servants and health service managers invoke bureaucratic and procedural arguments to justify actions that some people would regard as immoral. As Valverde (1996) argues, depraved actions can easily be sanctioned by liberal bureaucratic procedures.

Government still felt that their attack on asylum-seekers was insufficient to placate the hostile press. Further legislation was passed – the Immigration and Asylum (Treatment of Claimants, etc.) Act 2004. With 50 sections, the Act was nearly twice as long as when it was first presented to Parliament (Refugee Council, 2004). Many of the additions were introduced by the Home Secretary after passage through Commons and Lords committees, in a way that challenges the primacy of Parliament.

The 2004 legislation amends the Housing Act 1996 by stipulating that dispersed asylum-seekers will have a local connection with the local authority in which their NASS accommodation is located, as an attempt to prevent secondary migration of refugees. The legislation also allows for asylum-seekers to be removed from the UK to a third country (of which the asylum seeker is not a citizen), without entering the full asylum-determination procedures, or having a right of appeal in the UK (Refugee Council, 2004). Additionally, the Act provides for electronic monitoring of adult asylum-seekers – suggested by Ministers as a humane alternative to detention. Finally, the Act created a further class of person ineligible for support – a 'failed' asylum-seeker with family. Asylum-seeking families who have exhausted the appeals process lose their support if they fail, 'without reasonable excuse' to leave the UK voluntarily. (At the time of writing Parliament had overturned this section of the 2004 legislation).

As might be expected, hostile media articles continued. Early in 2005, Michael Howard, Leader of the Opposition, announced that he intended to make asylum and immigration an election issue, with some members of his party calling for a halt to immigration. The Conservative Party called for a quota system for asylum-seekers, with application being determined offshore, in a yet unspecified location. More worryingly, the Conservatives proposed the UK's withdrawal from the 1951 UN Convention Relating to the Status of Refugees. (This is a demand that resurfaces at regular intervals. It was articulated in the mid-1990s by Conservative politicians such as Michael Heseltine and privately by Jack Straw prior to the passage of the Immigration and Asylum Act 1999.[34]) Conservative Party campaign managers admitted that immigration was a 'dog whistle issue' that appeals to core supporters and is a metaphor for 'race'.

In response to Conservative proposals, the Government rushed to publish *Controlling Our Borders*, its own five-year strategy on asylum and immigration (HM Government, 2005a). This plan proposed further asylum legislation, now published as the Immigration, Asylum and Nationality Bill 2005. The new legislation will introduce major changes to the asylum application process, with applicants placed in one of nine streams. Government has also limited the period of settlement to those granted Convention refugee status to a period of five years, revocable at any time during this period. There is a clear expectation that those with refugee status would return if conditions improved in their home countries. (Previously, those with refugee status were granted indefinite leave to remain in the UK at the same time as their grant of refugee status.)

Europe

Throughout the period of time examined above, Europe-wide policy initiatives have also influenced UK policy. Before the 1997 Treaty of Amsterdam, most joint action on asylum was taken by European states acting through inter-governmental treaties and working groups, rather than through European Community institutions. Critics of this approach suggested that this was a deliberate attempt to avoid the democratic scrutiny of the European Parliament. The Schengen Agreement was one example of an inter-governmental treaty on immigration and asylum. When implemented in 1994, it provided for the increased policing of external borders, open borders between the nine Schengen states, a single Schengen visa, harmonised carriers' sanctions and orchestrated rules by which asylum-seekers have one chance of applying for asylum in a Schengen state. The 1990 Dublin Convention was signed soon after the Schengen Agreement. This, too was an inter-governmental agreement, determining which EU state was responsible for hearing an asylum application.[35]

The 1992 Treaty of Maastrict provided for greater inter-governmental cooperation on asylum. It formalised the structure of the European Union and empowered justice and home affairs ministers in EU states to further harmonise EU asylum policy. The Treaty gave legal backing to a three-pillared European Union. A central pillar of EC institutions is flanked by a second pillar of common foreign and security policy and a third pillar of cooperation in the fields of justice and home affairs. These two outer pillars are outside the

---

[34] Diary notes, 5 July 1999. Straw was reported as saying to Nick Hardwick, then Chief Executive of the Refugee Council, that unless the 1999 Act substantially reduced asylum numbers, the UK would consider withdrawal from the 1951 Convention.

[35] The UK and Ireland did not accede to the Schengen Agreement although both countries signed the Dublin Convention.

formal framework of the European Community. Actions taken are, therefore, not subject to European Community law. Until 2002, EU asylum and immigration policy lay within the third pillar of common justice and home affairs policy.

The 1997 Treaty of Amsterdam provided for asylum policy to be brought within the oversight of EC institutions within a five-year period. Much greater harmonisation of EU asylum policy was envisaged, but the UK, Ireland and Denmark were also granted permission to determine their own asylum policy. Since 2002, more asylum policy has been brought within the oversight of the European Community. The Council of Ministers of the EU leads on the development of policy and EC legislation, with EC legislation and policy determined by qualified majority voting. The European Commission's Justice and Home Affairs Directorate is also involved in the drafting of EU asylum policy. The European Parliament can scrutinise directives, and has amended proposals such as the draft directive on common asylum procedures.

The 1999 Tampere Summit was also a landmark. The written conclusions of this summit underlined the right to seek asylum and committed the EU to work towards a Common European Asylum System based on the full application of the 1951 UN Convention Relating to the Status of Refugees. The summit also initiated the European Refugee Fund, which aimed for greater sharing of the financial responsibility for supporting refugees. The Tampere Summit, therefore, gave much greater commitment to liberal international humanitarian law.

The Hague Programme of 2002 outlined future EC priorities on asylum and migration, namely a common asylum system, legal migration pathways, partnerships with counties outside the EU and the development of external processing centres, where asylum claims would be determined outside EU borders. At the same time, there has been a much greater conflation of asylum and security policy, with asylum-seekers being portrayed as a security threat in inter-European discussions.

As a result of the Treaty of Amsterdam and the extension of EC competency, a number of EC Directives on asylum have been issued. As directives, they have legal weight, obliging member states to amend their own primary legislation, if necessary. The European Council Directive on Temporary Protection entered force in August 2001. In 2003, a directive on family reunion and a directive laying down minimum standards for the reception of asylum-seekers were agreed (European Council, 2003a, 2003b). The latter outlines minimum rights to education, healthcare and the support of unaccompanied refugee children, *inter alia*, citing:

> Access to education shall not be postponed for more than three months from the date the application for asylum was lodged by the minor or the minor's parents.
>
> (Article 10, Council Directive, 2003/9/EC)

At the time of writing, the European Council and Commission were developing a directive on harmonised asylum procedures. The next ten years are likely to see considerable expansion of EC asylum law.

Conclusions

Much of the legislative and policy change discussed in this chapter has had a detrimental affect on the welfare of asylum-seeking children. It has also placed greater stresses on their parents, rendering many of them less able to provide the love and care that all children need.

There is growing evidence that many forced migrants are opting out of the asylum system. Their numbers include those who use other legal means to enter the UK, such as student visas or work permits. Other forced migrants arrive as clandestine entrants and remain in this irregular condition rather than apply for asylum. In researching this book, it was easy to locate children who were irregular *and* forced migrants. Their numbers included Albanians, Colombians and Zimbabweans.

Section 143 of the Nationality Immigration and Asylum Act 2002 makes facilitating the stay of an illegal immigrant a criminal offence. This law has resulted in some refugee organisations ceasing to provide assistance for those who cannot prove that they have legal residency. There is thus a real need for strategic thinking among child welfare, refugee and migrant organisations as to how to respond to vulnerable irregular migrants.

Most human rights organisations believe that European governments are cutting a broad swathe through the humanitarian principles of the 1951 UN Convention Relating to the Status of Refugees. Genuine asylum-seekers are being prevented from reaching safety. The citizenship rights of asylum-seekers, migrants and refugees have been reduced, with the asylum-seeker emerging as the ultimate outsider.

Asylum legislation and policy will continue to change, at a national and European level. In the immediate future the UK will have to decide whether to participate in a common European Asylum System and the harmonisation of the criteria for granting refugee status. Transit Processing Centres and Regional Protection Areas are back on the agenda. There is greater articulation of the suggestion that the UK withdraw from the 1951 Convention. Such a move would seriously undermine international human rights law and the United Nations itself.

Twenty years ago, if refugee advocacy organisations had been told that by 2005, asylum-seekers would have lost so many civil and social citizenship rights, these groups and networks would have expressed disbelief. Yet this has happened, in a slow process that has normalised inhumane treatment of one group of human beings, using the justification of laws and policies of a liberal state. The Asylum and Immigration Act 1996 started this process of normalisation of the inhumane. Yet it is neither normal nor moral to deny children basic shelter, sustenance and healthcare.

HOW UK CHILDREN VIEW THE REFUGEE IN THEIR MIDST

The previous chapter examined changes to asylum legislation and policy in the UK. The legislation itself has had a detrimental effect on race relations. Additionally, almost all the legislative change has been accompanied by negative media coverage. Drawing on ethnographic research undertaken in four schools, this chapter examines how public discourses about asylum and migration are interpreted by young people.

As described in other chapters, there has been a long history of educational interventions that aim for better inter-ethnic relations. Many refugee NGOs have seen schools as an opportunity to get their message across to a youth audience and have consequently produced teaching resources. This chapter also examines the efficacy of such curricular interventions.

What research tells us about racialised social interactions

Refugee children's experiences mirror what is happening in the wider community. A number of previous studies on the experiences of refugee pupils reveal that many experience racial harassment in their schools and neighbourhoods. In one study undertaken in east London 32 refugee children were interviewed. They included Bosnian, Kurdish, Somali and Vietnamese children. Nineteen of them reported they had suffered racial harassment and nine had moved school as a result (Richman, 1995). *Starting Again* analysed the experiences of asylum-seeking children settled in Glasgow. Worries about racism and personal safety were the worst things experienced by the children (Save the Children Scotland and Glasgow City Council, 2002).

Existing research on prejudice and racialised social interactions is multidisciplinary and includes psychological research on the development and regulation of prejudice in children, described later. There is also an extensive theoretical literature examining the transmission of racialised knowledge and the development of contemporary racisms (see, for example, Back, 1996; Balibar, 1991; Bhavnani and Phoenix, 1994; Dyer, 1997; Kumar, 2003; Solomos, 1993; Wetherell and Potter, 1992). Hewitt's work is among a number of ethnographic studies of racialised interactions among young people (Cohen, 1989; Hewitt, 1996, 2003). There is also a rather sparse criminological literature about racially motivated offenders (see, for example, Smith *et al.*, 2003).

Much of the psychological research examines the causes of prejudice – unjustified feelings of dislike towards all members of a particular group. These studies usually examine the individual and his or her inner microsystem, with research often undertaken in laboratory situations. Conversely, ethnographic studies and sociological interpretations of racism usually examine factors within children's macrosystem. Few studies attempt to be ecological in their approach examining individual, environmental and the broader socio-political factors that cause racism.

Long-standing psychological research indicates that even very young children make racialised judgements about dolls and pictures. Research has attempted to explain these attitudes, but there is little agreement among social psychologists as to the causes of ethnic prejudice in children. Neither is there much research about how prejudiced attitudes affect children's actual behaviours.

Inner state or maladjustment theories examine the role of personality in the development of prejudice, with findings suggesting that children who manifest most anger, hostility, frustration and anxiety as a result of authoritarian parenting styles are those most likely to develop prejudices (see, for example, Adorno *et al.*, 1950). However, maladjustment theories do not easily account for why children are prejudiced towards some groups and not others.

Social contact theories suggest that the absence of contact with particular ethnic groups increases the likelihood that children will develop prejudiced attitudes towards that group. A development of social contact theory is inference ladder theory, where in the absence of social interaction with members of ethnic minority groups, a single negative contact with someone from this group leads to generalisations and the development of prejudice. In the UK, there is some evidence to show that children in London and Manchester manifest less ethnic prejudice than children from areas where there is less ethnic diversity. Criminological data also indicate that there are fewer reported racial incidents in ethnically diverse cities than in rural areas (Smith cites 4.7 racial incidents per 1000 people in London and Manchester, compared with 19.5 in Cumbria in 1999; Smith *et al.*, 2003). In the UK, social contact theories have influenced a number of interventions by refugee advocacy groups. Some organisations may organise sports or arts activities that involve refugees and the majority population, or programmes where refugee speakers are taken into schools to talk to young people.

Social identity theories of prejudice suggest that some children have a strong desire to identify with an ingroup whose characteristics are perceived to be positive. These children have negative attitudes towards members of outgroups, who are viewed as having negative qualities (see Brown, 1995). Cognitive development theories of prejudice draw on staged notions of child development as well as social identity theory, asserting that children pass through stages where their cognitive development affects their attitudes towards the ingroup and outgroups (Aboud, 1988; Nesdale, 1999). Nesdale (1999) proposes that children pass through a stage of undifferentiated attitudes towards different ethnic groups (up to three years), a stage of ethnic awareness (from about three to seven years of age), a stage of ethnic preference (from about seven to ten years) and, finally, to the stage of ethnic prejudice. However, cognitive development theories of prejudice fall down in one major respect – there is no consensus at all about the ages at which children manifest greatest prejudice.

In some parts of the world, including areas of conflicts such as the Balkans, social identity and cognitive development theories of prejudice have influenced interventions to lessen prejudice. Decentring activities have been developed for educational professionals, whereby children are encouraged to understand the perspective of members of an outgroup. Other educational activities encourage the development of moral reasoning, for example by presenting children with scenarios where they have to make moral decisions.

Finally, among psychological theories of prejudice are social reflection theories, whereby children's prejudice reflects the attitudes of their parents, peers and society (see, for example, Tajfel, 1978). Regrettably, few British schools and NGOs include parents in educational interventions that aim to lessen prejudice.

Ethnographic studies in areas of inter-ethnic tension

Hewitt is one of the few academics who attempts ecological studies of racism. Some of his work was undertaken in an outer-city council housing estate characterised by marked housing segregation – it was an area where ethnic minority communities did not reside or even visit. This housing segregation has been perpetuated by policies enacted by the local authority during the 1960s and 1970s, whereby the children of deceased tenants could inherit their parents' council properties. Such policies prevented social housing passing to newcomers, and were commonplace until legislation deemed them discriminatory.

Hewitt's research led him to conclude that many white children had little social contact with children from ethnic minority backgrounds until they entered secondary school, by which time they were becoming aware of themselves as part of a specific peer group, and aware of others as members of an out-group. He suggests that the main agents of reproduction of racist attitudes were the peer group and the regulation of racist attitudes came more from the peer group than from parents. Hewitt argues that local authority anti-racist policies were widely interpreted by the majority community as being 'unfair to whites', stoked by coverage of anti-racist initiatives in the right-wing tabloid press. Two domains of school activity were also considered as unfair to whites: discipline and the way cultural differences were portrayed. Some schools dealt with disciplinary incidents in a way that stressed the school's anti-racist policy rather than asserting the fundamental wrong of the offence. Cultural events such as 'international evenings' make no attempt to represent the culture of the white working-class English and were also interpreted as being unfair.

Hewitt (1996) concludes that 15 years of multi-cultural and anti-racist education policies have changed the attitudes and behaviour of many school pupils but that there remains a core of racist youth. His study did include a number of young people who had committed racist offences, but there has been relatively little criminological research into racially motivated offences. Smith's team, working in Manchester, however, has drawn important conclusions, suggesting that racist offenders are young, with an average age of 24 years and lacking in cultural capital and with few opportunities for betterment. They postulate that the personal shame experienced by this excluded group becomes externalised into violence and directed at symbols of cosmopolitan culture and economic success – often new immigrants (Smith *et al.*, 2003). Much of Smith's work also examines societal violence, linking racism with a cultural acceptance of violence as a means of resolving conflicts.

Hewitt's later work, conducted in Liverpool and Kent, has led to the identification of a number of risk factors that make it more likely that tensions will develop. These include:

- localised high unemployment and bad housing
- negative portrayals for refugees in the local media, particularly concerns about crime
- inflammatory statements by local politicians
- British National Party activity in the local area
- ill-planned dispersal of asylum-seekers, particularly in relation to choice of accommodation and the development of community relations strategies
- little previous settlement by ethnic minority communities or high levels of ethnic segregation in housing
- overstretched public services, particularly healthcare and education, where the arrival of new migrants may have real impact
- failure by the police to pick up on growing tensions and to protect victims effectively
- failure of schools to challenge hostility to refugees from non-refugee pupils and their families (Hewitt, 1996, 2003, ICAR, 2004a; Rutter, 2003a).

While the studies above detail risk factors, comparatively little is known about how these factors cause changes in behaviour.

Interventions

A number of studies have examined the effectiveness of school-based interventions in challenging racism (Hewitt, 1996; Lemos, 2005). There has been a long history of educational interventions that aim for better inter-ethnic relations, such interventions including curricular and extra-curricular activities to promote good inter-ethnic relations, as well as sanctions against pupils who perpetrate racist bullying (Commission for Racial Equality, 2000; Runnymede Trust, 2003). To these ends the new citizenship curriculum has been advanced as an ideal opportunity to 'raise awareness about diversity' and today the English citizenship programme of study for secondary schools includes an obligation to teach about:

> the diversity of national, regional, religious and ethnic identities in the United Kingdom and the need for mutual respect and understanding.
> (Qualifications and Curriculum Authority, 2000)

Many non-governmental organisations have seen citizenship education as an opportunity to get their message across to a youth audience and have consequently produced teaching resources for this area of the curriculum (Refugee Council, 1998b; Rutter, 2004b; Save the Children, 2004). Such resources include *Refugees: We Left Because We Had To*, first published in 1991, and recommissioned as a third edition in 2003 (Rutter, 2004b). The book comprises background information, refugee testimony and activities and is targeted at young people aged 11–18.

In order to inform the development of a new edition of *Refugees: We Left Because We Had To*, research was undertaken in four schools in different parts of the UK. The research examined five areas:

- young people's views about asylum and migration
- how young people form conceptual boundaries between 'us' and 'them'
- media, family, peer, teacher, institutional and locality influences on young people's discourses about asylum and migration
- how young people's views about asylum and immigration are played out in everyday social interactions
- whether schools can act as mediating institutions, challenging popular hostility to refugees and migrants, and, if so, what makes a successful intervention.

In each school classroom observation of lessons on asylum and migration issues was undertaken. Initially, it was also intended to conduct focus group interviews to gather information about children's views on asylum. However, this was abandoned as the first focus group showed considerable self-regulation, with children guarded in expressing their opinions on refugees. It was decided to have more informal discussions with children. Interviews with key teacher informants were also undertaken.

The location of the schools proved a significant factor in determining racialised social interactions. School A was located in a prosperous area, although the locality had seen the closure of traditional manufacturing industries. The local community was largely white and there were few migrants or visible minorities.

Of all the schools that were visited, School B felt most welcoming to outsiders. It too was located in an area that had seen closure of manufacturing industries, including a large engineering factory that employed many local men. The environs around School B were defined and dominated by an inter-war council housing estate, where most of its pupils lived. This, combined with poor public transport, gave the impression of an isolated community on the edge of a large city. The locality in which the school was situated had seen some population change during the past five years, with the arrival of both refugees and labour migrants. This change had been seized on by the British

National Party, which had become more active in the area, contesting council seats and gaining some electoral success in 2005.

In School B refugees comprised about 5 per cent of pupil intake. The school was also notable in its small size, having just 600 children on the roll. It drew most of its pupils from a small number of feeder primary schools. Among all the children there were strong friendship groups that went back to primary school, as well as a sense of membership of their local community.

School C was located about 11 kilometres from School B. The area was not so self-contained and public transport was much better. The local population exhibited much more heterolocality in its connections, travelling outside the area for work, shopping and leisure. The school itself was much larger than School B and had much greater pupil mobility. Before 1994, the school's intake was largely white British and Irish. Like School B, there has been considerable recent population change. The largest group of newly arrived migrants was from West Africa and refugees were 12 per cent of the school intake.

School D was located in a town in south-east England. The area appeared prosperous. It was largely white although there were small Indian and Pakistani communities. Again, the British National Party was active in the local area and had gained a considerable number of votes in the most recent local elections. This episode had surprised local commentators who suggested that the area's prosperity made it an unlikely target of the British National Party.

Each school was categorised on a School Violence Scale of 1 to 10, using a check-list developed from Hewitt and Leonard's work on violence-resistant and violence-associated schools (Leonard *et al.*, 2003). Factors that were graded were proportions of pupils excluded for violent incidents, presence or absence of community police in the school, an assessment conducted during a lunchtime observation of children at play and teacher assessments of violence. Schools A, C and D were the most violence-associated. Pupil behaviour was least challenging in School B.

Children's discourses

The research findings indicated that children talked about asylum in different contexts: formal classroom situations, informally among peers and directly to their refugee peers.

In classroom contexts, most discussion about asylum related to the subject matter of lessons. Most children knew that refugees had fled from war or persecution and many children were able to name countries from which refugees had fled. Children often regulated what they said within the classroom. Teachers also regulated discussion about asylum. This was achieved by teachers limiting the opportunity for debate within lesson. One teacher stated that she was fearful of teaching about controversial issues such as asylum. If questions about refugees were asked of students, those children who teachers thought might express racist opinions were deliberately ignored or told to be silent. But both strategies had the effect of making some children feel that no-one wished to listed to their opinions.

Children also talked about asylum informally and pejoratively to tease, insult, or bully their peers, and interchangeably with other oppressive discourses, as another 'weapon in hand':

Your mum's an Afghan. Yeah, she shops at Shoe Fayre.[36]

More rarely, children talked about asylum with the aim of bullying refugee children, but again using anti-asylum discourses interchangeably with other racist, sexist, homophobic and class-prejudiced discourses. In particular, children voiced anti-asylum sentiments interchangeably with anti-Islamic and anti-Asian discourses. Among boys in particular, anti-asylum prejudice was infused with gender-related discourses. Asylum-seekers were seen as a danger to women, with boys stating that 'my sister won't be able to go out at night if they move here'.

Throughout the 1990s, asylum-seekers have comprised a minority of international migrants to the UK. Much larger numbers of EU nationals, work-permit holders and overseas students have arrived in the UK (Dobson *et al.*, 2001). Yet most media coverage about migration concerns asylum-seekers. This imbalance was reflected in the schools where teacher and pupil discourse about migration was framed solely in terms of asylum.

Children differentiated between asylum-seekers and refugees, reproducing media differentiation between these groups. The term 'asylum-seeker' was almost always used in a pejorative way. Refugees were viewed as people who needed help, often objects of pity. One child, when asked the difference between an asylum-seeker and a refugee stated:

We have to help refugees, but asylum-seekers have come to get free housing.

The research confirmed that children's views about refugees were rather fluid and often localised. Anti-asylum discourses changed over time, and children's discourses often reproduced what had been recently featured in the tabloid media. A visit to one school confirmed this link:

Refugees need medical help
Yes, helping refugees, that's where all our money goes. Refugees have got AIDS, that's where all our money goes, for them.
(Conversation recorded in December 2003, following articles in tabloid press, blaming HIV incidence on refugees)

Afghans and Iraqis appeared targets of the greatest animosity. In two of the schools the terms 'Afghan' and 'Iraqi' were used as insults, sometimes in situations that became violent. Focus on these groups may reflect the media coverage of the wars in these countries, as well as growing Islamophobia. While anti-Islamic sentiments were voiced by some children, conspicuously absent from children's discourses was the notion that 'British' or 'English

---

[36] Shoe Fayre is a discounted chain of shoe shops.

culture was threatened by migration, despite this being an issue that has been aired in the media. Perhaps children are more willing to accept the benefits of new cultural forms.

Much writing about media coverage of asylum issues has blamed the local and national print media as the main cause of growing public hostility to asylum-seekers. However, among under 16s, the relationship between hostile news stories and children's own views is more complex. The print media did have a role – they appeared to seed or introduce racialised discourses into friendship groups via older students and siblings. One boy recounted how his brother had told him that asylum-seekers ate donkeys. The print media also seemed to legitimise anti-asylum sentiments by attaching truthfulness to such sentiments:

It's true, miss, asylum-seekers eat donkeys, it was in the *Sun*.

Discourses of national self-interest ran through much of what children said about asylum-seekers. They questioned the housing and social support offered to asylum-seekers, often believing that the latter received priority treatment. This belief was as common in the two schools located in prosperous areas as it was in less affluent neigbourhoods. Charity begins at home, was a popular sentiment. Students did not see themselves as global citizens sharing the same world. Global citizenship and notions of common humanity appeared to be rather intangible concepts for most children:

When an asylum-seeker wants housing they get it straight away, they get new furniture and everything. The council pays for new mosques, they pay for everything.

There were spatial discourses about migration in three of the schools. Children saw particular schools or areas as 'their territory' and new migrants as being invaders. Such spatial discourses also related to children's constructions of the inner city. In one school located on the edge of London, children associated the city with crime and social problems:

If we have too many asylum-seekers it will get like London . . . You get your phone stolen, it's dangerous to walk about.

Indeed, children viewed cities such as London and Manchester as crime-ridden and cosmopolitan, with their problems caused by migration.

Children who articulated negative views about asylum-seekers were asked if they thought their views were racist. They did not think so, defining racism as negative views and actions against British blacks and Asians. Negative attitudes towards Iraqi refugees, for example were not viewed as racist. One boy explained that since Kosovars were white, it was legitimate to use the term Kosovan as a form of abuse, since it was not racist. This finding mirrors Rutland and colleagues' work on prejudice towards national groups, with children not considering anti-German sentiments to be racist (Rutland *et al.*, 2003).

In all four schools there were few moral discourses about asylum or migration. Teachers did not pose questions that asked about justice and whether the local or national treatment of asylum-seekers was right or wrong.

Consequently, children had few chances to develop moral reasoning in relation to debates about migration.

In all the classes visited about 20 per cent of children were sympathetic towards asylum-seekers and refugees, about 40 per cent uncommitted and a further 40 per cent hostile or very hostile. Given that most children knew that refugees had fled war or persecution, there appeared to be mismatch between this knowledge and empathy towards refugees. This finding suggests that humanitarian discourses or the hard-fact discourses invoked by many refugee advocacy groups will not change behaviours.

There were students who voiced support for refugees. They were concerned about their treatment at the hands of the media as well as their peers. Pupils in the two schools with refugee pupils articulated most support, suggesting that social contact with refugees might have changed attitudes. Girls outnumbered boys in voicing support for refugees in a ratio of about four to one. Hewitt's and Lemos's studies also note gendered responses to minority groups, with Hewitt talking about exceptional girls who challenged the easily voiced racist sentiments of their peers (Hewitt, 1996; Lemos, 2005).

Findings: social interactions

Concurrent with the findings of other previous research projects, refugee children in the case-study schools experienced bullying. (It was witnessed in two schools.) A child, new to the UK and probably a refugee, was pushed out of a queue by another pupil. The latter had a reputation as an insecure and attention-seeking child. The perpetrator was asked why he did it. He was not able to explain this. It is often assumed that the motives of racist bullies are simple, transparent and political. But that was not the case. The bully's reaction to a newcomer was intertwined with his own uncertainties about his identity.

Not all refugee children were targets of bullying. Children who were targets were those perceived to be different, or vulnerable, often because of newness, lacking fluency in English, or isolated. In one school Islamic dress marked some girls as being different. In another school, in a prosperous area, refugee children were deemed to be different because they lacked the latest fashion accessories. Here a refugee boy recounted how consumer pressures impacted on him:

> When England were playing in the European Cup, everyone was wearing England shirts. I begged my mum to buy me one. I kept asking her. She said they cost £25 and she could not afford it. In the end she got me a cheap England shirt from the market. I wore it to school and I was very proud. But they knew it was not a real England shirt and they kept calling me 'Oxfam' and 'beggar boy'. I did not wear the shirt again but I dare not tell my mum.

Of all the factors that made children vulnerable to bullying, pupil isolation appeared most significant. Many refugee pupils were not part of established friendship groups. Pupil isolation has different causes: housing mobility and arrival after friendship groups have been formed are two reasons, as is lack of fluency in English and the perception of 'difference'. But there are also economic causes of pupil isolation. At school, friendship groups are cemented by visits to the cinema, shopping trips and birthday parties. Such activities require money and as many refugee households are dependent on benefits, or employed in low paid jobs, their children are often excluded from such activities. The boundaries between 'us' and 'them' are thus caused by poverty, as well as housing mobility and lack of fluency in English.

As mentioned earlier, three of the schools were violence-associated. It was these schools' acceptance of low level violence and taunting that appeared to relate most closely to the bullying of newly arrived migrants. This seemed a much more significant factor than children's strong sense of membership of peer group. Indeed, in School B, where friendship groups were long-standing and there was a strong sense of identification with the local area, refugee children seemed to be most welcomed and integrated into school life. This finding challenges the pre-eminence of social identity theories. Indeed, the research indicated that that there is no simple correlation between a strong sense of membership of peer group with negative attitudes towards outsiders. Other factors, including school violence may intervene. School B also drew its pupils from an economically deprived catchment area. Much writing suggests that racism and prejudice towards outsiders are more prevalent in areas with high unemployment and poor housing. But again, the research findings contradicted this assumption.

The research highlighted the capacity of local critical incidents to increase inter-ethnic tension and hostility in schools. One research visit was undertaken after a fight between a local football team and an inner-London football team with many players from visible minority ethnic groups. A number of players in the local team were suspended, including the brother of a popular member of the school. Their suspension attracted considerable coverage in the local newspaper and was portrayed as being very unfair to 'local people'. ('Local people' is often used as a metaphor for white people, in both the media and political literature.) The London players were described as 'a team of asylum-seekers', probably inaccurately. Within the school, the incident was interpreted in a racialised manner and tensions grew between a group of white boys and another friendship group, mostly comprising boys of south-Asian origin. After an unrelated incident, the two groups of boys met after school and fought each other. The school responded with a decision not to mention the original conflict involving the football teams, but with tutor time and assembly talks devoted to talks about non-violent ways of resolving differences.

The school glossed over the conflict. Indeed none of the schools that were visited attempted to deal with conflicts that migration might cause. Euphemisms were used when talking about inter-ethnic tensions. Children were rarely encouraged to articulate their views on asylum and migration, because teachers feared the vehemence of their views. The emphasis of teaching was an attempt for people to be 'nice to each other'. But in doing this, children from the majority and non-migrant community felt that no-one listened to their views and that their opinions were not important. Children were thus unable to reflect on their opinions. There was a mismatch between school and the 'nasty' outside world. But children need to be prepared for political conflict in the outside world. Teachers need to improve their teaching of controversial issues and develop skills that draw on peace education pedagogies.[37]

Findings: interventions

Interviews with pupils and teachers aimed to evaluate some of the curricular and extra-curricular initiatives to make pupils more aware of migration and refugees. All these had been planned by teachers who were concerned about how refugees were portrayed in the media and treated in the environs of the school. In the four schools, these interventions comprised:

- Two citizenship lessons, taught as part of a unit on human rights, supplemented by some teaching in the history and geography curriculum; the teaching included the use of video testimony narrated by refugees.
- A six-week unit on diversity in the UK, of which one lesson was about refugees, supplemented by a speaker visit from a refugee organisation.
- Half-term work in citizenship and English on journeys, with input from a an actor and writer who was himself a refugee.
- A curriculum unit on race and diversity, with other inputs from geography, history and English, the latter focused on the portrayal of refugees in the media; the school also ran high profile Refugee Week events that involved contribution from all pupils.

Some of these lessons were observed with the intention of finding out how teaching might challenge popular hostility to refugees and migrants. From this respect the most effective teaching about refugees and migration started with personal experiences. This mirrors approaches taken in Holocaust education, where personal experiences also start much teaching. In doing this, the common humanity of refugees is stressed. Arts education – creative writing, poetry, testimony and the visual arts – appears to be successful in developing empathy and notions of common humanity. Geography teaching, however, seldom uses personal testimony. With its emphasis on population inflows and outflows and the study of the impact of migration, the geography curriculum appeared to create prejudice in one of the case-study schools.

Another key factor in determining the success of citizenship initiatives in lessening the hostility expressed towards asylum-seekers appears to be the potential of young people in being able to *do* something to support refugees, rather than passively absorb information. This was achieved in just one school, where children themselves planned and delivered a range of activities during Refugee Week, including school assemblies, fundraising events and

---

[37] For a discussion of peace education pedagogies see Barsh and Marlor (2000), Galtung (1996), Hicks (1988) and Stornfay-Stitiz (1993).

drama and dance performances on the theme of asylum. One drama production about welcoming newcomers was performed in feeder primary schools.

Such an approach involved active and participatory learning. In another school, in response to growing tensions in the area, the police, the race equality council and the local authority had organised a number of arts and sports workshops for new migrants as well as members of the settled, majority community. Children met at the weekend and after school and engaged in activities such as silk-screen printing and felt-making. Migrants, refugees and children from the settled community worked at these art projects in mixed groups. While participation in the activities was voluntary, there was a high uptake among the year group selected for the project. The degree of cooperation needed in activities such as football and felt-making appeared to break down barriers between 'them' and 'us'.

In one school with a majority white population, children were observed completing tasks that involved them reflecting on their personal and national identities. This was undertaken in English lessons and was coupled with readings about identity. One of the activities that they undertook comprised writing a booklet entitled *All About Me*. Inside the booklet were a number of pages devoted to reflecting on what it meant to be British. Some of the booklets were then made into a display. Most of the children appeared to have strong ideas about the components of their identity, which included symbols of a multi-ethnic society. For example, a number of children drew pictures of their school, representing black and white pupils. The children's work was successful in helping them develop inclusive and positive notions of Englishness.

While a strong sense of membership of an in-group was not felt to be the most significant factor in causing the development of prejudice views, decentring activities appeared effective in developing empathy towards refugees. Children were seen undertaking an activity called 'insiders and outsiders' where insiders set rules that everyone has to obey, before swapping roles (Rutter, 2004b: 154).

The allocation of time resources appears to be another key factor determining if a curricular initiative about refugees is successful or not. It appeared that at least 15 hours of teaching on migration was needed for it to affect children's views. Given the pressures of delivery in a packed curriculum, it is thus essential that teachers work in cross-curricular teams if they are to teach about migration and asylum in a way that challenges racism and develops children's moral reasoning.

Curricular initiatives were not successful where teachers did not have consensual authority, or had a very authoritarian teaching style. Informed debate cannot take place where a teacher struggles to control a class. Empathy towards refugees cannot develop where there is poor classroom behaviour. Children cannot be told to welcome refugees. Teacher expertise in managing potentially difficult discussions was another factor determining the success of interventions. Children need to be given the opportunity to express their opinions and feel that they are being heard. At the same time, a lesson should not become a platform for racism, and a too easily formed consensus on asylum needs to be challenged. Skills in teaching controversial issues take time to acquire, but are the key to determining the success or failure of educational projects on migration.

So, can curricular interventions such as *Refugees: We Left Because We Had To* make a difference? Sometimes, but schools need to consider other factors. They need to acknowledge that the causes of prejudice and racialised social interactions are multi-factorial and sometimes localised. Interventions must, therefore, be ecological. One issue stood out as being a major cause of bullying of newly arrived migrants: schools' acceptance of violence and taunting.

NATIONAL EDUCATION
POLICY AND THE ROLE
OF LOCAL AUTHORITIES

This chapter examines interventions to support the education of refugee children. It starts with a chronological analysis of key events and actors, arguing that the past 15 years have seen a disengagement by central government from policy making on refugee children. It has been local authorities that have conceptualised good educational practice for this group, with their ideas dominated by discourses of trauma. But while local authority staff invoke trauma talk, in many areas interventions to help refugee children comprise a minimum of English as an additional language (EAL) support and little more. Moreover, additional support systems for refugee children have developed in isolation from the special educational needs system, as well as race equality projects in education.

January 1989: the state of play

By the mid-1980s, multi-cultural education policies had been replaced by a new dominant discourse, that of anti-racist education. This movement, dominated by academia, advocacy groups such as the Runnymede Trust, activists and a number of local authority staff, called for minority groups to unify as British blacks and fight racism. Schools and local authorities began to develop policies to confront racism and promote equality of opportunity for groups such as African–Caribbean boys, who were judged to have negative experiences of schooling. Such anti-racist policies reviewed curriculum and teaching resources and the implementation of school discipline procedures and streaming and setting practices on particular minority communities.

Key texts of the period included Troyna's *Race Inequality in Education* (1987), Eggleston et al. *Education for Some* (1986) and Mac an Ghaill's *Young, Gifted and Black* (1988). These were research monographs that examined the educational experiences of children from minority ethnic communities, mostly focusing on the discrimination meted out to African-Caribbean boys. While claiming to present data on 'race', almost of these studies were notable in that they made no mention of refugee children such as the Vietnamese, Iranians or Tamils. Neither were refugee children's needs articulated by the advocacy groups and issue networks concerned with anti-racist education. Like multicultural education before it, anti-racist education invoked essentialist and reified notions of race. Racism, too, was constructed as a unified phenomenon and there was a failure to acknowledge the range of different racisms in the UK (Anthias and Yuval-Davies, 1992; Rattansi, 1992).

Refugee advocacy organisations led a largely separate existence to antiracist groups. The British Refugee Council (later the Refugee Council) was the main actor in the settlement of refugees and as an advocate for their rights. This NGO provided casework for new arrivals.[38] Its advocacy mostly comprised parliamentary lobbying – in 1989 it did not have a strong tradition of seeking to influence local government. In January 1989, asylum migration was neither a political issue nor a public discourse in the UK, unlike in Germany. Asylum applications were far fewer than in the 1990s (3998 asylum applications were lodged in 1988) (British Refugee Council, 1989a).

There was no published policy text that articulated the needs of refugee children and their education was not an issue that concerned teachers. Surprisingly, too, there was little institutional memory of Vietnamese settlement. Those few refugee children – mostly Tamils, Eritreans and Iranians – who entered English and Welsh schools usually received EAL support from teachers funded by Section 11 of the Local Government Act 1966.[39] This Home Office fund made monies available for local government, with legislation stipulating that it was for those local authorities which

> have to make special provision in the exercise of their functions in consequence of the presence within their areas of substantial numbers of immigrants from the Commonwealth whose language and customs differ from those of the community.
>
> (Section 11, Local Government Act, 1966)

By 1988, around 82 per cent of Section 11 monies was used in education, mostly EAL teaching in schools (Home Office, 1988). Local authorities used Section 11 to employ teams of teachers who were seconded to particular schools, or formed peripatetic teams. That Iranian and Eritrean children were not from Commonwealth countries did not affect practice in most local authorities, which in most cases turned a blind eye to the requirement that Section 11's target group was populations from the Commonwealth.

In 1988, the Home Office investigated the use Section 11 monies, a scrutiny that comprised research and consultation (Home Office, 1988). The British

---

[38] The Refugee Council ceased to offer casework in 1989, replacing this with an advice and referral service, whereby refugees are referred to other agencies.

[39] Section 11 was never activated in Scotland as Scottish local authorities argued that the additional needs of ethnic minority children in Scotland should best be met by the appropriate delivery of mainstream local authority services.

Refugee Council (1989b) made a detailed submission to the study, pushing for Section 11 funding to be made available to those from outside the Commonwealth. The Home Office eventually recommended that the Section 11 monies be made payable to all ethnic minorities 'suffering racial disadvantage' (Home Office, 1988: 25). How this recommendation was phrased is indicative of racial essentialism, as well as the emerging division between ethnic minority and refugee education:

> The definition [of groups entitled to Section 11 funding] should also cover groups such as the Vietnamese, Chinese (as of right without assumptions about coming via Hong Kong) and the Somalis. It is more difficult to reach a view on other ethnic groups such as the Ukrainians and Poles, or indeed the Scots, the Welsh and the Irish. The position in relation to refugees is particularly difficult. Some, like the Vietnamese, suffer racial disadvantage in the same way as Commonwealth groups. Others such as the Poles and Ukrainians have similar needs in terms of language and newness but are less likely to suffer racial disadvantage.
>
> (Home Office, 1988: 62–63)

The broadening of Section 11 funding required an amendment of legislation and was not implemented.

Central government discussion about minority ethnic education appeared to be largely restricted to the Section 11 team at the Home Office. This team noted that:

> There are no systematic arrangements for consultation with other government departments. DES (Department of Education and Science) are consulted more frequently than other government departments and administrators there usually seek the advice of HMI (Her Majesty's Inspectorate of Schools).
>
> (Home Office, 1988: 6)

The reticence of the Department for Education to engage in race issues was a consequence of a right-wing campaign to undermine anti-racist education (Klein, 1993: 80–85). This crusade was led by individuals such as Ray Honeyford and pressure groups such as the Campaign for Real Education and the Parental Alliance for Choice in Education. All were adept at mobilising the tabloid print media. Mrs Thatcher added to the demonisation of anti-racism with a speech to 1986 Conservative Party Conference, stating: 'Children who need to be able to count and multiply are learning anti-racist maths, whatever that may be.' With such negative media coverage no education minister would risk a career by promoting interventions targeted at minority ethnic children. After the 1985 Swann Report no Department of Education policy text on issues relating to race and education was published until 1996.

1989: a new period

The year 1989 marked a turning point, both regarding asylum migration and refugee education. The year saw the start of a significant migration of Somalis and Turkish Kurds to the UK. In 1989 2415 Turkish and 1850 Somali asylum applications were lodged in the UK, with other Somalis entered as a result of family reunion (Refugee Council, 1998a).

Nationally, 1989 marked the implementation of the Education Reform Act 1988. This legislation was the most significant change in education law since the Education Act 1944, and had five main strands:

- The introduction of a national curriculum in English and Welsh state schools.
- The devolution of school budgets from local authorities to individual schools under the local management of schools system (LMS).
- The weakening of local authorities' power with the introduction of two new types of school: the grant-maintained schools (GM) and the city technology colleges (CTCs). Both lay outside the control of local authorities and could determine their own admissions policy *inter alia*.
- Parental preference in choice of school.
- The abolition of the Inner London Education Authority (ILEA), a local education authority perceived as being supportive of the education of children from minority ethnic communities.

While the Education Reform Act 1988 did not apply to Scotland, schools there, too, saw the introduction of a national curriculum, devolution of school budgets and a weakening of the power of local authorities. The legislation significantly weakened the anti-racist education movement by diminishing the power of local authorities, which previously had driven much of this practice. In schools, implementing the National Curriculum made huge demands on teachers' time and in such a climate, anti-racist education was no longer a priority.

The potential effects of the Education Reform Act 1988 did concern the Refugee Council. Its Education and Training Working Group was apprehensive about the abolition of ILEA and the effect on community schools of the possible removal of free premises in mainstream schools, as a result of devolution of educational budgets (British Refugee Council, 1989c). The Refugee Council decided to mark the end of ILEA with a conference on refugee education. This was held in March 1990 and marked the start of stronger links between refugee organisations and local education authorities. A leaflet, *Refugee Education into the 1990s*, based on the themes of the conference was published afterwards (Refugee Council and World University Service, 1990). Like much future writing about refugee education, it assumed homogeneity of refugee groups. Significantly, it had no discussion of trauma or resilience. However, it was instrumental in establishing models of good practice in refugee education, developed in later reflective practice texts (see, for example, Bolloten and Spafford, 1998; Camden, London Borough of, 1996; Enfield, London Borough of, 1999; Refugee Council, 2000; Rutter, 2003a).

Although the above publication did not discuss the psychological needs of refugee children, by 1989 such discourses were being aired by some British educationalists. Notions of trauma had begun to enter popular culture (Furedi, 2003). As discussed in Chapter 3, there had also been an expansion of psychological research on refugee children, almost all of which concluded that refugee children exposed to organised violence experienced high psychiatric morbidity. These studies were instrumental in introducing discourses of trauma into debates about supporting refugee children.

1990–92: increases in asylum applications

The numbers of asylum-seeking and refugee children in schools increased in 1989 and 1990, with the arrival of more Somalis, Turkish Kurds, and Congolese and Angolan refugees. This was essentially a migration to London and until 1997 around 90 per cent of the UK's refugee children remained in the capital.

In 1990, a number of London local authorities began to examine how they would support refugee children in their schools. This was almost always prompted by questions raised by the limits of Section 11 funding. Some local authorities now felt that the numbers of refugee children were so large that their English-language learning needs could no longer be met through quietly diverting Section 11 monies. Questions were also raised about the effects of this diversion on more established minority ethnic communities.

In 1990, three London local authorities founded teams of teachers or advisors whose job was to support refugee children in schools and, in some cases, to develop school and local-authority policy on refugee education. In 1991 and 1992, more London local authorities appointed such staff. Today, over 35 local authorities employ refugee support teachers, although their ways of working vary. Some local authorities have integrated refugee support teams, where all the additional educational needs of refugee children, including EAL, are met within the team. Other staff, such as educational welfare officers, bilingual teaching assistants, or teachers and educational psychologists might also work in an integrated refugee support team. An alternative approach is a specialist refugee support teacher whose job is to work with refugee children whose needs go beyond that of learning English. Here EAL support is provided by teachers outside the Refugee Team. This is the most popular model of support, with 16 London local authorities working in this way in 2000. Alternatively, a number of local authorities employ new arrivals teachers who help find a school place for a child, settle the child in, then hand over responsibility for that child to the school and EAL staff. A fourth way of working involves employing a refugee advisor who provides information to teachers and other professional groups about refugee issues and support strategies, but does undertake any casework or direct support. Finally, a few local authorities have refugee support teachers who work with specific communities, for example Sudanese in Brighton.

In 1991 a group of refugee support teachers met and formed an issue network on refugee education, later named the Steering Group on Refugee Education. It was primarily a local authority network and there was little participation from NGOs, academia and, most crucially, from central government. The professional background of this issue group was significant: most came from an EAL background. Members of the group were significantly less senior in their responsibility than those who attended race equality issue networks. There was also very little cross-fertilisation of ideas between the race equality networks or the world of special educational needs. Despite its lack of power, the Steering Group on Refugee Education has been instrumental in defining good practice in refugee education. Since its inception, two discourses have dominated its meetings – oppositional policy discourse about the effects of asylum legislation on children, and discourses of trauma.

New actors

In 1991 two new NGOs were founded, both of which influenced discourses on refugee children. The Medical Foundation for the Care of Victims of Torture works with those who have survived torture and organised violence. Its services for children include individual psychotherapy, family therapy, art therapy and a befriending project for unaccompanied refugee children. The organisation also undertakes casework, to help refugees gain access to statutory services such as social housing, healthcare and education. It is one of the few organisations that offers quality casework, rather than advice and referral services to refugees. The difference between casework and advice work is important – casework involves a social worker assisting an individual in solving social problems, often in the long term, advice work comprises the relaying of information and often the referral of that person to another organisation.

In 1992, the Medical Foundation published *Integrating Refugee Children in Schools*, a leaflet targeted at teachers (Melzak and Warner, 1992). Widely distributed, this leaflet was instrumental in introducing discourses of trauma into schools. In the same year, the Medical Foundation started a teacher-training programme, mostly speaking at local authority-convened training events on refugees. It was in response to these interventions by the Medical Foundation that my own educational publications for the Refugee Council subsequently included discussions about how educational providers could meet the psychological needs of refugee children (Rutter, 1994). I also invoked discourses of trauma in my speaking engagements, as I noted that I received a more sympathetic response from my audience that if I presented a political critique of asylum policy.

The other NGO was Children of the Storm, founded at Hampstead School, London in 1992. Here a Somali child collapsed during breaktime, allegedly because the child's prior experience of armed conflict caused a flashback. This shocked a number of teachers who, led by the head of EAL, organised an after-school club for refugees. Sixth-form volunteers helped run the club and the school raised funds for it and other forms of support for refugee children. A charity – Children of the Storm – was then founded. It provided social welfare support for refugee children at Hampstead School and also encouraged the peer support of young refugees, an approach that no other institution was undertaking at this time (Children of the Storm, 1998). Children of the Storm attracted celebrity support and media attention. Refugee children were described in the national media in terms that caused shock and pity. Undoubtedly, the publicity that surrounded the early work of Children of the

Storm was also instrumental in introducing discourses of trauma into local authorities and schools.[40]

The third new actor in refugee education was located in central government. At this time the numbers of asylum-seeking children in central London bed and breakfast hostels began to rise. In March 1991, an inspector from Her Majesty's Inspectorate of Schools (HMI) made a visit to schools, hotels and NGOs in central London. The school inspector was shocked to meet refugees – a population who were new to her. A policy conference on refugee education was subsequently organised by HMI. After the conference a small team in the Department for Education was given responsibility for refugee children – the Traveller, Refugee and Intercultural Education Team. Its work for refugees comprised the administration of a specific grant for the education of Travellers and displaced persons.[41] It generated no policy text on refugees until 2001. It also had little interaction with other government departments and its representatives did not attend the Department of Employment's Refugee Working Group, nor the *ad hoc* Home Office Interagency Bosnia Programme Working Group.

The Bosnia Programme, the Local Government (Amendment) Act 1993 and racial essentialism

In 1991 and 1992, following the outbreak of war in Croatia and then Bosnia-Herzegovina, refugees from both states began to flee to the UK. In November 1992, the British Government granted temporary admission to 1000 former Bosnian concentration camp detainees plus their dependants.[42] This group were housed in reception centres and afterwards moved to social housing in a resettlement programme led by the Refugee Council. While there was much public sympathy towards the Bosnians, there was resentment among some refugee community organisations of the level of assistance and public sympathy this group was receiving. That the Bosnians were white at a time when most asylum-seekers were black was a reason advanced for this preferential treatment by a number of commentators.

The arrival of the Bosnians focused the Refugee Council's attention on the inadequacy of funding for EAL support. This organisation approached Neil

---

[40] The charity ceased to operate in 2000. The lessons to be learned from its demise are important. Children of the Storm was an example of support organised 'bottom-up', by professionals with a concern for the welfare of refugee children. Its work developed out of individual initiative rather than out of local authority planning. The weakness of such an *ad hoc* approach is that it is dependent on the on-going involvement of a small number of people (Watters and Ingleby, 2004).

[41] This was the Section 210 grant of the Education Reform Act 1988. In England the grant's money has now been pooled into the School Standards Fund.

[42] The Bosnia Programme was announced on the same day as the UK imposed a visa requirement on Bosnian nationals. While the programme enabled some vulnerable people to reach safety, the visa requirement prevented many more from reaching the UK.

Gerrard, a backbench Labour MP, and asked him to raise a private member's Bill to widen the Section 11 target group to all minority ethnic communities, rather than just those who had their origins in the New Commonwealth and Pakistan. He agreed to do this, the Home Office indicated that they would give support and the Local Government (Amendment) Act 1993 passed smoothly through Parliament.

However, this legislation was not universally welcomed. The Runnymede Trust, a respected race equality organisation, opposed its passage, as did the Commission for Racial Equality. That there would be greater demands on Section 11 monies was one reason that the Local Government (Amendment) Act 1993 was opposed. The opposition used racialised discourses. Because Section 11 had previously been restricted to support for those from the New Commonwealth and Pakistan, it was assumed by some organisations to be targeted at England and Wales's visible minorities. It was also assumed that Section 11 financed anti-discriminatory and 'race' equality work, although its funding guidelines made no such stipulation. When a group of white European refugees arrived, their eligibility for Section 11 funding was questioned because of their lack of blackness. The tensions exposed during the passage of the Local Government (Amendment) Act 1993 again highlighted the split between the advocacy coalitions concerned with refugee children and those concerned with British minority ethnic communities.

Section 11 cuts and stability of services

Soon after increasing the target population of Section11, the Home Office cut its budget. A fund of £130.8 million in 1993–94 was cut to £110.7 million in 1994–95. In the financial year 1993–94, Section 11 paid 75 per cent of staff salary costs; this was reduced to 57 per cent in the following year. Local authorities were obliged to find the remainder, often a substantial amount of money (Rutter, 1994). Section 11 funding was further reduced in 1995–96, with 55 per cent of its total funding transferred from the Home Office to the then Department of the Environment to be incorporated into a new urban regeneration programme called the Single Regeneration Budget. Local authorities were informed that they could bid to the Single Regeneration Budget for educational projects that worked with minority ethnic children. However, within a local authority bid, educational projects would have to compete against large-scale construction, transport and other high profile projects. There was no ring-fencing of money for projects with minority ethnic populations. In the end very few local authorities included any educational projects in their Single Regeneration Budget proposals. The transfer of Section 11 monies to the Single Regeneration budget indicates the risks of not protecting monies for minority ethnic education by ring-fencing. Today in Scotland, where expenditure on minority ethnic education is not ring-fenced, there are big disparities in expenditure between local authorities. Monies for asylum-seeking children are also not ring-fenced within the English Children's Services Grant (and the preceding Vulnerable Children Grant) and again resulting in spending disparities.

Teacher trade unions and organisations representing minority ethnic communities launched vigorous campaigns to defend Section 11. The Steering Group on Refugee Education was active in this lobbying. The inclusion of refugee advocacy groups in the campaigns to defend Section 11 healed some of the divisions caused by the Local Government (Amendment) Act 1993 and placed refugee educational issues more centrally within the anti-racist education movement.

The strength of the campaign on Section 11 took the Department of Education by surprise. It responded by forming a working group on the education of children from minority ethnic communities – a token gesture to placate advocacy groups. This was the Task Group on the Education of Minority Ethnic Children. Its membership did not include anyone with expertise on refugee issues, and neither did it debate refugee education.

In October 1995 Peter Lilley, then Conservative Secretary of State for Social Security, announced that benefits would be removed from asylum-seekers who had lodged their claims 'in country' rather than at the port of entry, as well as asylum appellants. This policy change was eventually incorporated into legislation with the passage of the Asylum and Immigration Act 1996. The effects on children of this legislation are analysed in Chapter 5. The implementation of this legislation marked the point when significant numbers of asylum-seekers began to be housed outside Greater London. As a result of this population movement, the shortcomings of the Section 11 funding mechanism became more obvious. For refugee children, the lack of contingency funding was crucial: the Section 11 grant relied on a triennial bid to allocate funds, and children whose arrival in a local authority was unforeseen had no funding for EAL support. This problem was most acute in local authorities with the smallest numbers of staff, add therefore the least potential to redeploy teaching resources.

The allocation of Section 11 monies was based on historical precedent and there has been no open debate about how much funding is really needed to meet any additional educational needs of ethnic minority groups (Rutter and Stanton, 2001). Indeed, the adequacy of such funding was a discourse that was entirely absent from government, local authority or advocacy group text up until 1999, when the Home Office published guidance on bidding for additional educational costs of Kosovar children evacuated in the 1999 Humanitarian Evacuation Programme (Home Office, 1999b). For these children, local authorities were invited to reclaim additional costs up to a maximum of £2415 per year. Significantly, few local authorities bid for the maximum funding:

> If we had bid for the full amount, we would have set up a two-tier Ethnic Minority Achievement Service. Kosovars would have received a Rolls Royce service and everyone else . . . well, the equivalent of a battered Ford Escort. This would not have gone down well locally.
> (Deputy Head of a large local authority Ethnic Minority Achievement Service, northern England)

The Section 11 cuts in England and Wales also destabilised local authority work with refugee children. From 1994 onwards many local authorities began to issue temporary contracts to teachers whose posts were funded by Section 11. At this time, many staff left their posts. As mentioned previously, many educational projects for refugees were the result of bottom-up initiatives rather than top-down planning. When personnel move on, as many did in the period 1994–98, a number of initiatives were lost.

1997: new government, same education policies

As discussed earlier, the mid-1980s saw the ending of the post-war educational consensus. New Right educational discourses of this period assumed the weight of legislation with the passage of the Education Reform Act 1988. Further policy changes introduced the publication of school inspection reports and the results of national test and GCSE results, thus making schools 'accountable' to parents. Throughout the 1990s the dominant mantra emanating from central government concerned the need to 'raise standards'.

In 1997 a Labour government came to power with a manifesto commitment to increase educational expenditure and school standards. Two Labour administrations have re-introduced some discussion about equality and inclusion, and funded programmes such as Sure Start, initially targeted at the most needy under-fives. But at the same time Labour administrations have fully embraced the neo-liberal reforms of the preceding Conservative governments. In England, school league tables remain and the private sector has a greater role in education than ever before. The rhetoric about raising standards persists and the all-important measures of this policy are national test and GCSE results published annually in school league tables (Gillborn and Youdell, 2000).

Central government has not coherently engaged with debates about inequality and social class. Policy on issues of educational equality is marginalised and distinctly 'add-on' in its approach. As an appendage to the mainstream of education policy, policy on refugee education often runs contrary to it. One example of this is the Government's commitment to increase the number of academies as providers of secondary school education. Financed by private and public funds, academies operate as private trusts and are independent of local authority control. Crucially, academies can operate their own admissions procedures. One new academy, located in south-east London, which had previously had a school population comprising about 25 per cent refugees, chose to bar entry to all mid-term admissions in the year prior to launch as an academy.

Post-1997 Labour governments have also continued to sideline local authorities. Indeed, Government seems to operate a policy of 'local authority bad, private sector and school good'. One early victim of this approach was the Section 11 Fund. Soon after winning the 1997 election, the Home Secretary and the Secretary of State for Education published a consultation on the future of Section 11, with the suggestion that Section 11 monies move from the Home Office to the Department for Education. With Government committed to increasing school expenditure, the devolution of Section 11 monies directly to schools was the likely outcome of the consultation exercise

(Home Office, 1997). Indeed, Section 11 was replaced by the Ethnic Minority Achievement Grant (EMAG) in April 1998 with the Department for Education stipulating that a maximum of £150,000 or 15 per cent of the monies could be retained by local authorities, with the remainder going to school budgets. Additionally, total funding decreased at a time when the numbers of children requiring EAL support continued to increase. A Section 11 fund of £130.8 million in 1993–94 was cut to an EMAG fund of £83 million in 1998–99.

Today central government provides just over 50 per cent of the EMAG, while local authorities contribute the remainder. The allocation of the EMAG is still based on historical precedent, but the Department for Education and Skills is slowly moving towards a formula funding system (Department for Education and Skills, 2003b). In future, the size of the grant will be determined by the numbers of children with English as an additional language or who are a nationally underachieving ethnic minority group, with a small weight attached to the numbers of children in receipt of free school meals.[43] But the reliance on historical precedent to allocate funds means that today's funding does not match need. London local authorities, which have received the majority of post-1989 international migrants, receive proportionally less funding per child than do some northern local authorities with older established ethnic minority populations. This discrepancy is likely to continue for a long time.

Before 1998, local authorities employed peripatetic teams of EAL teachers and bilingual classroom assistants. While Scottish and Welsh local authorities continue to do so, the stipulation that 85 per cent of the EMAG has to be devolved to schools has meant staff changes in England. Some local authorities still employ EAL teachers directly, allowing schools to purchase their services. Other local authorities give most of the EMAG to schools who then employ their own EAL staff. While school funding is meant to be determined by need, in practice historical precedent again determines the levels of funding that schools get. It is politically awkward for a local authority to cut schools' EMAG funds – even when target pupil numbers fall. To do so would also involve EMAG-funded teachers losing their jobs or being uprooted from their usual places of employment. For these reasons, the full devolution of EMAG funds is an unjust arrangement in areas experiencing high levels of mobility among migrants (Rutter, 2003a).

Since 1998, the focus of EMAG funding changed to that of promoting achievement, rather than removing barriers to learning. The inclusion of non-classroom-based elements to support children was effectively ended. Indeed, the Department for Education refused to fund two educational psychologists and a social worker who were based in Enfield's highly respected

---

[43] Nationally underachieving ethnic minority groups are children of Black African, Black Caribbean, Pakistani and Bangladeshi origins, as well as children of black and white origin. Children of Turkish origin are not included. The change in grant allocation will move at a rate of 0.05 per cent of grant per year, so it will take a long time to move towards a formula-based allocation of the Ethnic Minority Achievement Grant (Department for Education and Skills, 2003b).

Refugee Support Team. This was despite their evaluations, which indicated that the complex needs of refugee children were best met by multi-disciplinary teams (Rutter, 2003a).

The devolution of Section 11 monies from local authorities to schools also weakened many excellent local authority projects and ultimately harmed the educational prospects of refugee children. In Greater London alone, seven local authorities made their refugee support teachers redundant in 1998 and 1999. The loss of these teams weakened local authority coordination on refugee children. Local authorities also lost voices within the central bureaucracy who were sympathetic to refugee populations, at a time when Children Act 1989 and National Assistance Act 1948 obligations had constructed asylum-seekers as a political problem.

Pupil mobility debates

As discussed in Chapter 5, the Asylum and Immigration (Appeals) Act 1993, the Asylum and Immigration Act 1996 and the Housing Act 1996 resulted in asylum-seekers losing their entitlement to permanent social housing. From 1993 onwards asylum-seeking children's mobility increased (Dobson *et al.*, 2000; Power *et al.*, 1998). The 1993 and 1996 legislation also increased the very uneven distribution of refugee children among the schools within a particular local authority.

Pupil mobility and the dispersal of asylum-seekers encouraged some local authorities to develop a new framework for supporting refugee children – the induction of new arrivals model of support. A new arrivals teacher helps find a school place for a child, ensures the family have access to other statutory services, settles the child into school, then hands over responsibility for that child to the school and EAL staff.

Continued lobbying from local authorities on pupil mobility, as well as publicity afforded to the research of Janet Dobson forced the Department for Education and Skills to take action. In 2003, they published non-statutory guidance on supporting mobile pupils (DfES, 2003a). This proposed that schools employ induction mentors to ease the integration of children who enter school mid-term. But this response is a further example of the real lack of coherence in central government's engagement on issues of inequality and social class. Central government failed to provide any targeted funding for the proposed induction mentors. More crucially, too, the Department for Education did not engage with other central government departments and thus did not tackle the root causes of much pupil mobility – shortages in social housing and the effects of asylum policy.

New Eastern European refugees

During much of 1997 and 1998, organisations concerned with the welfare of refugee children became increasingly preoccupied with the support meted out to new groups of Eastern European asylum-seekers: Kosovar Albanians and Roma. In 1998 around 7980 asylum applications from the Federal Republic of Yugoslavia were lodged in the UK, almost all of whom were Kosovar Albanians. Among them were 1549 unaccompanied children.

Many Kosovars arrived in the UK as clandestine entrants, having travelled hidden in lorries. The nature of their entry determined where they settled; local authorities in which sea ports and freight deports were situated often hosted Kosovan populations. Local authorities through which motorways passed also received Kosovan refugees. The Children Act 1989 and the National Assistance Act 1948 then provided the legal basis for support for asylum-seekers, including unaccompanied children,[44] obliging the local authority that first received them to offer support. This 'local connection' prevented most Kosovars from moving to London, as they would not receive sustenance and accommodation if they moved.

The arrival of Kosovars highlighted the inadequacy of support for unaccompanied refugee children. In England and Wales, the Children Act 1989 makes a local authority social services department responsible for supporting all 'children in need' living within its boundaries. There are two care options:

- The child may be formally 'looked after' or 'accommodated' under the provisions of Section 20 of the Children Act 1989. A 'looked after' child is entitled to a named social worker, care plan, independent visitor, education plan and support after leaving care. The usual care arrangements for looked-after children are fostering, residential care or supported housing where children are regularly visited by social workers. Fostering is most frequently used for younger children.
- The child/young person may be supported under the provisions of Section 17 of the Children Act 1989.

Until very recently a refugee child's age usually determined their support. Under 16s tended to receive support under Section 20, while 16- and 17-year-olds received Section 17 support (Free, 2005). The poor quality of Section 17 care was a concern articulated in much action research undertaken by NGOs (see, for example, Kidane, 2001; Munoz, 1999; Stanley, 2002). Recently, government policy has changed with a Department of Health circular (LAC 13) stating that the majority of unaccompanied refugee children are likely to need Section 20 support (Department of Health, 2003). Additionally, a Judicial Review, now known as the Hillingdon Judgement, found that Section 17-were supported young people had essentially been 'looked after' as defined by Section 20 and were thus entitled to leaving care support under the Children (Leaving Care) Act 2000. Today, most unaccompanied refugee children should be given support under Section 20 of the Children Act 1989, although in practice this is not always the case (Free, 2005).

---

[44] The UNHCR defines unaccompanied children as 'those who are separated from both parents and are not being cared for by an adult who, by law or custom has responsibility to do so' (from Refugee Children: Guidelines on Protection and Care; UNHCR, 2005). The UN Convention on the Rights of the Child and the Children Act 1989 define a child as anyone under the age of 18 years.

Action research also highlighted the unsatisfactory educational experiences of many unaccompanied refugee children (Stanley, 2002). Access to education is an issue: many 14- and 15-year-olds arriving in the UK failed to secure a school place. Research undertaken in the London Borough of Camden in 1998 indicated that at least 50 per cent of 16–19-year-old refugees were not in school or college, including the majority of young Kosovars (McDonald, 1998).

The first migration of Czech and Slovak Roma started in 1997. In both states, Roma had been the victims of increases in racist violence. They also faced considerable poverty and poor quality, overcrowded accommodation, some without running water or electricity. In the Czech Republic 70–80 per cent of Roma are unemployed. Most Czech Roma children have been effectively confined to special schools for children with learning difficulties. Similar levels of unemployment, as well as the same educational segregation, are experienced by the 500,000 Roma living in Slovakia (European Roma Rights Centre, 1997; Refugee Council, 1999b).

Many Roma made road journeys to the UK, entering through the port of Dover. Unlike many other migratory movements, most Roma asylum-seekers comprised family groups. In Dover, many Roma were housed in cheap hotels in the Folkestone Road area, which became known as 'asylum alley'.

Elected members of Kent County Council were active in lobbying central government for more money to support asylum-seekers as well as campaigning for amendments to the Asylum and Immigration Act 1996. Sir Sandy Bruce-Lockhart, then leader of Kent County Council, argued for a national dispersal system, as he felt that Kent had become responsible for disproportionate numbers of asylum-seekers. (The number of asylum-seekers per head of population was, in reality, far lower than almost all London local authorities.) The language he used to describe asylum-seekers was not inflammatory, rather a bureaucratic discourse, but it had the effect of constructing asylum-seekers as a costly population to maintain. This discourse was later magnified by less sympathetic elements of the national and local press, alongside other hostile media commentary. Local newspapers were the most antagonistic, with Roma referred to as 'human sewage' in one Kent paper. The coverage was so extreme that the Kent police warned the editor of *Dover Express* that he faced being charged with incitement to racial hatred.

Tensions did rise in Dover and schools were often a focus of it. Some parents in this largely white town viewed Roma children as problematic, needy and lacking English. They argued that the needs of the Roma and subsequent demands on teacher time would hamper the progress of their own children. Kent County Council was also subject to criticism by parents and some teachers for failing to make sufficient EAL support available. In the face of opposition, some schools in Kent made extraordinary efforts to welcome asylum-seeking children. But other schools, often under pressure from parents hostile to the Roma, refused to offer school places. In mid-1998, some 990 asylum-seeking children were without a school place (Kent County Council, 1998).

Schools with surplus places were breaking the law by refusing to admit refugee children. Kent County Council, too, contravened educational and race relations legislation in its failure to make school places available. It, too, invoked bureaucratic and budgetary discourses, thus masking the intention of not wanting to be seen to be too welcoming to the Roma. The Department for Education also failed in its duty, refusing to take a robust line with Kent County Council.[45] One interpretation of the Department for Education's failure to take action was that it, too, did not want central government to be seen to be making a public stance favourable to asylum-seekers.

The Commission for Racial Equality (CRE) was lobbied by the Refugee Council, the latter requesting a formal investigation of Kent schools, using Race Relations Act 1976 powers. However, the CRE also took no action.

The failure of Kent County Council to provide school places was discussed in issue networks such as the Steering Group on Refugee Education. Soon, teachers sympathetic to refugees volunteered information about other local authorities that were also failing to provide school places for refugee children. In one London local authority there were more than 700 children out of school in 1999. A neighbouring London local authority was unable to provide school places for 190 children of which 83 per cent were from minority ethnic communities. Nationally at least eleven local authorities were depriving large numbers of refugee children of a basic human right – their education.

But not only were local authorities failing to provide school places, they were also organising alternative educational provision for refugee children. At least eight local authorities ran alternative classes for children without school places. Such an initiative might be commendable if the education provided was full-time and children were exposed to a varied curriculum. However, the reality of 'alternative provision' was far from ideal. In two London local authorities it comprised three hours education per day delivered by one teacher. This schooling was delivered in a church hall.

In a Midland city, where the migrant population comprised asylum-seekers and children of overseas students, the local authority set up a unit called the International School. This was a portable classroom on the playing field of a secondary school. All children newly arrived in the UK spent one year in the International School, irrespective of their fluency in English. They did not have access to sports facilities or laboratories. A number of the students' parents were dissatisfied with this arrangement, moving their children to schools in neighbouring authorities. The Refugee Council lobbied the local authority, citing race relations case law, in particular the 1986 Calderdale Judgment.[46] But the local authority justified this unit, stating:

> We have a very mobile population of new arrivals. Head teachers don't like this and have refused to enrol them. We checked out the legality of

---

[45] Throughout this period, I kept civil servants at the Department for Education informed of the situation in Kent. In November 1998 I met Charles Clarke, then minister at the Department for Education. This issue was discussed, but no action was taken.

[46] This was case law generated by a Commission for Racial Equality investigation into the English language support offered to children in Calderdale, a local authority in Yorkshire (see Chapter 5 and Commission for Racial Equality, 1986).

the International School very carefully with the local authority solicitor.

(Deputy Head of the EAL service, Midland local authority)

The failure to provide a school place – a basic human right under the UN Convention on the Rights of the Child – became a normalised bureaucratic practice in a country that views itself as a liberal democracy. Local government officers called on bureaucratic and procedural arguments to justify actions that some people would regard as immoral.

The legislation of 1999 and 2002

The Labour Government inherited an asylum-support system that both local government and refugee advocacy groups regarded as chaotic. The Immigration and Asylum Act 1999 was an attempt to deal with this legacy. It profoundly changed the way that asylum-seekers were housed and supported in the UK; its impact on children is discussed in Chapter 5.

To prepare for dispersal, the UK was divided into regional groupings termed 'asylum consortia'. Some of the asylum consortia set up educational working groups. During 2000 and 2001 the Refugee Council lobbied the asylum consortia, proposing inter-authority projects, such as collaborative interpreting services or projects that worked with specific vulnerable groups. Inter-authority traveller education projects were held up as examples of collaboration. But to date, collaboration has been restricted to conferences and training events. The 'talking about trauma' model of support for refugee children has become the norm.

Further legislation followed with passage of the Nationality, Immigration and Asylum Act 2002 discussed in Chapter 5. Opposition to this act focused on the separate education of children within accommodation centres. That many asylum-seeking children failed to secure a school place at all was not discussed, despite its being another form of separation and affecting a far larger group than ever would be educated in accommodation centres. (Plans to build accommodation centres were quietly shelved in June 2005.)

The forcefulness of the campaign against separate education surprised both the Home Office and the Department for Education and Skills (DfES), with each department blaming each other for not anticipating the opposition:

We told Education about accommodation centres. They knew it was in the legislation. They didn't comment. If we had been told that it (separate education) would have caused such a furore, I think the Home Office would have reviewed this proposal.

(Home Office civil servant)

With the education of refugee children finally receiving media coverage, central government was forced to be seen to be active. OFSTED (2003b) published research findings from visits to 37 schools, highlighting much good practice. The complacent message that emanated from this publication was that all was rosy in the world of refugee education.

In England, the DfES introduced the Vulnerable Children Grant (now part of the Children's Services Grant) in late 2002. Comprising £84 million in 2003, this new fund supports travellers, asylum-seeking children and other children out of school (DfES, 2003c). Unlike the Ethnic Minority Achievement Grant, its monies do not have to be devolved to schools. However, there is no ring-fencing of funds for different groups, consequently there is variation in the way that local authorities use this money. At local-authority level the use of the Vulnerable Children Grant to support asylum-seekers depends on the presence of vocal refugee advocates within the local government bureaucracy. Where there are no determined advocates, monies are not allocated to this group, whether they are present in significant numbers or not.

In 2003, DfES commissioned a website on 'international new arrivals', now located on the website of the Qualifications and Curriculum Authority. In the same year it published non-statutory guidance on the education of asylum-seeking children (DfES, 2004a). At the same time, at least 2000 refugee children are unable to secure a school place, with the DfES failing to take robust action to ensure this basic human right is met. There has been no central government action to improve the educational experiences of Somali children – one of the most underachieving minority groups in the UK. Websites are no substitute for robust action and are a further example of central government's incoherent and add-on approach to issues of child inequality.

The end of local authorities?

The process of weakening local authority involvement in education has continued in England. Here, mainstream finance for education has been broken down into two separate funds since 2003. Around 90 per cent of monies comprise the 'school block' and go directly to schools. The remaining 10 per cent comprise the 'local authority block' and are allocated for the funding of local authority support services. For some local authorities, this has meant a cut in central expenditure and has limited their capacity to employ central teams to support refugee children and to coordinate welfare interventions.

Child welfare advocacy groups have continued to be critical of the incoherent approach to child poverty in the UK. Briefly, in 2004, the Government appeared to engage with this issue publishing *Every Child Matters*, a Green Paper on children's services, followed by the Children Act 2004. Both the Green Paper and legislation were prompted by the inquiry into the prolonged neglect, torture and eventual murder of Victoria Climbié, an eight-year-old migrant from the Ivory Coast. Prior to her death on 25 February 2000, Victoria Climbié and her carers had extensive contacts with hospitals, the police and social services, all of whom had failed to intervene to protect her or share information with each other (Lord Laming, 2003).

The Children Act 2004 requires statutory service providers – healthcare, education, social services and the police – to share information about vulnerable children. The Children Act 2004 also requires the integration of children's services by 2008. Each local authority is required to set up a children's trust, bringing together social services, education, primary health trusts,[47] the police, youth offenders teams and relevant parts of the local learning and skills councils.[48] The new children's trusts will be led by a chief executive and a board of trustees. When operational, they will plan and commission services for children. It is argued that this structure will improve communication between different agencies as well as better enable multi-disciplinary child support work, enabling, for example, social workers to be based in schools.

Children's trusts have been piloted, but there is little evidence of greater grassroots multi-disciplinary work to support the most vulnerable children. Crucially, too, the new children's trusts raise questions about local democracy, as well as the privatisation of welfare services. Put together with the Education Act 2002 and *Higher Standards Better Schools for All*, the 2005 education White Paper, they herald the end of the local education authority (HM Government, 2005b). In future, schools may receive a basic capitation from central government – the present schools block. Children's trusts may hold and allocate all remaining money for children's services, including special educational needs, health visiting services, school improvement advice and so on. An evaluation of the 35 pilot children's trusts suggests that a number of them are already planning to broaden the commissioning of children's services, inviting the private sector to tender for services (University of East Anglia, 2004).

Children's trusts sit outside the structures of local government and local democracy. Local citizens cannot vote to change children's trust policies and they have no right to select board members. With less transparent and accessible mechanisms of democracy, local pressure groups, including refugee community groups, may find it more difficult to lobby children's trusts on behalf of their members. Much vigilance is needed if the needs of refugee children are not to be quietly forgotten by children's trusts.

Alongside the children's trusts sit extended schools (new community schools in Scotland). By 2010 all schools in England will be expected to offer a range of 'extended' activities that might include additional schooling, homework clubs, arts and leisure activities for pupils, adult education, childcare and welfare support for children and their parents. The pilot extended schools have been evaluated, with this study highlighting two important issues. First, there is little agreement as to what should be included in extended schools programmes. Related to this there is an unresolved tension – whether extended schools should promote achievement or promote child welfare.

---

[47] Primary health trusts plan and commission primary healthcare.
[48] Learning and skills councils plan and commission post-16 education and training. They are independent of local authorities.

Central government disengagement

The media have driven the formulation of asylum policy within the context of influence – Home Office ministers, political advisers and an elite group of civil servants. Asylum policy, while sometimes clothed in the language of public good, has had one intended outcome: Government needs to be seen to be taking firm action to stem the tide of asylum-seekers.

As shown earlier there is little tradition of inter-departmental cooperation on refugee settlement issues. Settlement policy – education and health policy included – has usually been determined at a much lower level than asylum policy, with less ministerial participation and the involvement of lower grade civil servants. Using the policy trajectory model, most settlement policy is determined outside the 'asylum context of influence' by civil servants inter-preting Government text on asylum policy – the need to be tough – rather than by direct cross-departmental instruction (Bowe and Ball, 1992). Educa-tion policy for refugee children is determined by lower grade civil servants *interpreting* text on asylum policy. Given the perceived need to be seen to be tough, no Department for Education minister or civil servant would risk their careers by promoting large-scale interventions targeted at refugee children. There have been, therefore, no explicit central government policy directives on refugee education in the period 1989–2001. Since 2001, the few central government educational interventions for refugees have been secretive, with refugee children hidden from view by euphemistic terminology such as 'new arrival' and 'mobile pupil'.

In England, Scotland and Wales, mainstream education legislation and policy does not account for refugee children (or other vulnerable groups). Within the education context of influence, there is little debate about the needs of vulnerable children. Policy on social welfare and inclusion appears to be 'add-on'.

Central government structures and policy initiatives have also widened the split between the education of refugees and minority ethnic communities. This split has its roots in essentialist and reified notions of race invoked by the multi-cultural education and later the anti-racist education movements. Section 11 of the Local Government Act 1966, targeted at communities from the 'New Commonwealth and Pakistan', as well as structures within the Department for Education – the separation of the refugee team from ethnic minority achievement team – have also institutionalised the racialised divide between refugee education and the education of children from minority ethnic communities.

While the majority – probably 95 per cent – of the UK's refugee children is resident in England, child refugee populations also live in a number of Scottish and Welsh cities. Cardiff has a significant Somali population (dat-ing back over 100 years), swelled in the 1990s by the arrival of Somali refugees. Glasgow, Cardiff, Swansea, Newport and Wrexham have also received asylum-seeking populations dispersed by the National Asylum Support Service (Home Office, 2005a). The Welsh Assembly does not have legislative powers and the legislative framework for education and child welfare is similar to that in England. However, the Welsh Assembly has chosen not to devolve its monies for the teaching of English as an additional language to school.

Education is a fully devolved power in Scotland, with the Scottish Parliament passing its own legislation since inauguration in 1999. Parliament is supported by the Scottish Executive. In relation to issues affecting minority ethnic pupils, the Scottish Executive's Education Department has shown much of the disengagement manifest by the DfES in England.

To date, only Glasgow City Council has provided accommodation for asylum-seekers dispersed by NASS. In reality, it is the education department of Glasgow City Council that determines education policy for refugee children in Scotland. Glasgow City Council receives a *per caput* grant from the Home Office for its housing and support of asylum-seekers. Unlike in England this grant also funds asylum-seeking children's additional educational needs. Asylum-seeking children are offered EAL support in schools, funded by NASS rather than the Scottish Executive. Once immigration status has been determined and that child afforded Convention refugee status or leave to remain, EAL support ends. Migrant children who are not asylum-seekers supported by NASS receive more limited EAL support in school.

Despite the different legislative framework, educational issues affecting refugee children in Scotland and Wales are remarkably similar. Trauma discourses dominate, preventing analysis of other pre-migration or post-migration issues that influence children's progress. Somali children are among the groups who are underachieving. Scottish and Welsh schools, too, are not good at developing the academic literacy of children with more fluent English.

Constructing the hegemony

In the absence of central government engagement on refugee education, it has been local authorities and NGOs that have filled the policy vacuum. A central argument of this book concerns the hegemonic construction of the refugee child as traumatised. Key NGOs have been influential in constructing this hegemony. They include the Refugee Council, the Scottish Refugee Council, the Medical Foundation for the Care of Victims of Torture, the National Children's Bureau, the Children's Society, Save the Children, Children of the Storm and Salisbury World.

Many of these organisations advocate for refugees' rights and have thus been forced to mobilise humanitarian discourses, mostly the discourse of trauma, to argue for the sympathetic treatment of asylum-seekers. Additionally, the language of trauma has been invoked as an argument for greater healthcare and welfare resources. For local authorities, too, there is a financial incentive to label refugee children as traumatised.

A number of policy texts have been influential in constructing educational views about refugees – educational regimes of truth. Mostly published by NGOs and local government, they are listed in the Bibliography. A thematic analysis based on Foucault was undertaken and is given in Table 7.1. It yields important information about how the needs of refugee children are viewed by the education system.

Table 7.1 Themes articulated in 43 UK-published policy texts on refugee education

Theme	% of texts
EAL needs and pedagogy	39
Trauma and post-traumatic stress disorder	36
Need for in-service training on refugees	36
Securing free school meals, uniform grants and school transport grants	31
Heterogeneity of refugee populations	25
Difficulties securing access to school places	22
Home–school liaison	22
Destitution of refugee families	19
Translation and interpreting needs	19
Racial harassment and bullying of children	19
Need for induction procedures in schools	17
Vulnerability and needs of unaccompanied refugee children	17
Needs of children who arrive late in their educational careers	17
Physical health needs	14
Inadequacy of statutory funding	14
Home language issues	11
Ways of working with other support agencies	11
Somali children	11
Uneven distribution of refugee children between schools	11
Pre-migration experiences, other than trauma	8
Pedagogic issues other than EAL	8
Post-16 provision	6
Resilience and vulnerability	6
Gendered experiences of schooling for refugees	3
Special educational needs system	3

The discourse analysis indicated that key themes changed with time. Crucially, little British writing about refugee children before 1992 mentioned trauma. Discussion of refugee children's underachievement was absent prior to 2003. All of the texts present refugees as being a clearly demarcated group. None of the texts suggest that some forced migrants may also be irregular migrants, or might have economic motives for migration.

Around 75 per cent of the documents assumed an homogeneity of pre-migration and post-migration experiences. Those who wrote these documents did not appear to see refugee children 'ecologically' (see Chapter One). Only Somali and Turkish children received any separate discussion, although this was limited to a small number of local authority documents, generally written to secure funding. There was very limited discussion of pre-migration factors other than trauma. Prior education experiences were barely mentioned, apart from interrupted schooling. Very few texts discussed pre-migration background in relation to language, gender, ethnicity or social class. Social class, either before migration or after receives no mention at all. This is surprising, as class stratification is dominant explanation for children's educational progression.

Many texts stressed the need for training, with the suggestion that refugee children were different from other children –and in order to meet their needs teachers would need new skills. Seldom is this argument applied other groups of vulnerable children, such as UK-born children who have witnessed domestic violence. In many texts refugee children emerged as the exotic other, for whom teachers were ill-equipped to support without additional training.

Most documents articulated narrow conceptualisations of refugee children's needs: EAL support, trauma interventions, induction into a new educational system and measure to prevent racist bullying. Many documents, too, made policy and practice recommendations. However, they were usually of a very general nature and avoided political issues such as the treatment of asylum-seekers by Government or the lack of funding for EAL.

> Schools can play a vital role in identifying the needs and promoting the well-being of these (unaccompanied) children.
>
> (Camden, 1996: 2).

No-one would dispute that schools can promote the well-being of children, but such an assertion does not explain how to do this. Rather it is an example of an humanitarian discourse, as theorised by Harrell-Bond in her study of Ugandan refugees in southern Sudan (see Harrell-Bond, 1986 and page 143). Trauma discourses of a general nature are the same 'compassion speak' described by Harrell-Bond. They make educational staff feel that they care about refugees, but mask difficult questions about the way refugees are treated. Indeed, such questions were largely absent from the texts, including the uneven distribution of refugee children within local authority schools and the inadequacy of educational funding.

Local authority interventions

Local authority staff, mostly refugee support teachers, have also influenced educational understandings of refugee children. Within local authorities there appear to be a number of different conceptualisations of refugee children's needs:

- The trauma approach: that refugee children are a psychologically vulnerable group and need the interventions of specialist mental health providers.
- The special educational needs approach: that some refugee children have special educational needs as a result of past experiences, principally emotional and behavioural difficulties.
- The ecological resilience approach: that refugee children need protective factors put in place in order for them to develop resilience. Local authorities who adopt such an approach typically organise a wide range of different support services for refugee children: induction, EAL, host community awareness raising activities, home language classes, art therapy, horticultural therapy and links with mental health providers.
- The induction approach: that refugee children, often a mobile population, need a planned induction to a new education system.
- The race equality approach: informed by anti-racist education movement and discussion about 'race equality after the publication of the Macpherson

Report (Macpherson, 1999). Here refugee children's needs are seen as the need to ensure equality of opportunity in education.
* The EAL approach: that refugee children's needs are principally the need to learn English.

Using field notes and local authorities' own published policy text from the period 2000–04, conceptualisations of refugee children's needs were analysed. None of the above conceptualisations are mutually exclusive. It should also be noted that local authorities are not monolithic institutions, and there is often struggle between senior officers about approaches to take to support refugee children. It was also sometimes difficult to determine which conceptualisation was dominant. The results of this analysis are shown in Figure 7.1.

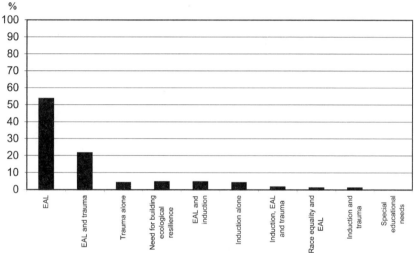

Figure 7.1 Local authority's conceptualisations of refugee children's needs.

Refugee children's needs were largely viewed as needing EAL support in 54 per cent of local authorities. Some of this group comprised local authorities with small refugee populations and no specialist refugee support teachers. A number were local authorities with larger refugee populations that argued that refugee children had to use mainstream services. Surprisingly, a large number of local authorities that conceived refugee children's needs as primarily the need to learn English were located in London. Many had received training on the psychological profiles of refugee children. But that did not change conceptualisations of need. Many of these local authorities were characterised by a response that comprised talking about trauma, but delivering EAL support as before.

The trauma approach was dominant in 12 London local authorities and 16 local authorities outside London. All but one had small refugee support teams, often employing staff on basic teacher's salary. Some of the refugee teams that advocated the trauma framework were located near refugee mental health charities or medical schools. Perhaps, too, viewing refugee children as a traumatised group is symptomatic of relative powerlessness to affect change within an education department. As discussed in the next chapter, trauma talk may be the strategy adopted by street-level bureaucrats – in this case EAL teachers – in situations of powerlessness and the financial limitations of funding for EAL. Discourses of trauma make a person appear caring towards the victim. This deflects from hard political questions about EAL funding or the refugee policy of local government.

Only five local authorities used conceptualisations of resilience to inform their support to refugee children. Unusually, the refugee support teachers in four of these local authorities were male – perhaps resilience may be more appealing to 'tough males'. One of the refugee support teachers was forceful in his rejection of a trauma paradigm, referring to the work of Summerfield and Bracken (Bracken, 1998; Summerfield, 1998). Additionally, all of the refugee teachers were employed at senior level. They had much more power to enact a wide range of ecological interventions in their local authority.

One London local authority and seven outside London adopted an induction approach. Typically they employed new arrivals teachers and had well-planned procedures for dealing with new arrivals. In five of these local authorities, this induction system had been set up in response to dispersal by NASS and was only made available to children who had been dispersed by it. Other groups of international migrants did not receive support and there seems little recognition that forced migrants may not always enter the asylum determination system. Such a determination of service by immigration status is arguably undesirable when migration patterns are complex.

Only one local authority based its work on conceptualisations of race equality. This was a shire county, where a local authority race equality officer was given responsibility for coodinating support for refugee children. That so few local authorities viewed refugee children's needs from the perspective of racialised minorities is reflective of essentialist and reified notions of race dominant in education, and the sidelining of the experiences of ethnic groups such as Albanian, Turkish and Vietnamese refugees.

No local authority conceptualised refugee children as having special educational needs, despite the dominance of the trauma discourses. This was a surprising finding, given that many educationalists appeared to equate refugeeness with post-traumatic stress disorder, thus the inability to function at school, thus a special educational need. But there has been a failure of refugee education specialists to engage with the world of special educational needs. Far fewer special needs teachers and educational psychologists have received training on refugee issues, and far fewer of them, reliant on their own special needs data, describe refugee children as being traumatised.

Policy into practice

So how do conceptualisations of refugee children's needs determine local authority interventions? Using local authority policy text, field notes and the minutes of the Steering Group on Refugee Education, the support offered by local authorities in Greater London was analysed for the period January 2000–December 2004. The results are shown in Table 7.2.

Table 7.2 Interventions to support refugee children in 31 London local authorities

Intervention	No. local authorities
EAL support only	9
EAL support and in-service training on refugees	9
Development of written local authority policy on refugees	7
Inclusion of refugee children in Education Development Plan 2002–07	13
EAL support and interventions listed below	13
Direct involvement of refugee support teacher in supporting refugee children's social needs	11
Employment of new arrivals teachers	1
Employment of refugee support teacher(s) within Ethnic Minority Achievement Teams	14
Setting-up of educational project for asylum-seeking and refugee children outside Ethnic Minority Achievement Teams	1
Employment of educational social worker to coordinate admissions for newly arrived asylum-seekers	5
Commissioning of child mental health support specifically for refugee children from the NHS, educational psychology service or a non-governmental organisation	4
Sustained work with special educational needs and educational psychology teams	4
Awareness-raising events for refugee children's peers	5
Delivery of training for centrally employed local authority staff	12
Delivery of school-based training	6
Production of pedagogic material	4
Assistance with school policy development	4
Employment of bilingual teachers and assistants[49]	6
Work to bring community groups into school	4
Promotion of home language teaching	3
Local authority funding of community arts or sports projects with refugee children	3
Local authority-funded refugee youth projects	2
Post-16 support	3
Early years work	4
Delivery of induction courses in schools	5
Targeted alternative provision in the absence of school places	8
Summer schools for refugees	2

The above analysis shows that only a small number of local authorities have developed broad ranging work to develop refugee children's resilience. Such interventions are usually not embedded in bureaucratic structures of local authority, and when staff move, they are often lost. The analysis also shows that many local authorities with large refugee populations have not changed practice in response to the post-1989 arrival of refugees. While educationalists invoke discourses of trauma, in 18 London local authorities support for refugee children comprises EAL teaching and little more.

---

[49] All six employed Somali speakers and one employed an Albanian speaker.

8

SCHOOL PRACTICES

This chapter analyses the school experiences of refugee children. Researched in five schools, it examines how their practices influence children's adaptation and progress. All five schools were mixed comprehensive schools located in urban areas in different parts of England. One school was a Roman Catholic voluntary-aided school, the remaining four schools were community schools. School records indicated that all were educating small numbers of refugee pupils in the 1970s and 1980s. At this time it was School Two that had the largest population of refugees, mostly Chileans, Poles and Vietnamese, although today it had the smallest refugee intake.

The refugee population in the five schools ranged from 5 per cent to 55 per cent of the total school roll. The largest refugee groups were from Somalia and Turkey (many of whom were Kurds) but there were refugee children from more than 45 nations in the five schools.

School One had 600 pupils on roll. The local authority in which the school was located is very ethnically diverse and contains extremes of wealth and poverty, with local authority housing interspersed with expensive properties. In the immediate environs of the school there is also a great deal of temporary accommodation: hostels and hotels for homeless families as well as privately rented temporary accommodation.

By the early 1990s, the school was experiencing falling rolls as a consequence of its poor reputation. Consequently, it had surplus spaces and started to admit refugee children from the temporary accommodation near the school. The level of pupil mobility in the school was high; in a year about 40 per cent of all pupils either enrolled at the school or left. Among refugee pupils, almost none remained in the school for their five years of compulsory secondary education. School One had a rather troubled recent history with school inspectors deeming its educational standard to be unacceptable.

OFSTED[50] placed the school in 'special measures' in the late 1990s and many teachers left at this time. An outcome of high teacher mobility is that few teachers in this school knew much about the home circumstances of children, or had detailed knowledge of the local area.

School Two was a voluntary-aided Roman Catholic School with about 1000 pupils on roll. The catchment area of the school comprised local authority housing estates and streets of Victorian terraces, many of which were rented and badly maintained. Nearly 40 per cent of the children in the school were in receipt of free school meals, a reflection of the poverty of the area. About 8 per cent of pupils were refugees, mostly from Latin America, Vietnam, Sudan, the Democratic Republic of Congo (DRC) and Angola. Pupil mobility within the school was lower – about 8 per cent per year. Staff turnover was also much lower. Links with children's homes were also strong, often facilitated by priests and local churches. Teachers in this school did appear to have a realistic knowledge of children's home circumstances, although this was sometimes framed in the language of deficit.

School Three had 1300 pupils on roll. It was located close to a large outer-city council estate and drew most of its non-refugee pupils from there. Of the five schools, this institution had the lowest proportion of refugee children. The majority of children who attended the school were white and working class, with few remaining in education after 16. Pupil mobility was 14 per cent. The school had a reputation as an institution that did not secure good examination results and like School One also had poor inspection reports. Similarly, the school had experienced difficulties in retaining teachers.

School Four was located in an area containing extremes of wealth and poverty. There were over 900 pupils on roll, of which half spoke English as an additional language and nearly half had special educational needs. Pupil mobility was high, with 20 per cent of children enrolling or leaving every academic year.

School Four was popular with local parents in the 1970s but during the 1980s its reputation was dented. Then in the mid-1990s, the local authority closed another secondary school, judged to be failing. Since then, School Four has gained the reputation as the 'failing' school in the area and has experienced a further fall in the school roll. However, School Four's reputation did not extend to refugee parents. Both Somali and Congolese parents chose to send their children to this school, judging it to be supportive of their needs. (Refugee parents whose children attended School One and School Five, also schools which were less popular with parents from more settled communities, also made positive choices to send their children to these schools.) These

---

[50] OFSTED inspects all English schools, usually at five-year intervals. Schools that fail their inspection may be placed in 'special measures' or judged to have 'serious weaknesses'.

findings challenge assumptions that it is only middle-class parents who possess agency and the means to exercise choice in education.

School Five was a mixed comprehensive school with nearly 1200 pupils on roll. The school was located in an area dominated by Victorian terraces and the surrounding streets gave an appearance of stability and moderate prosperity. However, the pupil intake did not represent the local population. Nearly 70 per cent of children were in receipt of free school meals. Ward level ethnicity data from the 2001 Census indicated that 76 per cent of the local population were white UK or Irish, while only 8 per cent of the school population were from these groups.

Pupil mobility increased in the late 1990s, with a 1999 school estimate suggesting a mobility rate of over 1000 per cent per annum. This means that every week 25 children either left or enrolled at the school. The head of EAL estimated that 55 per cent of pupils were refugees and 80 per cent spoke English as an additional language.

Annually since 1995 less than 20 per cent of students at School Five had gained five grade A*–C grades at GCSE. But there were four other schools in this position within the local authority. Because of this, School Five has escaped the label of a 'sink school' and had not experienced falling rolls. But there was very marked ethnic segregation within the local authority. White parents preferred certain schools. Two local schools had acquired the reputation as being the schools for African–Caribbean pupils. 'They see us as the Somali and Turkish school,' said a senior teacher in School Five, explaining that Turkish parents and children expressed a preference for the school. A parent governor in the school stated, 'The place has got a local reputation as being the refugee school. Lots of white parents avoid the school because of this'.

Commonalities among the schools

School Two was not typical of institutions attended by refugee children in the UK, although the remaining four institutions were more typical. In many ways these four schools were very similar. There were disproportionate numbers of UK-born children with complex social, psychological and educational needs. There was high pupil mobility, as well as high teacher mobility. In each school, teaching staff comprised a small core of skilled and dedicated older teachers, many of whom had worked in the school for long periods. But the majority of teaching staff in these schools were young and inexperienced, or overseas trained. In three of the schools, teachers lacked a knowledge of children's home circumstances, a factor partly caused by pupil and teacher mobility.

In each of the four schools, unpopularity with more affluent and settled families had increased during the 1990s as a result of the policy of parental choice in education, and publication of inspection reports and examination league tables. Hence they had gaps on roll and were able to admit refugee pupils who arrived outside the usual school admissions cycle. There has been some academic research on the uneven distribution of vulnerable children across a local authority, but this issue is rarely discussed in policy text (see Dobson and Pooley, 2004; Lodge, 1998; Mott, 2000). This is also an issue that central government has failed to confront. For the Department for Education and Skills an examination of this issue would mean admitting that parental choice does not work for all communities. For those who have constructed policy debates on refugee children – local authority staff – unpopular schools are all too easily equated with 'bad' schools. But it is the 'bad' schools that have often been most welcoming to refugee children. Labelling schools as unpopular tends to upset committed teachers.

An uneven distribution of refugee pupils between schools can also be caused by schools refusing to admit refugee children, despite having surplus spaces. Such an illegal practice has its foundation in the belief that a refugee child is problematic, expensive to educate, or will not secure the required five grade A*–Cs at GCSE. This is usually a covert process, the family told that there are no spaces:

> The head teacher has decided he is only going to take ten refugee children in a year. If more children come, he tells them there are no spaces . . . He has told me this. He says that he is acting in everyone's best interests, he doesn't have the facilities to teach them English.
> (Interview with a refugee support teacher in the local authority in which School Three was located)

In most English local authorities there are a small number of 'unpopular' schools whose intake contains a disproportionate number of troubled children. These schools usually have a culture that does not support learning. Highly motivated refugees soon become acculturated into the dominant behaviours in these schools. In four of the schools, pupil behaviour was poor and field notes include accounts of fights. At the end of one day of research, a fight between a group of Turkish and Somali students was witnessed. This later escalated, with weapons fetched and older brothers summoned. In two of the schools there appeared to be an underlying atmosphere of aggression, an observation also noted in school inspection reports.

Another commonality was high levels of racially motivated violence in the environs of four of the schools. The British National Party was active in the environs of one school; here a young Somali had been recently murdered by a gang of white youths. There were also inter-ethnic tensions in all five local authorities. In one, there had been conflict between young Somalis and young Bengalis. The police, youth service and a mediating project had been involved and the conflicts had been largely resolved. In four local authorities there were long-standing and rather fluid tensions involving Turkish Kurds, mainland Turks and Turkish Cypriots. Sometimes the conflicts were between Kurds, mainlanders and Cypriots. At other times, young men mobilised under the banner of being Turkish, and against Somalis, white and African–Caribbean youth. At times these tensions erupted into violence, sometimes within school premises. Schools denied there was an ethnic element to such fights, despite children perceiving this to be so. There had been no attempts at conflict resolution. These tensions continued to affect children's schooling, particularly their perceptions of safety and ability to identify themselves as Kurdish or Turkish.

The refugee children

As mentioned earlier, the children came from a wide range of national groups, with the largest being from Somalia, Turkey, the Democratic Republic of Congo, Sudan, Eritrea, Vietnam, Colombia, Albania, Kosovo and Sri Lanka, although the origins of the children differed between schools. Children's class origins were also diverse. Most of the Sudanese and Eritrean children were from the educated and urban elite. However, many of the Albanian, Colombian, Turkish and Vietnamese children came from households where fathers held unskilled or semi-skilled jobs.

The children: achievement and progression

Data on Congolese, Somali and Turkish and Kurdish children's test and GCSE results were analysed (other national groups were not present in sufficiently large numbers to draw valid conclusions). Data on children who had been in the UK for less than five years were examined, leaving a sample of 432 children. Achievement data from 2002 showed:

- In national tests at 14 years, around 11 per cent of Congolese children achieved Level 5 or above in English and maths (the expected level).
- Around 11 per cent of Congolese children secured five grade A*–Cs at GCSE.
- At 14 years, 4.5 per cent of Somali children achieved Level 5 or above in English and mathematics.
- No Somali children secured five grade A*–Cs at GCSE.
- At 14 years 18.2 per cent of Turkish and Kurdish children achieved Level 5 or above in English and mathematics.
- Around 3 per cent of Turkish and Kurdish children gained five grade A*–C at GCSE.
- At 14 years around 42 per cent of white UK and Irish children secured Level 5 or above in English and mathematics.
- Around 33 per cent of white UK and Irish children secured five grade A*–C at GCSE.

Reading test data were available for children.[51] Standard deviations around the mean reading age for each ethnic group were also calculated:

- Congolese children had a mean reading age 42 months behind their chronological age.

---

[51] Different reading tests were used in the schools. Four of the schools used the London Reading Test to estimate reading age, a test that was developed for use in multi-ethnic urban areas. One school used the Schonell reading test and a word comprehension test.

- Somali children had a mean reading age 28.2 months behind their chronological age. However, 9.8 per cent of Somali children had reading ages equal to or above their chronological age.
- Turkish/Kurdish children had a mean reading age 44 months behind their chronological age. Only 3 per cent of these children had reading ages equal to or above their chronological ages.
- White UK and Irish children had a mean reading age 11 months behind their chronological age, although 37 per cent of children had a reading age higher than their chronological age.

There was much more deviation around the mean reading age for Somalis, indicative of an achieving elite among Somalis.

Teacher records showed that about 25 per cent of Congolese and Somali children were not developing fluency in English. It is expected that a child will progress through the four-stage model of learning English at the rate of one stage per year, and acquire native-speaker fluency in 5–7 years (see Glossary). School data indicated that many Congolese and Somali children remained at early stages of English language despite having been in the UK for more than five years. The causes of this are examined in Chapters 9 and 10.

There was no significant difference in levels of achievement for male and female Congolese and Somali students in tests and GCSEs.[52] Neither did special needs data show any gendered differences. That there was no difference in boys' and girls' achievement was an unexpected finding, as a number of books and reports have constructed Somali boys as a problem group (Harris, 2004; Kahin, 1997). Nationally, there are also differences in boys' and girls' achievement – the largest gender gap being among white working-class and African–Caribbean students.

There were gender differences in achievement data among the Turkish and Kurdish community. In tests at 14 years, 13 per cent of boys gained the target grades compared with 22 per cent of girls, but at GCSE there was no significant gendered difference in achievement.

Congolese, Somali, and Turkish and Kurdish children's level of achievement was similar in the five schools. These children appeared to be underachieving in relation to other minority groups, including children of African–Caribbean and Bangladeshi origin, as well as white UK and Irish children. Only School Four had managed any sustained improvement in refugee children's achievement – an improvement in Somali children's GCSE performance from 0 per cent gaining five grade A*–C at GCSE in 2002 to 36 per cent in 2004. In all other schools Congolese, Somali, Turkish and Kurdish test and GCSE performance showed no sustained improvement.

---

[52] Statistical tests showed that the differences that did occur were due to chance alone.

Special educational needs (SEN)

Special educational needs are conditions that impede a child's learning and are generally grouped as (i) communication and interaction difficulties, which include language and literacy problems; (ii) cognition and learning difficulties, including specific difficulties such as dyslexia, as well as more generalised learning difficulties; (iii) behavioural, emotional and social difficulties; and (iv) sensory, physical or medical difficulties. Children with English as an additional language are not considered to have special educational needs.

In England, the Education Act 1993, the Education Act 1996, the Special Educational Needs and Disability Act 2001 and the Special Educational Needs Code of Practice provide the legal basis for the special educational needs system (DfES, 2001). Schools provide a graded approach to support, with children assessed as having the least severe difficulties supported within the school – perhaps by a classroom assistant or a special teaching programme. This type of response is termed 'School Action'. Children with more severe difficulties who need support from agencies outside the school are assessed as needing 'School Action Plus'. The greatest level of intervention is provided when a child receives a Statement of Special Educational Needs. This is a legal document, giving a diagnosis of a child's condition, as well as specifying the type of additional support a child should receive. Across England around 22 per cent of children have special educational needs (at all levels), although the proportions vary between schools.

All English schools employ special educational needs coordinators (SENCO) – teachers who have usually undertaken further training. Their job includes the assessment of children's needs, as well as the coordination of support for all children with special educational needs. The five schools had special needs departments of varying sizes. The level of qualification, experience and commitment of the special needs teachers (and classroom assistants) was also varied. Three schools had strong departments, while the remaining two schools had departments beset by high staff turnover and the employment of unqualified staff.

An analysis of special educational needs data for Congolese, Somali, Turkish and Kurdish children was undertaken and is given below.

Congolese

Around 56 per cent of Congolese children in the five schools had special educational needs, compared with 35 per cent of all children. Across the five schools, there was no significant difference in the proportions of Congolese children with special educational needs. Approximately 52 per cent of all Congolese children were listed as having speech and communication difficulties. This over-representation is discussed in Chapter 9.

Somalis

Around 44 per cent of all Somali children had special educational needs, compared with 35 per cent of all children. High proportions of Somali children were diagnosed with 'language and literacy difficulties'. This issue is discussed in Chapter 10. Only 3.7 per cent of Somali children were deemed to have social, emotional and behavioural difficulties. This was a far smaller proportion than white UK and Irish children, as well as children of African–Caribbean origin. It was also surprisingly low given a research literature on Somalis that stresses psychiatric morbidity.[53]

For Somali children there were also major differences in schools practices:

- School One: 22 per cent of Somali children had special educational needs, compared with 35 per cent of all children.
- School Four: 78 per cent of Somali children had special educational needs, compared with 41 per cent of all children.
- School Five: 31 per cent of Somali children had special educational needs, compared with 35 per cent of all children.

The Somali population was much more mobile in the environs around School One, with many living in temporary accommodation. School records, including special needs assessments, rarely followed these children as they moved school, despite legal obligations to do so. There were also real differences in how special educational needs coordinators assessed children in the five schools. In one school, children with English as an additional language experienced very long delays in assessment because it was assumed that their prime need was to learn English.

Turkish and Kurdish children

About 43 per cent of all Turkish and Kurdish children had special educational needs. Most of this group were diagnosed as having language and literacy difficulties at a school action level of support; only three of Turkish and Kurdish children had statements of special educational needs.

As with Somali children there were differences in practice among the schools:

- School One: 22 per cent of Turkish and Kurdish children had special educational needs, compared with 35 per cent of all children.
- School Three: 41 per cent of Turkish and Kurdish children had special educational needs, compared with 39 per cent of all children.
- School Five: 51 per cent of Turkish and Kurdish children had special educational needs, compared with 35 per cent of all children. Far larger proportions of Turkish and Kurdish boys had special educational needs: 53 per cent of boys compared with 44 per cent of girls.

---

[53] See Harris (2004) for a summary of existing research literature on Somalis.

There was an unexpected distribution of Turkish and Kurdish children with special educational needs in School Five, with few mainland Turkish or Turkish Kurdish children with special needs in Year 7 of that school. But in later years 49 per cent of Turkish and Kurdish children had special educational needs. When asked about this, an EAL teacher stated that the school had received a letter from the local authority that suggested that too many Turkish and Kurdish children were being diagnosed as having special educational needs. For the Year 7 intake the school had decided not assess Turkish or Kurdish students for special educational needs, unless their problems were severe.

The proportions, diagnosis and support for Congolese, Somali, Turkish and Kurdish children were compared with their white UK and Irish peers. In four schools Somali, Turkish and Kurdish children were more likely to have a special educational need, but less likely to have a Statement of Special Educational Needs or be at a School Action Plus level of support than a white child. Therefore Congolese, Somali and Turkish children were receiving a diagnosis, but limited support.

Data indicated discrepancies in special needs practices within schools. Consider 'Adam', a 15-year-old student who had spent ten years living in the UK. He was deemed to have special needs: language and literacy and reading age were judged to be those of a 10-year-old. 'Abdillahi', Adam's twin brother had a reading age of 8.07 years and appeared more vulnerable than his twin, but was not judged to have special educational needs.

In the five schools it was UK-born children that manifested the most disturbed behaviour and came from the most troubled homes. Across all five schools, very few refugee children were deemed to have emotional and behavioural difficulties – just 2.2 per cent of refugee children from all national groups received this diagnosis, in comparison with 5.7 per cent of white UK and Irish children. Across the schools there were no significant differences in the ration of refugee and non-refugee with emotional and behavioural difficulties. This makes it less likely that pupil mobility or misdiagnosis account for the lesser representation of refugee pupils among those with emotional and behavioural difficulties. The special educational needs system is the means by which children who are judged to have disturbed behaviour are assessed and supported. Although many refugee children were described as being traumatised by their teachers, special educational needs data did not support this assertion. Neither did classroom observation data and interviews with children. There were a small number of refugee children who were clearly not functioning at school, but most refugee children were largely not a traumatised and homogeneous group of policy text.

How teachers talk about refugee children

Previous chapters have examined how refugee children have been homogenised and labelled. Given that the school is the prime support institution, an examination of teachers' discourses concerning refugee children is of importance in understanding the process of labelling. It also throws light on how teachers interpret and recreate policy text (Bowe and Ball, 1992). The discourse analysis used a sample of 32 children from the DRC, Somalia, Sudan, Turkey and Vietnam. Their class tutor was asked to describe their main needs. Separately an EAL teacher was asked the same questions. The replies were coded and the results are given in Table 8.1.

Table 8.1 Teachers' descriptors of refugee children

Descriptor	No. children by EAL teacher	No. children by class teacher
Trauma	10	3
Emotional and behavioural difficulties	7	11
Isolation/social skills	3	4
Health problems, disability	2	1
Speech delay, communication	1	1
Language/literacy	4	5
Learning difficulties	2	4
Interrupted education	4	0
No support for learning at home	0	1
Attendance	2	4
Talented	2	2
Motivated/hardworking	4	5
Passive	2	2
No problems/average	3	4
Cultural conflict	0	2
Family problems	3	5
Family separation	3	0
Poor housing/socio-economic	2	1
Hunger	3	0

The results indicated that in most cases similar attributes were used by EAL and class teachers to describe refugee children. However, there were key differences. 'Traumatised' was the most frequent descriptor attached to refugee children by EAL teachers, while class teachers talked about 'emotional and behavioural difficulties'. Thus EAL teachers saw refugee children from the framework of trauma, while mainstream classroom teachers saw refugee children from the framework of special educational needs. Within schools, just as in local authorities, there were two discourse communities – those invoking trauma and those using the language of special educational needs. As detailed in Chapter 7, this discursive split has been caused by the failure of refugee education specialists to engage with special educational needs teachers.

Within the schools, the descriptor of 'traumatised' was sometimes used in a contradictory manner. There were instances where achieving and seemingly well-adjusted children were described as being traumatised. PTSD implies an inability to function, but one child was described as 'traumatised . . . hardworking and highly motivated, you could not wish for a better pupil'.

The Somali children were viewed as being most traumatised. None of the Vietnamese children were described as traumatised, despite one child having had a very difficult journey to the UK: many people died of thirst on a sea voyage, including the child's beloved uncle. All of the Vietnamese children, also, had previously resided in camps in Hong Kong, places known for violence and stress.

In all five schools Congolese, Somali, and Turkish and Kurdish children were underachieving in relation to their white peers. But this was not an issue that was articulated, despite the availability of the statistics. The achievement data on Congolese, Somali and Turkish and Kurdish children had been accessible for ten years but schools had seemingly ignored them.

There was little teacher discourse about differences in teaching strategies between the home-country and the UK. Indeed, in four schools teachers rarely discussed children's home country experiences. There was virtually no talk of pre-migration factors that may influence children's education in the UK, for example in one school EAL teachers did not know that some children, whom they identified as being Somali, were Bravanese rather than ethnic Somali. High staff turnover may have acted as a factor that prevented the accumulation of detailed knowledge about children's background and circumstances, but there was a culture of teacher inertia and a reluctance to question and research children's backgrounds.

Three teachers commented on refugee children being hungry and in two instances stealing food from their peers. It is surprising to come across such accounts of child poverty in 21st-century Britain. But apart from this, few teachers had clear ideas about children's home circumstances.

Teachers talked about refugee children more generally. These conversations usually took place informally, in settings such as staff rooms, as well as more formally in meetings. The ways teachers talked about refugee children fell into a number of discourse types:

- refugee-related ecological discourses – talk about the social conditions affecting the lives of individual refugee children, their background experiences and how this may affect their adaptation
- bureaucratic discourses – about educational funding, for example
- professional/academic discourses – for example, talk about curriculum, language acquisition, or theoretical discussions of trauma or resilience
- moral discourses – talk of right and wrong
- political discourses – for example, critical discussions of asylum or educational policy
- humanitarian discourses – discourses of pity.

These typologies draw from Foucauldian discourse analysis as well as debates within social policy – debates about the interactions between bureaucratic and professional behaviour within organisations (see, for example, Mashaw, 1983). The discursive formations were different from those used by refugee advocacy groups described in Chapter 1, although both teachers and refugee groups invoked humanitarian discourses of trauma. Among teachers, bureaucratic and humanitarian discourses were the most common. Professional and academic discourses were very rare – teachers did not talk about how they might adapt their teaching for children who might have little prior education. Neither was there any debate among EAL specialists about trauma versus resilience as academic concepts.

Moral and political discourses were equally rare. There was no talk of the rights or wrongs of their local authorities' treatment of asylum-seekers, or national immigration policy. The only moral discourse that was aired concerned asylum-seekers themselves. In three schools a number of teachers voiced concerns about whether some refugee families were 'bogus' or 'genuine'. There was a clear tension in some teachers between the messages they had received from refugee advocacy groups, such as the Refugee Council, and their judgment about individual families:

> People are asking questions about some of the Turkish and Kurdish families. They keep taking holidays in Turkey. They can't be persecuted if they are doing this.

Refugee-related ecological discourses were also infrequent. There was some limited discussion about individual refugee children, usually complaints about children's behaviour or poor work. Very rarely was there any dialogue about the pre-migration lives of children or their home conditions in the UK.

The most common bureaucratic discourses about refugees were those that concerned pupil mobility and the financial pressures of admitting refugee pupils. (If a child arrived and left between the annual school census, the school would not receive funding for that child.) EAL teachers talked about the inadequacies of government funding for their work, albeit in a very general way. They rarely discussed campaigning on this issue or how limited public monies for their work affected decisions about which children to support.

Almost all humanitarian discourses invoked vague and non-academic descriptions of traumatised children, and as noted above, were most frequent among EAL specialists:

> Omaar is such a traumatised little lad, he is so tiny and vulnerable.

Arguably, the trauma discourses fulfilled a key need in teachers. Faced with little power to develop broad-ranging support for refugees and limited EAL staffing, trauma discourses induced a sense of being caring. Trauma discourses are survival strategies used by street-level bureaucrats, 'techniques to salvage service and decision-making values' (Lipsky, 1980: 7).

Policy text from local government and refugee advocacy groups uses the language of trauma. Using Bowe and Ball's policy trajectory model, these documents interpreted in the *context of practice* – in this case, schools. Here text is received, interpreted and recreated, with trauma discourses predominating, because of the feel-good factor (Bowe and Ball, 1992: 9). A message that this school is caring then feeds back to local government, school inspectors and eventually to central government.

Twenty years ago, Barbara Harrell-Bond, an anthropologist and a founding mother of refugee studies, published a critique of humanitarian interventions to support Ugandan refugees living in settlements in southern Sudan. Her study exposed the ineffectiveness of many international aid programmes, arguing that poor quality services are often hidden behind the rhetoric of compassion. She writes:

> Humanitarian assistance is governed by compassion and compassion has its own mode of reasoning . . . It is the moral loading of humanitarian assistance which denies the need for review and prevents scrutiny. It is not simply that compassion overshadows logic and fact, although it often appears to do so, but rather that the assumptions that lie behind compassion are based on false premise.
>
> (Harrell-Bond, 1986: 26)

Trauma discourses in schools are essentially the same 'compassion speak' described by Harrell-Bond. They make teachers feel that they care about refugees. They make teachers feel good in the face of limited public funds. But schools go on working in the same ways as before, delivering very limited EAL support. There is no challenge to the status quo.

Interventions to support refugee children: School Four

Teacher discourse influenced interventions to support refugee children. Unsurprisingly, the school with staff most aware of refugee children's backgrounds had the most developed support for refugee children. This school was located in a local authority with a long-standing refugee support team. Teachers from this team had been visiting the school from the early 1990s, to conduct training and to help individual children. Unlike many local authorities there was a harmonious relationship between the local authority refugee support team and school staff. The refugee support team's work was also widely understood by staff in the school.

By the mid-1990s, the numbers of refugee children increased in the school. Lobbied by the local authority refugee team, the school designated one of the school's EAL teachers as refugee pupil coordinator. This post was located within a large learning support department, comprising EAL and special educational needs staff. The EAL team comprised a team leader, refugee pupil coordinator, two further EAL teachers and three bilingual classroom assistants. The latter included Somali and Albanian speakers. Although titled classroom assistants, much of their work involved supporting parents from these communities. Similarly the refugee coordinator also assisted parents. Such work involved taking on cases, as a social worker would do so, and helping parents gain access to healthcare, decent housing, English lessons and other forms of support. This work lay outside their stipulated role and formal job description. It involved advocacy on behalf of parents, advocacy which sometimes saw the refugee coordinator in conflict with her own employer – the local authority.

Within the school, the EAL team had invested time in developing induction systems. All new arrivals from overseas were interviewed and their educational needs were rigorously assessed before starting the school. Children who lacked fluency in English were placed in classes with a pupil who spoke their language. Where appropriate, students were placed in a part-time induction programme, running for one day every week. Here students were introduced to the routines of the school, as well as study skills and information technology. The induction programme also helped students learn their first English.

Refugee Week was celebrated within the school, with all pupils being involved in activities such as assemblies and displays. The school employed a counsellor and also worked with local refugee mental health specialists. The EAL team had also forged links with a number of mother tongue and supplementary schools – refugee and non-refugee – who used school premises on Saturdays. These links have benefited the school, as well as creating a feeling among refugee parents that the school belonged to them.

More broadly, the EAL department also offered some in-class support for the most vulnerable students, as well as partnership teaching with other teachers, whereby an EAL specialist worked collaboratively with the class teacher to plan and to deliver the lesson. From the perspective of refugee pupils, the EAL department in this school was different in a number of crucial ways. It was much larger than in most schools, including institutions where the proportions of bilingual pupils are higher. The department had a well-defined working relationship with local authority staff, including the refugee support team. Within the school, the EAL department had forged good working relationships with the special needs department and there were regular discussions about teaching approaches. The department had also been able to employ well-qualified classroom assistants with relevant language skills.

Despite high pupil and staff mobility, many teachers knew about children's family circumstances. The school implemented a system where all teachers had access to brief records about each child's background. Securing knowledge about children was also embedded within the ethos of the school. Staff asked questions where they did not know about children's backgrounds. More than this, many teachers seemed to have the ability to place themselves in the shoes of the children they taught.

The school was the only one of the five schools that had a written policy on refugee children. All schools are required to produce a school development plan – a strategic document that sets performance targets. Schools are also obliged to publish a race equality policy, a requirement of the Race Relations (Amendment) Act 2000. The school had targeted Somali pupils in its development plan, part of a long section on improving provision for bilingual and ethnic minority pupils. Its race equality policy mentioned refugee pupils and committed the school to engage in Refugee Week activities as a means of improving race relations.

Interventions in the remaining four schools

The pattern of support for refugee children was very different in the remaining four schools. In two, interventions comprised EAL support alone. In one of the schools, where 70 per cent of pupils came from minority ethnic communities, the Ethnic Minority Achievement Team was staffed by 1.5

teachers, both of whom were often asked to perform other duties, including covering for absent colleagues.

In the other school, EAL support was provided by peripatetic teachers employed by the local authority. At the start of the research, there was poor coordination between the local authority EAL team and school staff. Within the school, local authority EAL staff had little say in the placement of bilingual children within teaching groups and there was a tendency to put all children with EAL in low ability classes or 'sets.'[54] Later, there was a change of personnel within the local authority's EAL team. A more senior and charismatic teacher started visiting the school to give EAL support. She also had much more knowledge about refugee issues and organised some meetings with senior management within the school to discuss the experiences of refugee children. Plans were made for staff training and for a summer holiday club for bilingual children. A number of key school letters were translated into Turkish and Somali. But at the same time, the school was receiving adverse publicity because of poor GCSE results. The head teacher and senior staff then resigned and were replaced by a new management team. Securing better GCSE results and preparing for the next school inspection became the absolute priority. Plans for staff training and the summer holiday project were stopped.

The remaining two schools had organised targeted, but very different support for refugee children. Both institutions had seen a growing number of refugee children enrol during the early 1990s. One of the schools responded quickly. Its head teacher secured a small grant from central government for a programme of support for refugees. There was some initial staff training, which led to the school reviewing its induction system for refugees. The school also organised a pupil befriending system for new arrivals. Issues concerning migration and human rights were included in the English, drama, art and religious education curriculum. The school also attempted, not always successfully, to build links with child and adolescent mental health services. All this was achieved with little support from the local authority, which did not employ a refugee specialist at this time.

During the early 1990s, almost all the teachers in this school had a high level of awareness about issues facing refugee children. The level of kindness and sympathy towards the children also seemed high. However, academic standards were not high; GCSE results fell markedly during the period 1992–95. Following a very poor school inspection report, the head teacher and a number of experienced senior teachers resigned. A new head teacher was appointed and judged it to be a priority to attract more middle-class pupils to

---

[54] Able children had limits placed on their progress because of this practice. In line with setting, many GCSE boards offer 'tiered' GCSE courses, with students sitting the same subject at different ability levels. A teacher has to decide the level at which a student should be entered, effectively capping the grade that can be achieved. In mathematics, students may sit papers at higher, intermediate or foundation tier and the foundation tier cannot yield more than a grade D at GCSE. In this school refugee students with good mathematical skills were entered in 'foundation' tiers because the foundation classes were the ones where all bilingual children were placed.

the school. For this to be achieved the institution must not be seen as the 'refugee school'. One teacher commented:

> The head teacher does want to change the demographic of the school – attracting more As, Bs and C1s.[55] That is why we changed the uniform. They (the senior management team) don't see refugees as improving the school. That's why we don't want to go out of our way to support them, in case more want to come here.

Projects to support refugees were effectively dismantled and the school reverted to an EAL-only model of support for refugee children.

The final school was late to respond to the arrival of refugee children. The school saw marked demographic change in the early 1990s, and by 1995 around 80 per cent of all children in the school spoke English as an additional language. Despite this, only two EAL teachers were employed by the school. Apart from minimal EAL support, the only targeted intervention throughout the late 1990s was a GCSE Turkish course.

In 1999 the local authority decided to employ two refugee support teachers. Although they did very little direct work in schools, they did raise the profile of refugee children in the local authority, for example by speaking at head teacher meetings. In 2001, a new head teacher was appointed at the school. Improving GCSE results and getting through the next school inspection were priorities. A pre-GCSE coaching programme was put in place, targeted at children on the C/D grade borderline. (Two other case study schools also instituted such programmes.) However, virtually no refugee children were enrolled on the coaching programme, because they were designated to be 'beyond recovery'. Gillborn and Youdell write extensively about the effects of the 'A–C economy' on the way schools deliver their support. Their study suggests that in face of pressures targets on GCSE results, many schools are now adopting a triage system. All additional support is targeted at children who are on the C/D borderline. Those deemed unlikely to secure pass grades are written off, and this group includes a disproportionate number of children from minority ethnic communities (Gillborn and Youdell, 2000).

The new head teacher became concerned about the under-achievement of Turkish pupils and undertook a review of provision for them. A separate pre-GCSE coaching programme targeted at Turkish-speaking students was organised. More students were encouraged to enrol for a Turkish GCSE.

Funding for EAL support was very limited. Instead, the school decided to use other monies for mentoring to expand its support for children with English as an additional language. It set up a programme for new arrivals led by an EAL teacher but staffed by mentors. Bilingual children identified as most vulnerable were placed in a separate teaching group of about 20 pupils. Some children had little or no prior education; some had learning or behavioural difficulties. Children did make progress in this new arrivals group. However, the calibre of many of the mentors was poor; many were not

---

[55] From the Registrar-General's social classes: the professional, managerial classes and skilled workers.

educated to degree level and had received little or no additional training about refugee and bilingual children. There was also high turnover among this group of staff.

Other refugee children were supported in a small group teaching scheme. Each year group was provided with a one-hour per week withdrawal group for children with English as an additional language and other educational and social needs. The groups comprised about five pupils and were taught by an EAL teacher. But students had to wait for such support, as names for the withdrawal programme were drawn up on a termly basis.

Limitations on progress

The aforementioned accounts are from five different schools. In four of them, most refugee children were receiving EAL support and little else. This is effectively central government education policy for refugee children.

In all the schools refugee children's hegemonic construction as 'traumatised' also impedes analysis of their pre-migration backgrounds as well as masking the significance of post-migration experiences. In four of the schools there was no work to support parents as children's prime carers: parents who often speak little English themselves and face challenges securing healthcare, decent housing and work. Here too there was a view, held by many teachers, that projects to support refugee children would impede the school's prime aim of securing good GCSE results. Such programmes might attract too many refugees. It was also suggested that energy put into supporting refugee children of work might detract from teaching and administrative duties. The dominance of the school effectiveness movement within government contributes to the marginalisation of programmes to support refugee children. School effectiveness – measured by the proportions of children who secure five grade A*–Cs as GCSE – is seen as the means to improving the life chances of vulnerable children. Schools must get the GCSE results at all costs. Little consideration is given to family and community interventions and measures that may address social inequalities. Consequently, schools feel that their role does not extend outside the classroom.

An estimated 15 per cent of the refugee children had missed more than one year of their schooling. Many Somali and a small number of Congolese children had little or no prior education before arrival in the UK. Yet even this group received limited support. For 'Abdi' this support amounted to 18 hours in-class support during his first half term in the school, when he was taught to read, write, use a ruler and other very basic skills. After this, he was effectively abandoned and spent many lessons copying, colouring in pictures, daydreaming or disrupting the class. The level of small group teaching offered to 'Abdi' and other children with an interrupted prior education was insufficient to teach him the skills and concepts needed to make educational progress in a secondary school.

In all five schools, most in-class EAL support was targeted at children who had been in the UK for less than a term. Students who had achieved survival English rarely received extra support. It was left to the mainstream teacher to develop the English language skills of these children and to compensate for gaps in children's conceptual understanding. This would be a reasonable proposition of the remainder if the class were fluent English speakers, well-behaved and attentive. But the classes in which many of the children were placed were full of other pupils with multiple educational and psycho-social needs. In the case study schools there were too many pressures on most classroom teachers to enable them to give much additional help to bilingual children.

In the lessons observed there were few attempts by teachers to provide models of good academic writing and few activities where children's writing skills might be developed. Even able students had poor writing skills and seemed unable to express themselves in an academic register, instead using a playground register in written text. This finding was consistent with high proportions of Somali, and Turkish and Kurdish children who were diagnosed as having 'language and literacy difficulties'. In most cases, rather than having intrinsic learning difficulties, children's progress was limited by a lack of EAL support and too many pressures placed on most of their classroom teachers.

In many cases, too, lessons were inaccessible to children with limited fluency in English. The language used was too complex for most Stage-2 or Stage-3 language learners.[56] Classroom observation notes remark on the lack of visual cues in lessons in all five case study schools. Lessons observed included a history lesson on medieval England taught to a class of 21 11-year-olds, of whom 11 were newly arrived in the UK. The primary sources used in the lesson were extracts from William Langland's *Piers Plowman*, a poem written in Middle English. No visual sources were used. A geography lesson to the same class also used no visual cues. Lessons that did not provide social context or visual cues were very frequent in all five schools, despite most linguistic research showing that an understanding of social context speeds a child's acquisition of a new language.

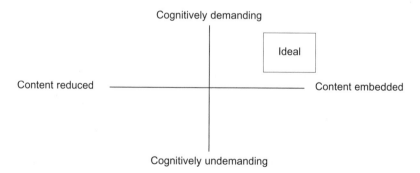

Figure 8.1 Cummins' quadrant of developing language competency.
Source: Cummins (1981b).

---

[56] See Glossary for information about the EAL language learning stages.

Cummins is among the socio-linguists who have examined factors that limit or enhance children's second-language learning. He suggests that children must understand the social context of their learning in a second language if they are to make progress. Context is enhanced through providing visual cues, using body language and relating learning to children's previous experiences (Cummins, 1981b; Cummins and Swain, 1986). He also proposes that teaching tasks must be cognitively demanding if language competency is to be developed, putting forward his often quoted quadrant of developing language competency. Despite this, much teaching in the five schools was cognitively undemanding, abstract and lacking in visual cues and context, thus limiting children's progress (see Figure 8.1).

The delivery of English language support

In the five schools, support for children with English as an additional language was given by EAL teachers and bilingual classroom assistants, both funded by the Ethnic Minority Achievement Grant. All the schools also used non-bilingual classroom assistants attached to academic departments to help children within the classroom. But their services were not well utilised, for example in one lesson the classroom assistant sat at the back of the room for the first 40 minutes while the teacher went through whole drills to reinforce children's understanding particular French verbs. Secondary schools need to re-evaluate the role of classroom assistants. Perhaps some of the monies spent on their employment could be better used to fund home–school social workers.

English as an additional language teachers coordinated and provided most of the limited EAL support. Today such an educational input can be delivered in different ways:

- In class, with an EAL teacher or classroom assistant helping targeted children with their work.
- Through partnership teaching, where the EAL teacher works with the class teacher, planning lessons and teaching materials together and perhaps team teaching a lesson (DfE, 1991). This approach can be costly in terms of staff time.
- Withdrawal groups outside the classroom. Many educationalists argue that this is a suitable intervention for children who are total beginners in English or have little or no previous schooling and lack literacy in their home language. Withdrawal can also be used to help students with coursework or help more advanced language learners with specific problems, for example, certain English tense forms.
- At a distance, by planning lessons and teaching material with individual classroom teachers. This type of input aims to develop the skills of other staff to deliver lessons that are accessible to bilingual children.

In each of the schools, EAL teachers were asked how they divided up their time between withdrawal, in-class support and the strategic development of the skills of other staff. The answers confirmed the very limited nature of EAL

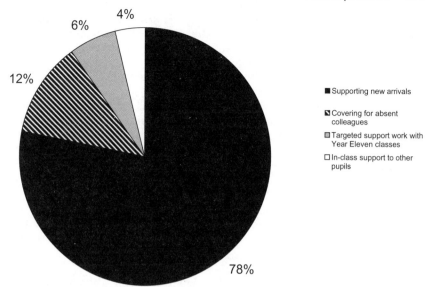

Figure 8.2 Per cent of scheduled lesson time spent on different tasks in School One.

support in schools. Figure 8.2 shows practice in School One, which employed two EAL teachers.

School One experienced high pupil mobility and up to ten new bilingual students were admitted every week. Much of the Head of EAL's time was spent interviewing them, finding out key information about their education and linguistic history, assessing their fluency in English, recording these data on a spreadsheet and communicating key information to staff and the local authority. This teacher had been in the school for 14 years and talked about how her work had changed during this period. In the 1980s she had been able to give more support to more advanced learners of English and she saw the demands of high pupil mobility limiting her work with this group.

Once children's fluency in English had been assessed, children were placed in a mainstream class. Here a child who was a beginner might get some in-class support during their first term. This was given in an *ad hoc* manner – EAL teachers were not busy with other tasks. Consequently, it was difficult to calculate how many hours of in-class support a child received, but at max-imum it amounted to a total of eight hours of support.

The two EAL teachers had much discretion about who would receive EAL support. Two factors influenced who would receive in-class support: children who were identified as potentially troublesome appeared more likely to get support and for this reason boys were given more support than girls. One EAL teacher told how Somalis and Albanians were identified as disruptive and thus received more help. Client preference was also a factor: a child who was seen to be a 'genuine' refugee and who was clever, well behaved and grateful also appeared more likely to get support. Children who were viewed as neither troublesome, clever or the grateful victim appeared to be ignored.

School One grouped its students by ability in Years 8 to 11. In most subjects children were divided into three ability sets. From the late 1990s, the new head teacher requested that the EAL teachers spent more time in the top and middle sets of Year-11 classes in order to boost the proportions of children securing five grade A*–C grades at GCSE. Other year groups were largely ignored. It was a triage system, similar to the accounts given in Gillborn and Youdell's research (Gillborn and Youdell, 2000).

Despite pressures on their time, the two EAL teachers in School One had developed a range of teaching resources for classroom use with children with little or no English. These were available to all staff to whom they also gave informal advice on teaching strategies. But this type of strategic development was sporadic and reactive. The head of EAL stated:

> There are many teachers who don't use our resources. Those who tend to work with us are usually keen young recent graduates . . . It is very difficult to work with whole departments . . . Staff turnover means that at the start of every year you almost have to start again with some departments.

The pattern of focus on new arrivals with little English was also evident in the other case study schools. It is also reproduced across London and in other parts of the UK which have experienced international migration coupled with high pupil mobility. Central government is aware of this issue:

> One of the findings of the Ofsted report on the introduction of the Ethnic Minority Achievement Grant (EMAG), *Managing Support for the Attainment of Pupils from Minority Ethnic Groups*, published in 2001, was that the increase in new arrivals in almost all the 12 local education authorities visited meant that some schools had stopped providing regular support for more advanced learners of English as an additional language (EAL). This issue is not confined to these 12 local authorities . . . Such an evaluation has resonance for many schools facing conflicting demands. Inevitably, many schools conclude that the needs of those bilingual pupils whose English is more advanced are less urgent than those who struggle to understand the curriculum. Facing the problem of deciding those needs to which to give priority, schools have to answer some key questions. For how long do bilingual learners need additional support? What is the nature of their support need? How does it differ from the language needs of English mother tongue speakers? And what is the best way of meeting this need given the available resources?
>
> (OFSTED, 2003a)

Government's response has not been to discuss the size of the Ethnic Minority Achievement Grant, but to suggest that class teachers need to be better at delivering lessons that extend the language skills of children with English as an additional language. While there is much room for improvement in teaching skills, Government should also acknowledge that teaching is a demanding job and that there are limits to the amount of individual coaching a child can receive in a class of 25 students.

Conclusions

An examination of the case study schools showed good practice. One school had substantially changed its practices in response to the arrival of refugee pupils. The school had done this in a manner that attempted to meet the ecological needs of the whole child, and in a way that increased refugee children's resilience. This was the only school that had shown any sustained improvement in refugee children's test and GCSE results. The remaining schools had continued to deliver EAL support to new arrivals and little else. This was also support given in isolation to the special educational needs system. In the remaining four schools notions of meeting the ecological and holistic needs of the refugee child, as well as promoting resilience were extremely marginalised concepts.

In all five schools Congolese, Somali, Turkish and Kurdish children were largely failing to make the progress expected of them. There were different reasons for this underachievement, some of which related to the pre-migration experiences of children or post-migration factors outside the school. These issues are explored in the next three chapters. But a major factor that did constrain children's progress was the limited nature of English language support in the school. Many refugee children were consequently diagnosed as having language or literacy difficulties and usually left school with few qualifications.

That refugee children received such limited help appeared discriminatory. In the United States, a key legal case established the discriminatory nature of such a policy response. In 1970, Chinese-American community activists filed a lawsuit against the San Francisco School Board after parents expressed concern about the level of English language support their children were receiving. *Lau v Nichols* resulted in the San Francisco School Board agreeing to provide bilingual education for Chinese, Filipino, and Hispanic children.

So why is there little pressure for change in the UK? The answers partly lie in Government's unwillingness to be seen as being supportive of refugees. But why has the discontent of EAL teachers in the context of practice not been manifest as sustained political action? Why are there no lawsuits that argue that Government is thus discriminating against minority ethnic communities? To answer this we need to examine the discourses and actions of our street-level bureaucrats – EAL teachers. Michael Lipsky in his bottom-up analysis of the policy making process argued that:

> the decisions of street level bureaucrats, the routines they establish, and the devices they invent to cope with uncertainties and work pressures, effectively become the public policy they carry out.
>
> (Lipsky, 1980)

Minimal EAL support for new arrivals has become education policy for refugee children. Lipsky examined the strategies used by staff to prioritise scarce public resources. Triage systems and client preference are all too familiar responses (Lipsky, 1980: 105–110). Lipsky also analysed how a highly motivated street-level bureaucrat dealt with the contradictions of being a committed public sector worker and having to ration scarce public resources. He suggests that alienation or advocacy are strategies that public sector workers invoke as a response to such pressures (Lipsky, 1980: 71–80). A few EAL teachers who worked in the case study schools did experience alienation. They expressed dissatisfaction with their jobs and the way that they were managed. Alienation was also manifest in the high levels of staff turnover – the endless quest for a better job.

Two EAL staff opted for advocacy. They were involved in refugee campaigns. They also took on casework, helping refugee children and their families with immigration, housing and welfare rights problems. These staff risked burnout. But most EAL teachers were neither alienated workers, nor 'activist advocates'. They were compassionate individuals, but individuals who did not argue for more resources. Trauma discourses, because they invoked a sense of being compassionate, were survival strategies that they mobilised to appease their conscience and salvage their public sector values. Trauma discourses were codes for the powerlesness of teachers. More crucially, trauma discourses camouflaged a poor quality education that so many refugee children received. It is very difficult to be critical of a system staffed by personnel who appear to be so caring.

PART THREE:
COMMUNITY CASE
STUDIES

THE ELUSIVENESS OF INTEGRATION: THE EDUCATIONAL EXPERIENCES OF CONGOLESE REFUGEE CHILDREN

The last years of the 20th century saw the arrival of a Congolese community in the UK. The majority of this new African diaspora have their origins in the Democratic Republic of Congo (formerly Zaire). A smaller number of people from Congo-Brazzaville (the Republic of Congo) have also arrived in the UK, most of them after 1997. No accurate demographic data exist on the size of these two national groups, but it is likely that at least 15,000 people from the Democratic Republic of Congo (DRC) now live in Greater London alone, with other researchers giving higher estimates (Rutter, 2004a: 217; Styan, 2003).

Congolese children are a significant group in schools in parts of London, particularly in the London boroughs of Camden, Islington, Haringey and Newham. Until 2003, there were no data or articulation of specific problems encountered by these children. Indeed, the assumption made by refugee agencies was that the Congolese community were well educated and their children were generally 'doing well' at school. This chapter disproves this complacent belief and argues that Congolese children's lack of educational progress is largely caused by specific linguistic and social factors.

Causes of flight

The DRC achieved independence from Belgium in 1960. Between 1965 and 1997 the country experienced the dictatorial rule of President Mobutu and almost all opposition was suppressed. In 1989, student demonstrations were held in Kinshasa and Lubumbashi against increases in the cost of living. Over 50 students were killed and others forced to flee the country. The repression of students and political opposition continued throughout 1990 and 1991. It was this that caused the first Congolese asylum-seekers to flee to the UK.

Mobutu left Zaire for cancer treatment in 1996 and died in 1997. Soon after rebels, led by Laurent Kabila, grouped in north-east Zaire and formed the Alliance des Forces Democratiques pour la Liberation du Congo-Zaire (AFDL). They swept though Zaire and, in 1997, entered the capital and seized power. Zaire was renamed the Democratic Republic of Congo. The new regime announced that elections would be held in April 1999. However, a ban was soon imposed on all political activity and key opposition leaders were not integrated into the new Government.

In 1998, another rebellion started in eastern Congo, with a new group – the *Rassamblement Congolaise pour la Democratie* – seeking to oust the Government. Since then there has been intense conflict in many parts of eastern Congo. Human rights violations are as serious as in Mobutu's time. At least 3.3 million people have been killed or have died of starvation and disease caused by the breakdown of food supply and health services. Although a peace agreement has been signed, parts of eastern DRC continue to experience conflict. Local warlords play on ethnic differences. Their illegal control of diamonds, coltan and other mineral wealth prolong the war by paying for small arms. The DRC is a failed state in every sense: outside the environs of Kinshasa central government has little control and public services such as healthcare, education, water and sanitation are virtually non-existent.

Congo-Brazzaville has also experienced conflict and the flight of refugees. The country gained its independence in 1960 but the first democratic elections were not held until 1992. But the following year saw fighting between government forces and the opposition over disputed parliamentary elections. In 1997, Denis Sassou-Nguesso toppled Pascal Lissouba, the elected president. Civil war soon engulfed the country, with supporters of Lissouba fighting government forces and allied militia. Fighting flared up again in late 1998. After peace talks in 1999 the fighting ceased and over 800,000 displaced people returned home. In March 2002 fighting flared up again after Sassou-Nguesso won a landslide victory in elections. All sides in the conflict have been engaged in killing and looting. There are many arbitrary arrests. Journalists and human rights activists are threatened. Brazzaville lies in ruins and refugees have fled over the River Congo to neighbouring Kinshasa, as well as to Europe.

Community leaders based in London have identified different migratory movements to the UK. The first arrivals from the DRC comprised political opponents of the Mobutu regime, journalists and student activists, particularly those studying in Kinshasa and Lubumbashi. Soon after a second migration – 'people from lower socio-economic classes' – began to seek asylum in the UK. This group of people were largely from Kinshasa and their arrival appeared to be mediated by existing social networks in the UK (Koser, 1997). Their motives for migration were also complex; security and the existence of a welfare safety net appear to be pull factors:

Letters went home saying that it was not bad in the UK, you could get treated if you were sick, schools were OK.

(Congolese community leader, London)

Asylum applications from the DRC decreased in 1993, although they have increased since 1999. Post-1999 arrivals include those associated with the Mobutu regime. However, greater numbers of recent arrivals are former traders and business people – the new commercial class – who have come from all parts of the DRC. Advice workers in two Congolese community organisations have stated that:

> The recent arrivals we see are mostly from outside Kinshasa. They come from families that have money, but are not well-educated. These people mostly went to private schools. When the (Mobutu) government fell, these people made a lot of money. They stayed on in the Congo, and ran their businesses, but now the situation has got much worse and they have decided they must go. They have come from all parts of the Congo, all over, sometimes from towns deep in the forest.

The UK has also admitted Congolese in resettlement programmes organised through UNHCR. This group have their origins in the eastern parts of the DRC and have fled intense fighting. These experiences as well as their linguistic background make them a very different population from the Congolese who came in 1990 and 1991.

The arrival of Congolese in the UK illustrates the complexity of migratory movements and the lack of demarcation between forced and voluntary migration. Their migration has involved different social classes migrating at different times – with better educated pioneer migrants arriving first, afterwards facilitating the migration of less wealthy and often less well-educated co-nationals. Thus the educational profile of refugee and migrant communities can change over a period of time – an issue to which policy makers need to respond.

The Congolese people: social class, ethnicity and language

Class identity plays a role in the lives of Congolese, in Africa or in exile since the DRC has become an increasingly class-stratified society (Nzongola-Ntalaja, 2002; Schatzberg, 1988). Class identities reproduce themselves in exile where there is often a tension between the activists who lead refugee organisations and the less educated Congolese. Nevertheless, there is little discussion about class among the large refugee agencies. The DRC is also a patriarchal society and rarely do women occupy positions of authority. About 30 per cent of boys progress to secondary education, but only 10 per cent of girls do so (US Department of State, 2002). In the UK, Congolese women are more likely to have had little or no education than men, an issue which may prevent mothers being involved in their children's schooling.

An understanding of Congolese children's educational experiences in the UK requires knowledge of their linguistic background. The population of the DRC is diverse and there are over 200 ethnic groups resident in the country, the largest being the Kikongo, Luba and Mongo. While ethnic allegiance plays a part in politics in the DRC, a legacy of both Patrice Lumumba and Mobutu is a sense of Congolese national identity.

French is the official language of the DRC and most books and print media are in the French language. It is the official medium of education, although in school classrooms teachers will frequently use the local language. Fluency in French depends on how long a person has spent at school. The use of French is associated with high social status, more so in the DRC than the more urbanised Congo-Brazzaville.

Four other languages had official status in the DRC of Mobutu's time: Kiswahili, Tshiluba, Kikongo and Lingala. Of these languages, Lingala is the most widely spoken. It is also the most widely spoken language among Congolese living in the UK. Here very few families – only those from the most highly educated elite – use French as a home language.

Lingala developed from the Mangala language, spoken by the Ngala who lived on the River Congo near Mbandaka and Nouvelle Anvers. River trade ensured that the language spread upriver and downriver long before European colonists arrived. Throughout the 19th century this trading pidgin[57] developed into Lingala and was later scripted in the Roman alphabet and standardised. Both grammar, vocabulary and word formation were changed as a result of this process.

Army recruitment in middle Congo ensured that Lingala became the language of the army – new recruits were required to know 600 words of Lingala (Dalby, 1998). Lingala was the only language used by Mobutu in his popular addresses. Truck drivers further extended Lingala's prevalence, as did its use as in popular music. Today Lingala is the dominant language of middle Congo, Kinshasa, and many other urban areas. In Kinshasa, Lingala has replaced Kikongo as the most widely spoken language. But many of Kinshasa's inhabitants are trilingual, speaking Lingala, Kikongo and French. In cities such as Kinshasa, people will use different languages in different situations. French is the language used among the educated elite. Lingala (and sometimes Kikongo) is the language of the home and the street. Parents and children, however, will use borrowed French words in everyday speech.

There is a now a standard form of Lingala in the DRC, taught in schools and used in newspapers and radio. Standard Lingala differs from 'street Lingala' – the spoken form. The latter has many regional variations, as a result of contact with other languages. Congolese children in the UK will have relatively little contact with standard Lingala, but will reproduce the street Lingala of their families.

The main ethnic group in Congo-Brazzaville are also the Kikongo, comprising about 48 per cent of the population, mostly living in the south of the country. Congo-Brazzaville is one of the most urbanised countries in Africa, with 85 per cent of the population living in Brazzaville or Pointe Noire. French is also the official language of Congo-Brazzaville and the medium of

---

[57] A pidgin language develops when speakers of two different languages need to communicate, but without the conditions for in-depth language learning. Pidgins usually have limited vocabularies – just enough for the circumstances in which they are used. Creoles are the offspring of pidgin languages and develop when a pidgin becomes the first language of some people (Dalby, 1998).

education, although in classrooms teachers will frequently use the local language. School enrolment is much higher than in the neighbouring DRC, a reflection of a more urbanised population. In 1997, UN estimations of literacy rates in Congo-Brazzaville were 89 per cent for males and 79 per cent for females, consequently the use of French is more widespread. Other major languages include Lingala and Kikongo and its variants. Kituba is widely spoken in Brazzaville. This is a creolised version of Kikongo and has been influenced by French and Lingala.

The Congolese community in the UK

Almost all Congolese living in the UK are asylum migrants. However, the treatment of asylum-seekers from the DRC and Congo-Brazzaville has been a cause for concern to refugee and human rights organisations for many years. Despite the grave deterioration in the security situation post-1997, the Home Office continues to refuse most asylum applications (see Tables 9.1 and 9.2). In August 1998 the Home Office suspended the removal of 'failed' Congolese asylum-seekers and has extended this suspension of removal at periodic intervals since then. Government considered it too unsafe to remove them. This policy effectively left over 3500 people in limbo. One community informant stated:

> We have hundreds of clients who have been refused asylum and been refused appeals, but the Home Office keeps giving them six month extensions on their stays and extending their IS96s. [IS96 is a Home Office form acknowledging its bearer is an asylum-seeker and giving temporary admission to the UK.]

Local authority refugee coordinators have commented on the worry this causes families, with anxieties often affecting the welfare of children. Although some Congolese were granted permanent residence in the UK in October 2003, in a file-clearing exercise, many more Congolese asylum applicants remain in this indeterminate state.

Table 9.1 Asylum applications and decisions, Democratic Republic of Congo

Year	Applications	Refugee status (%)	ELR/HP/DL	Refusal (%)
1989	525	81	3	16
1990	2590	9	4	87
1991	7010	1	1	99
1992	880	1	1	99
1993	635	1	1	99
1994	775	1	1	99
1995	935	1	1	98
1996	680	1	3	96
1997	690	7	13	80
1998	660	2	77	21
1999	1240	15	40	45
2000	1030	11	14	75
2001	1385	13	14	73

2002	2315	4	11	85
2003	1540	5	10	85
2004	1460	3	10	87
2005	1060	8	22	70

Table 9.2 Asylum applications and decisions, Congo Brazzaville

Year	Applications	Refugee Status (%)	ELR/HP/DL	Refusal (%)
2002	600	8	13	79
2003	355	0	10	90
2004	165	4	9	87
2005	70	0	0	100

Source: Home Office Asylum Statistics. Since April 2003, Exceptional Leave to Remain (ELR) has been replaced with Humanitarian Protection (HP) and Discretionary Leave (DL). There have been very few grants of HP for Congolese.

The 2001 Census showed that 81 per cent of the UK's Congolese lived in Greater London. Within London, the greatest populations of those born in the DRC and Congo-Brazzaville were resident in the London boroughs of Newham and Haringey. Other local authorities with significant Congolese communities are Barking and Dagenham, Croydon, Merton, Camden, Islington, Hackney and Redbridge (Office of National Statistics, 2002). An analysis of school language statistics in 2002 showed 2786 Congolese children in schools in Greater London, with 34 per cent of them at schools in Haringey. The numbers of Congolese children in Haringey and Islington schools have increased since the late 1990s, suggesting some secondary migration of Congolese families to this part of London.

Two studies of Congolese refugees have been undertaken: a large-scale needs analysis of refugees in Haringey and the earlier survey in Islington (Haringey, London Borough of, 1997; Healthy Islington 2000; 1994a). Both research projects included data about refugees pre-migration experiences and current needs. However, both surveys used a snowballing technique to select their sample for interview. Congolese community leaders were asked to find refugees for interview. Snowballing as a way of sampling refugees has attracted criticism as the sample selected for interview may be biased towards those associated with community groups (Bloch, 1999). The sample may not include 'hidden' elements of refugee communities – those working full time, the less well-educated, those from different political groups, minority populations within refugee communities, those fearful of authorities and those who have disappeared after a negative asylum decision.

Both surveys identify issues relevant to children's education and welfare:

- Around 47.8 per cent of the Congolese in the Haringey sample had started a university course, a proportion much higher than any other group surveyed. But 17.39 per cent of those interviewed also had no education at all (a proportion also higher than many of the other refugee groups surveyed). The Congolese in Haringey fell into two groups: the well-educated and those who have had little or no education.

- Around 23 per cent of Congolese could not read and write French and 45 per cent could not read and write Lingala.

Community informants describe the stigma of illiteracy, as well as the status associated with speaking French. It should be noted that throughout the UK there are very few English language courses targeted at those who are not literate in their home language – most college teaching assumes prior literacy.

The research conducted in Haringey indicated that unemployment was a major issue facing Congolese in London. Since this research was undertaken, more Congolese resident in London have secured work, often facilitated by their social networks. Outside London unemployment among the Congolese remains high (Greater London Authority, 2005). Most Congolese are employed in low paid, service-sector jobs, for example as cleaners. Private security firms and London Transport were other major employers – there is a team of Congolese 'fluffers' who nightly clean dust from London's underground train tracks.

There has also been research on health issues affecting the Congolese (Healthy Islington 2000, 1994a). These include sickle cell anaemia and HIV/AIDS. In the DRC the rate of HIV infection is estimated at 20 per cent of the adult population and about 10 per cent of all infants have been vertically infected with HIV (Royal College of Paediatrics and Child Health, 1999). In the UK, anti-retroviral drugs have extended the life expectancy of those with AIDS. As well as drug treatment, a range of social support is available to individuals and families affected by HIV/AIDS. However, community informants indicate that many Congolese adults are not taking up HIV testing, treatment and social support because of fears of stigmatisation. The fear that HIV/AIDS will prevent an award of refugee status or leave to remain is also a significant factor that stops the uptake of testing and treatment and can only worsen as a result of press coverage calling for HIV tests for all asylum-seekers:

> People will not come forward and say they have AIDS or are HIV positive. They just say 'I don't feel well.' I went to a meeting with Ugandans and people were saying they were HIV positive. You would never get that with the Congolese.
>
> (Congolese worker at a community group)

There are a number of community groups which support Congolese living in the UK, mostly based in Greater London. The close cultural and linguistic links mean that Congolese from the DRC and Congo-Brazzaville use the same community organisations. All of the funded Congolese community groups are working with young people. This is in contrast to most other refugee organisations, where work with children is rather infrequent, usually because emergency issues such as immigration and housing take higher priority. In London, Congolese community groups are running youth clubs, sports and cultural activities and parent–child mediation. The London Borough of Haringey places a 'parental outreach worker' in one community organisation, who support parents and carers and develops links between them and their children's schools.

In addition to community groups, there are a number of other foci of Congolese community life. These include shops run by the Congolese and four London-based news publications, including *L'Eclaireur*, a political paper.

There is also a vibrant Congolese music scene in London and performances attract a big attendance (Styan, 2003).

Churches also play a major role in the lives of many Congolese in the UK. Indeed, the leisure activities of many families mostly consisted of church attendance. A small number of Congolese attend Roman Catholic churches, but the majority of church-going Congolese go to African-led Evangelical, Pentecostal or charismatic congregations. There are over 30 such churches serving the Congolese community in London, and other congregations in Birmingham and the North West. The Pastor is usually supported by the congregation's donations and many of these churches have links with congregations in Africa.

Church attendance appears to be stronger among Congolese who are less well-educated. That such a large proportion of Congolese do attend church reflects the need for comfort and support. However, some community leaders express concerns about the role of churches – in particular requirements to make financial donations to the pastor, as well as the messianic and spiritual aspects of religious practice.

Media attention was focused on these churches in 2005, following the conviction for child cruelty of three Congolese refugees resident in the UK. An eight-year-old orphan girl was tortured by her relatives after being accused of witchcraft. Following the conviction, a Metropolitan Police report alleging that hundreds of African children were being trafficked into the UK to be sacrificed in religious ceremonies was leaked to the BBC ('Boys used for human sacrifice', Angus Stickler, BBC News, 16.6.05). The report was based on hearsay and later withdrawn by the Metropolitan Police. However, child exorcism does sometimes take place in the UK – within many communities. Community leaders, journalists, academics and aid agencies have raised concerns about this for a number of years, but with no response from statutory services (see, for example, 'Child witches in Congo', Jeremy Vine, BBC News, 12.10.99). Sometimes exorcism takes place in a church, more frequently a child is taken to a spiritual healer, whose services may be advertised in newspapers such as the *Evening Standard* and *The Voice*.

Whether in the DRC or in the UK, belief in spiritual possession thrives in conditions of poverty, poor education and where people feel they have little control over their lives. Sita Kisanga, one of the three Congolese convicted for child cruelty, had been a refugee in Angola before coming to the UK. She was illiterate, unemployed and unsupported by social welfare agencies. Arguably, the abuse of children and the exploitation of vulnerable people by pastors and spiritual healers will only cease when people feel secure in their financial and immigration status within the UK.

Congolese children's education and welfare

Until recently there has been no research about the experiences of Congolese children in the UK, or in other western European countries. However, in 2002, staff employed in a refugee education team in a London local authority began to document concerns about Congolese children:

- the under-achievement of Congolese children, in national tests and in GCSEs
- the apparent over-representation of Congolese children among those diagnosed with special educational needs.

Research was commissioned in response to these concerns. At the same time the local authority funded a Congolese community worker to run home language classes at a number of primary schools. Here he taught children Lingala and French, as well as using music, art and drama to develop both language skills and social confidence.

The research had five components. First, there was an analysis of statistical data – test and special educational needs data – as well as their progression through different stages of learning English. Second, classroom observation and interviews were undertaken with 14 Congolese students who attended four case study schools. Third, teachers in these schools were interviewed, as were parents, carers and key informants (Rutter, 2004a). Finally, a questionnaire was sent to other local authorities. Throughout, findings were discussed with informants from the Congolese community during different stages of the research. The findings are outlined below.

Pre-migration education

For a small number of children an absence of education limited their progression. Two of the children had fled from towns in central Congo that had experienced armed conflict and breakdown of state services. Neither child had attended school in the DRC. One child had fled to the USA aged 11 where he had attended school before coming to London. Another girl left the DRC aged 13. The head of EAL described her needs:

> I had to teach her to use a pencil, ruler and scissors when she first arrived. Her finer psychomotor skills are still very poor. I don't know if she has learning difficulties or not, her previous experiences might mask something like that. She seems so disorientated and lost around any equipment. Sometimes she just doesn't know whether she is coming or going.

Post-migration: language issues

Children were asked about languages spoken at home, access to books, magazines and videos in their home languages and attendance at community schools. All 14 children stated that Lingala was the only language they used at home, suggesting that their parents or carers are not from the elite first migration. But none of the Congolese children could read and write in Lingala or French. Only one Congolese child stated that there were French magazines[58] in his home. In the local authority in which the research was undertaken the majority (73 per cent) of all Congolese children listed Lingala as their first language, with very few speaking French at home.

Security of first language was an issue, with 50 per cent of the sample of 14 children lacking a secure first language. These children appeared to speak a mixture of Lingala, Kikongo and English at home, with some words borrowed from French. Two children of secondary school age were unable to name their home languages and a language assessment of one of the children noted:

> Linguistically E is, in my opinion, operating in three languages, Lingala, French and English. She has real difficulties making logical connections in language-based activities.

English language learning

An analysis of the English language learning levels of Congolese children produced significant data. Most schools assess the English language needs of bilingual pupils using a four-stage assessment model, given in the Glossary. Stage One language learners are beginners, while Stage Four language learners approach the fluency of a native speaker. The consensus among EAL teachers is that children should progress through one language learning stage per year of schooling.

The research showed that 17 per cent of all Congolese children were Stage one language learners, compared with 10 per cent of all bilingual children within that local authority. About 22 per cent of all Congolese children were Stage two language learners, compared with 6 per cent of all bilingual children. About 35 per cent of all Congolese children were Stage three language learners, compared with 27 per cent of all bilingual children and 26 per cent of all Congolese children were Stage four language learners, compared with 56 per cent of all bilingual children. The figures indicate that a much greater proportion of Congolese children were in the early stages of language development than bilingual children as a whole. In both primary and secondary schools there were significant numbers of Congolese children who had spent all of their education in the UK but remained at the earlier stages of English language learning.

Post-migration: data on achievement

In national tests at seven years Congolese children's achievement was comparable to the local authority average. (One might, however, expect the

---

[58] There are four French-language Congolese political and lifestyle magazines published in London.

greatest underachievement at this age, caused by children entering school without English.)

In national tests at eleven years Congolese children achieved less than the local authority average in English, mathematics and science. But the most marked levels of underachievement were in tests at 14 years and in GCSE examinations. In the year of the research, just 21 per cent of Congolese children achieved the expected Level 5 or above in mathematics, compared with 62 per cent of pupils as a whole. At GCSE, approximately 25 per cent of Congolese pupils achieved five Grade A*–C in the period 2000–02, compared with 52 per cent of all pupils. Although there was a weak positive correlation between length of time in the UK and achievement in these tests, Congolese children who had been in the UK for all or most of their lives underachieved in relation to pupils as a whole.

One other UK local authority collected data on Congolese children's achievement. This showed similar levels of underachievement. Five other local authorities noted their own concerns about Congolese children's achievements in tests and GCSEs, although none had conducted their own statistical analysis. Surprisingly, three local authorities stated that they had no concerns about Congolese children's achievement, including one local authority that was forceful in its denial that Congolese children might be underachieving. This local authority had one of the largest populations of Congolese children in the UK. But an examination of its school data – available in the form of spreadsheets which identified children's country of origin and home language – showed marked underachievement among Congolese children. The spreadsheet data were presented to the local authority statistics office. Here, data on Congolese children's achievement were subsumed within the category 'Black African' and failed to show marked levels of underachievement. It could be argued that such a presentation of data gave the local authority an excuse for inaction.

Despite the underachievement of many Congolese children, all local authorities who were contacted were able to identify high achievers among their Congolese students. In the local authority where the research was conducted there were Congolese pupils who had positive experiences of school and were achieving at levels comparable with or better than children of their age. These pupils are mostly female and usually listed French as their home language. For some of these 'achieving girls' the traditional Congolese expectations of women was a major concern:

> At home, women are not expected to go to university. Their job is to stay at home and look after the children. Here it is different, but I had problems explaining this to my mum. I think she expected me to stay at home with her, but now it is alright and she accepts that I am going to university this year.

There is an extensive literature on changing gender roles in refugee communities (see Buijs, 1993; Camino and Krulfeld, 1994; Kay, 1987). Indeed, states of change in gender relations seem to be central to the process of refugee acculturation. However, there is very little research on the gendered nature of school experience for refugee girls. This is surprising, given concern about boys' supposed educational underachievement in the UK, and data that are interpreted as showing girls of all ethnic groups outperforming boys[59] (Gillborn and Mirza, 1998). Clearly, this is an area that requires further research.

Special needs

Special educational needs data were also examined. Crucially, 50 per cent of Congolese students were judged to have special educational needs compared with 22 per cent of pupils as a whole. Almost all the students with special educational needs were listed as having cognitive and learning difficulties, often with poor language development. In one primary school around seven of eight Congolese children had speech delay and associated cognitive difficulties.

Of the 36 places in specialist speech and language units in the local authority, 12 were occupied by Congolese children, all boys. Those children who did have emotional and behavioural difficulties were usually included for 'poor social skills', lack of confidence and 'low self-esteem', rather than very challenging behaviour. This lack of confidence appears to be closely associated with children's communication difficulties. While it might be expected that some Congolese children would experience emotional and behavioural difficulties, as a result of persecution, loss of family and changes in exile, that so many Congolese children were experiencing speech and communication difficulties and cognitive difficulties was wholly unexpected. The significance of these findings is discussed at the end of this chapter.

Racialised experiences of school

The research highlighted a number of other themes, with disaffection with school emerging as an issue in one school. Here, disproportionate numbers of Congolese children had been excluded from school for alleged poor behaviour. These exclusions were temporary, usually for a week or less. Three of the pupils, all girls, had been excluded repeatedly, both at primary and secondary school. In this school almost all Congolese pupils exhibited high levels of disaffection and perceived that they were being treated differently because of their ethnic origins:

> Miss X, she sends out black girls when they kiss their teeth, but if a white girl says fuck, or something like that in a lesson, swearing, she does nothing.

The different treatment of black pupils in this school was also noted in recent school inspection reports. A culture of resistance to education was developing

---

[59] The research uses the DfES's very broad ethnicity categories, such as Black African, making meaningful conclusions about refugee children's achievement impossible to calculate.

in this school, in a process that mirrored Sewell's study of the educational experiences of black boys (Sewell, 1997).

Home–school links

Home–school liaison emerged as a problem, from the perspective of both parents and teachers. Homework diaries and school records were examined during the research with 50 per cent of the sample rarely, if ever, undertaking homework. Two of the children had notes in their school records which stated 'there is no educational support at home'. Parental absence from the home due to work and parental exhaustion may have acted as factors that prevented support for homework.

In two of the schools, Congolese parents were not viewed as being partners in their child's learning. Indeed, a few teachers appeared to view Congolese parents as secretive, difficult, and as parents who appeared to frustrate the best efforts of teachers:

> The Congolese seem a very secretive community who keep themselves to themselves.

> To be honest I don't know who these children go home with every night.

Parents articulated their own worries about poor links with their children's schools. They explained this as being caused by language barriers, parental work patterns, lack of confidence in dealing with authorities and a lack of parental knowledge about the UK education system. Despite both sides acknowledging that home–school liaison is a problem, both school and home appear to blame each other for this, acting as protagonists, rather than partners. Of course, poor home–school partnership is not a problem confined to the Congolese community, as much research shows, but this antagonism needs to be broken down if Congolese parents are to be genuinely involved in their children's education (Crozier, 2000).

Parental coping and family welfare issues

As discussed in Chapter 3, the ability of parents to give quality care to refugee children is probably the most important factor that determines whether a child will successfully adapt to life in the UK. Family separation is considered a risk factor that decreases resilience among refugee children (UNHCR, 1994). Significant proportions of Congolese children had experienced changes to household structure, as a result of flight and exile, with children living with carers who were not their parents. In the four case study schools about 34 per cent of all Congolese children had experienced a change of carer, mostly living with 'aunts and uncles' in private foster-care arrangements unknown to social services and often the children's teachers.[60] Most of the children experiencing changes to their care arrangements manifested unsettled behaviour.

There was an apparent over-representation of Congolese children on many local authority child protection registers, most usually for harsh physical punishment or neglect. Community informants cited the demands of work and the loss of support of the extended family as a major cause of child neglect:

> Parents are working at all times of the day. Mothers are cleaning and sometimes leave their children at home while they go out to work. Here you can't do that, but they (the Congolese) don't understand that.

> Congolese parents sometimes get accused of neglecting their children. But if they lose their extended family and community support they can't cope.

Work patterns of Congolese parents resulted in some children being continually late for school, because parents left home early in the morning, leaving children to get themselves and siblings to school on time.

Three families had been referred to social services for domestic violence. There is research evidence that suggests that domestic violence increases early in exile, as a result of over-crowded living conditions as well as changing gender roles in a new country (Burnett and Peel, 2001; Kay, 1987). For the children involved, family conflict caused enormous stress to the children, perhaps more than flight from the home country. Another family had had contact with social services because of the death of one parent from AIDS and the HIV positive status of the remaining parent.

Despite the involvement of social services, very few of the more vulnerable families appeared to be receiving welfare support, from either local authority social workers or NGOs. The exception was the family affected by HIV, in contact with healthcare providers, social services and an AIDS charity.

Intergenerational conflict

This emerged as a theme throughout the research – children who were interviewed talked about not being allowed out with friends. Intergenerational conflict centred on children's perceptions that their parents did not understand how children were brought up in the UK and were consequently too strict. Despite this, children had developed their own strategies for coping with the often opposing cultural expectations of home and peers and most seemed able to straddle the worlds of home and school with ease.

Congolese adults talked about the lack of respect that UK children

---

[60] The Children Act 1989 requires local authority social service departments be informed of private fostering arrangements.

exhibited to parents and teachers. They also described how their children manipulated the greater power afforded to them in the UK to their own advantage:

> Parents can feel very disempowered by their lack of education and their lack of English. They may see their roles change in the family if their children speak English and they don't . . . this can lead to conflict in the family.
>
> (Congolese mother who is active in a community group)

Leisure time

Live music is a part of Congolese life in London and many of the Congolese children talked about parties and bands they had heard. But lack of access to leisure and play activity was an issue highlighted by parents and children. (School records from the schools that took part in the research indicated that all but one Congolese child were living in a flat, presumably without a garden.) Parents and children described being able to play outside in Africa, but not in London:

> You can let children out to play on the streets at home. But here you cannot do that because of the cars. Back home everyone takes care of the children, but not here. You can't expect your neighbours to keep an eye on the children.

> I don't go out, when I come home that is it, just television or helping my mum.

Future prospects

Children were asked about their plans. They were asked where they expected to be living at 25 and their career plans. Most children had a fairly clear idea about their intended future careers, although most were less certain where they might be living as young adults. As might be expected older students were clearer about their career aspirations. Many children wanted professional skills, as teachers, doctors, nurses and lawyers. This may reflect the status given to these but may also be a planning decision that would enable children to return to the home country with a profession (Marshall, 1991, 1992):

> I want to be a nurse, because I can find a job here or in the Congo.

One child, a newly arrived Congolese girl, expressed an immediate desire to return to the DRC. But the majority of children had rather dualistic notions of home and were uncertain where they would be living in future. Some of the older Congolese children appeared to see themselves as temporary exiles, with the DRC being home, even though they had few memories of it, rather than as young, black and British. This influenced their career planning as described earlier.

Most children seemed content with the ambivalent notion of 'home'. What did seem to worry a number of children, as well as their parents, was their future immediately after school, both expressing concerns about earning a living:

> After GCSE some Congolese children go to the Job Centre and sign. There is no job. They are left on the street. We are worried about their future.

> My son is 17, he isn't at college, he does not work, he does not know what he wants to do. He sits at home all day or stays on the streets.

Conclusions

After 15 years in a new city, many Congolese were a community still struggling to survive. Most adults had acquired spoken English and many were employed, albeit in badly paid jobs, often working anti-social hours. Adults were appreciative of a secure income, but were also forceful in their belief that these low paid jobs did not comprise integration into UK society, but were a temporary measure. Congolese parents wanted better for their children, but their very working patterns impacted on the welfare of their children.

The research showed significant under-achievement of Congolese children in tests at 14 years and in GCSE examinations. Significant groups of Congolese children in primary and secondary schools were not progressing through the stages of acquiring English language fluency. But perhaps the most surprising conclusion is the disproportionate numbers of children with speech and communication difficulties and associated cognitive difficulties. The cause of this lies in the linguistic and social background of Congolese children in the UK.

Lingala is the dominant language among the Congolese community in London. In most families, it is 'street' Lingala that is spoken in the home, sometimes mixed with French and Kikongo, rather than the standard form of Lingala or French. The absence of books and magazines in standardised Lingala means that street forms of the language will continue to dominate in London. Congolese children speak 'street' Lingala at home and English at school. This *diglossia* affects their linguistic and cognitive development at school.

Linguists suggest that children have different types of language competency: thinking, speaking, writing, listening and reading. Linguistic thresholds theory suggests these competencies may differ between first and second languages and affect children's learning. Thresholds theory may be portrayed as a house with three floors (Baker, 1996). On the top floor are 'balanced' bilinguals who have age-appropriate and equal competencies in both languages and may experience cognitive advantages. On the middle floor are less balanced or 'dominant' bilinguals. These are children who have age-appropriate competence in one but not two languages. On the bottom floor are 'limited' bilinguals, a group lacking high levels of competence in either language. The danger of terming some children limited bilinguals is that it tends to locate language under-development in internal, individual factors, rather than external societal factors. In *Bilingualism or Not*, Skutnabb-Kangas (1981) argues that if children's languages competencies are relatively undeveloped, it is usually political and social conditions that cause this under-development. When suitable conditions are provided language competence can easy develop.

Limited bilinguals may be at a cognitive disadvantage in school. Cummins suggests that a child's second language competence is partly dependent on the level of competence achieved in the first language. The more developed the first language, the easier it is to develop the second language because the child can transfer concepts and meanings from one language to another (Cummins, 1977, 1981a).

The research in London showed that many Congolese children were entering the education system as limited bilinguals. They arrived at school speaking dialectised 'street' Lingala, interspersed with French and Kikongo vocabulary. Parental employment contributed to undeveloped language among young Congolese children, with parents who worked long hours being too tired to support their children's language development. That children with the severest language and cognitive delay were all boys may indicate that girls' language development was promoted by their closer association with their mother.

The fragility of many Congolese children's first language does not support the learning of a second language. As their early English is not well developed they risk falling behind in their learning, as neither the home language nor English is sufficient for classroom learning and complex cognitive tasks. Hence, the disproportionate numbers of Congolese children with special educational needs, as a result of cognitive and learning difficulties as well as poor speech development and a lack of social confidence.

The research also showed that some refugee children's needs are broader than the need for 'English and therapy' as portrayed in much literature about them. That a specific linguistic issue caused Congolese children's under-achievement highlights the danger of homogenising refugee children as a group. Policy makers need to engage in some disaggregation of this bureaucratic label. Instead of discussing the underachievement of *refugee* children, policy makers need to focus on the underachievement of particular groups such as the Congolese. A child's background and experiences in their home country need to be considered; different national groups of children have different linguistic, educational and social experiences. Educational interventions need to focus on particular groups, rather than refugee children as a whole.

The research also highlighted issues of relevance to those concerned with refugee integration. As discussed in Chapter 5, the Home Office, as well as the Department for Education and Skills (DfES) have advanced policy that is designed to promote refugee integration (Home Office, 2000b, 2004b). Ager and Strang (2004), in research commissioned by the Home Office, propose indicators of refugee integration. For refugee children these include the proportions who secure five grade A*–Cs at GCSE and for adults the indicators include average annual earnings compared with the majority community. By these definitions the Congolese are not a community which has achieved integration – even after 15 years in the UK. The educational outcomes of Congolese children suggest that they too will be confined to the same low paid jobs as their parents, jobs that many other people do not want to do. For the Congolese, warm words about integration and achievement are a façade, and camouflage their function in the UK – as migrant labour undertaking society's most unpopular jobs.

THE SOMALIS: CULTURES
OF SURVIVAL

Somalis are the largest refugee community in the UK and comprised an estimated 22 per cent of all refugee children in 2002 (Rutter, 2003a). This chapter examines the life experiences of young Somalis, focusing on their schooling, arguing that their lack of progress has many causes. Interventions to promote Somali school achievement must, therefore, be flexible and eco-logical in their approach.

The Somali people: ethnicity, clan and language

Over 80 per cent of the pre-war population of Somalia identified themselves as ethnic Somalis. Despite strong ethnic, linguistic and cultural unity, clan affiliation remains a divisive factor in Somali society. There are four major clan families (Dir, Daarood, Issaq and Hawiiye) plus minority clans. Each clan family is divided up into many clans, sub-clans and branches, down to the level of extended families. There are also two minority clans – the Digil and Rahanweyn – and a number of occupational caste groups. The Digil, Rahan-weyn and the occupational caste groups have been the targets of widespread prejudice.

Over 20 per cent of the 1991 population of Somalia belonged to ethnic minority groups, the largest of which are the Bantu, living around the Juba river. In pre-war Mogadishu nearly 40 per cent of the inhabitants comprised ethnic minorities, the most significant being the Bravanese, who also live in other southern coastal towns. This group trace their ancestry back to Yemen and coastal Kenya, and are usually physically distinct from their ethnic Somali compatriots. The Bravanese speak a dialect of Swahili called Chimini or Brava within the home. Other southern minority groups include the Benadiris, the Banjuni, the *reer* Hamar and the Tunni. Both Bravanese and Benadiris have been targets of violence and continued harassment since the start of the civil war and many have fled as refugees – to Kenya, the Gulf States or Europe (Cassanelli, 1994: 24). By 1999, the Bravanese refugee community in the UK was estimated at 7000 people. There are also small numbers of Benadiris, Banjuni and Tunni (Banafunzi, 1996: 332; Bolloten and Spafford, 1996)

Somali is the first spoken language of ethnic Somalis. It became the official language of Somalia in 1973, after being transcribed into a written form, using Roman script in the early 1970s. Previously Arabic, English and Italian were used in written communication, and English was the language of administration between 1960 and 1973. There is a strong oral tradition of story telling and Somali culture places greater emphasis on the spoken word; a university-educated Somali stating:

> I'm an oral person. I like talking, I don't like reading and writing that much. I don't like form filling.

The Somali language is heavily dialectised, with not all dialects being mutually intelligible. The dialectisation of Somali is an educational issue in the UK: few children have attended school in Somalia, thus few understand standard Somali. Yet bilingual books are written in standard Somali. Additionally the codification of Somali is incomplete, and there is considerable fluctuation in spelling the language. (Codification has effectively been halted by the war.)

Causes of flight

The UK's Somali community dates back nearly 100 years, when sailors from British Somaliland settled in the port cities of London, Liverpool and Cardiff. The community grew in size after the Second World War, as more Somalis joined the merchant navy or migrated to work in industrial cities such as Manchester, Birmingham and Sheffield. The 1950s and 1960s also saw a small and elite migration of students. Until the 1960s, the Somali community was predominantly male, with wives being left at home to look after property and livestock.

Somalia won its independence in 1960, when British and Italian Somaliland were united. While the first governments were parliamentary democracies, a coup of 1969 installed a military government led by Mohammed Siad Barre.

Three opposition parties started to organise by 1982, each drawing support from particular clan families. All soon committed themselves to armed struggle. In retaliation for attacks on the northern Issaq clan, the Somali National Movement (SNM) launched a military offensive in 1988, entering a number of northern cities. The Government responded with extreme force, destroying the cities of Burao and Hargeisa. Shelling and the aerial bombardment killed over 72,000 people in Hargeisa alone. Around 400,000 refugees fled from northern Somalia at this time, mostly to camps in Ethiopia. A number of these refugees subsequently sought asylum in the UK, often joining relatives already living here.

In 1990, the civil war moved south and members of the Hawiye clan family were targeted. They too fled as refugees, with some seeking asylum in the UK. In early 1991 Siad Barre was overthrown as opposition forces marched into Mogadishu and in May 1991, the SNM declared independence in the north. Since 1991 there has been a fragile peace in the Republic of Somaliland.[61] But in southern Somalia, political opposition failed to unite and the conflict worsened. The war continues to the present, although there has been an attempt to establish a transitional government. Nearly one million people have been forced into exile or are internally displaced. Almost all Somali children who have lived in Somalia before coming to the UK will have been exposed to organised violence.

Siad Barre's assault on northern towns, followed by the collapse of the Somali government has gravely affected education. In the north – now the Republic of Somaliland – most urban schools were destroyed in 1988 and for over three years many children were unable to attend school. There have been attempts to restore state education in the towns but many teachers are still working without books. In southern Somalia, education has been completely destroyed by the fighting. Although a few primary schools have reopened in Mogadishu, the only form of education for many children is the *madrassah*.[62] Children who have come directly from southern Somalia usually have had little or no education; those who have come via Kenya or Yemen may also have had many interruptions to their schooling.

Somalis in the UK

Many Somalis have had complex journeys to the UK, often living in third countries for protracted periods: for example, Kenya, Ethiopia and Yemen (usually in camps), or other Gulf States. Somalis who have gained refugee status or citizenship in another EU country have formed a significant group entering the UK since 2000, settling in particular cities such as Leicester, London, Manchester and Sheffield. Most of this group have their origins in Somaliland.[63] Thus the Somali population in the UK comprises different migratory movements:

- pre-1988 migrants who mostly came from northern Somalia
- refugees who have travelled directly from Somalia
- asylum-seekers and refugees who have spent protracted periods of time living in other countries
- Somalis who have previously been resident in other EU countries
- children born in the UK to parents from the above groups.

Between 1988 and 2003 about 58,630 asylum applications from Somalia were lodged in the UK and recent asylum statistics are given in Table 10.1. Accurate

---

[61] Somaliland was still an unrecognised state in 2005.
[62] A Q'uranic school.
[63] Leicester Council estimated there were 1091 Somali children in their schools in 2003, almost all from other EU nations.

demographic data about Somalis are absent. The 2001 Census gave 43,532 persons as being born in Somalia – a likely under-enumeration[64] (Office of National Statistics, 2002). Significant numbers of children have been born in the UK to Somali parents.

Table 10.1 Asylum applications and decisions, Somalia

Year	Applications	Refugee status (%)	ELR (%)	Refusal
2000	5020	47	32	21
2001	6500	35	24	41
2002	6540	35	12	53
2003	5090	27	9	64
2004	2590	14	15	71
2005	1770	29	14	67

Source: Home Office Asylum Statistics. Since April 2003, Exceptional Leave to Remain (ELR) has been replaced with Humanitarian Protection (HP) and Discretionary Leave (DL). There have been very few grants of HP for Congolese.

Until late 1998 almost all Somali asylum-seekers were granted refugee status or leave to remain in the UK. Since then, the proportions refused permission to remain has increased substantially and stood at 72 per cent of initial decisions in 2004. A re-interpretation by the Home Office of what constitutes 'persecution' within the terms of the 1951 UN Convention Relating to the Status of Refugees has caused more Somalis to be refused asylum; with the Home Office deciding that those granted refugee status had to be persecuted by a state authority. (There is virtually no functioning state in southern Somalia.) A 1998 House of Lords Appeal also established a precedent. *R v Secretary of State for the Home Department ex parte Adan* held that in order to be successful, an asylum applicant would have to show that he or she faced a risk 'over and above' those inherent in a civil war (Harris, 2004). It should be noted that many Somalis appeal against negative asylum decisions; in 2004 approximately 43 per cent of Somali appellants were successful and allowed to remain in the UK.

The Home Office has announced the formation of a task group on reducing Somali asylum applications. It also recently attempted the return of failed Somali asylum applications to Tanzania and Somaliland. In May and June 2004 the British Government also tried to remove a number of Somalis to Mogadishu – at a time of increased factional fighting in many parts of this devastated city.

Research on Somalis

The Somalis are the most widely documented refugee group in the UK although most writing about them is grey literature – mostly local authority

---

[64] Population number is the most important factor used to allocate local authority and health funding. That there appears to be such major under-enumeration among Somalis has economic consequences for local authorities and health authorities.

needs analyses – produced to try to secure central and local government resources for this community (see, for example, Ahmed, 1998, East London Schools Fund, 1999; Harris, 2004; Harrow, London Borough of, 1999). In the UK, Somalis are the only refugee group that has a significant separate literature, distinct from general 'refugee' policy research. In this way, they are the only group that has escaped the process of homogenisation.

Literature on Somali refugees highlights changes in the socio-economic profile of the community. Somali refugees who arrived in 1989–91 were predominately urban and middle class – a 1991 survey of Somali refugees in Tower Hamlets concluded that 75 per cent had completed secondary education (Tower Hamlets, London Borough of, 1992). More recent arrivals include men and women who have received little or no education in Somalia: a 1997 survey concluded that around 50.6 per cent of Somali adults had no literacy in any language (Haringey, London Borough of 1997: 116).

Social welfare issues emerge from research, mostly importantly, unemployment and extreme poverty. Despite dense social networks, unemployment among Somali refugees remains very high, with studies conducted in the 1990s citing unemployment rates between 70 and 97 per cent for Somali men (Ahmed, 1991, 1998: 19; Tower Hamlets, London Borough of, 1992: 38). There is some recent evidence of greater success in the job market, although male unemployment among Somalis is probably in excess of 75 per cent. Indeed, an analysis of the 2001 Census suggested that just 13.8 per cent of adult Somalis were in employment. The experiences of the Somali community challenge the assumption in much migration research that social capital in the form of social networks leads to employment and eventual integration.

Somali family size is larger than the UK average, with five or six children common. However, there is little social housing for larger families and overcrowded accommodation is also an issue highlighted in many studies (Ahmed, 1991, 1998: 19; Healthy Islington 2000, 1994b: 17; Tower Hamlets, London Borough of, 1992: 38). Clearly there are educational implications – it is difficult to study in an overcrowded house. (Although not researched among Somalis, recent UK studies have also indicated a correlation between large family size and lower levels of educational achievement among younger family members.) There are a disproportionate number of single female heads of household with figures of between 20 and 70 per cent of Somali households being headed by women cited in research. This may be as a result of men being killed in Somalia, families being split up (some men are still working in the Gulf states) and also divorce. Family separation has been identified as an issue in a number of studies often because of the psychological sequelae for those separated from their spouses, children or their usual carers (East London Schools Fund, 1999).

Literature about Somalis also cites racial harassment as being a universal experience. At least four Somalis have been murdered in racially motivated attacks in the UK. Almost all the literature about Somali children describes the racial harassment of this group.

Much research on Somalis mentions specific health problems, including war injuries and malnutrition sustained in east African camps. Female genital mutilation and the abuse of *qat*, a leaf chewed for its amphetamine-like qualities, are also health issues cited in literature. Female genital mutilation takes three forms – circumcision, excision and infibulation – the most severe form being infibulation, which involves the removal of the clitoris, labia minora and part or all of the labia majora (Dorkenoo and Elworthy, 1994). Most women in Somalia are infibulated, usually at between five and ten years old. Before 1991, a number of women's organisations in Somalia worked to ban this practice, although their work has been undone by the war. In the comparative peace of Somaliland this work has continued.

In the UK, legislation prohibiting female genital mutilation came into force in 1985, with the Prohibition of Female Circumcision Act 1985 and the Female Genital Mutilation Act 2003. More and more Somalis, both women and men, have been outspoken in their opposition to female genital mutilation. Female genital mutilation has been incorporated into local authority child protection protocols and there have been nearly 40 cases where there has been action to protect girls at risk. The operation affects a girls' schooling as those who have been infibulated are often unwilling to take part in physical education. Girls may frequently be absent as menstruation can be painful. It will also take an infibulated girl a very long time to pass urine: in schools where children have little privacy this can lead to questions, teasing and desperate embarrassment.

Identity and belonging

London hosts the largest Somali community and in 2002 Somalis were the largest refugee groups in schools in 15 London local authorities (see Figure 10.1). Outside London the largest communities are in Liverpool, Manchester, Sheffield, Cardiff, Leicester and Birmingham.

Clan identity affects settlement patterns in the UK. In London, Newham and Tower Hamlets remain solidly northern and Issaq, while Camden's Somali community are mostly southerners, mostly Darood (Griffiths, 2002: 104). That clan determines settlement pattern in the UK and schools in the same city may well have different populations of Somali children, with dissimilar prior experiences. For example, a Somali child born in the UK to Issaq parents will have different life experiences from a child who arrived from Mogadishu in 2004.

In the UK, clan affiliation is less important among the pre-1988 migrant communities but it is still very important among newly arrived refugees. Memories of war and atrocities perpetrated by particular warlords can scar social relations between Somalis. El-Solh's research indicates that in London, in conditions of dislocation and poverty, clan allegiance is the only viable form of solidarity and support (El-Solh, 1991; Griffiths, 1997: 5-10). Many of the UK's 120 or so Somali community groups have been set up by male clan elders and work with specific clans or sub-clans – a fact that has been used by local authorities to argue against funding Somali community groups. Indeed, identification with the clan is usually viewed as a negative by many working in local authorities. But an alternative approach would view clan solidarity as a means by which Somalis provide mutual support and advice. Additionally,

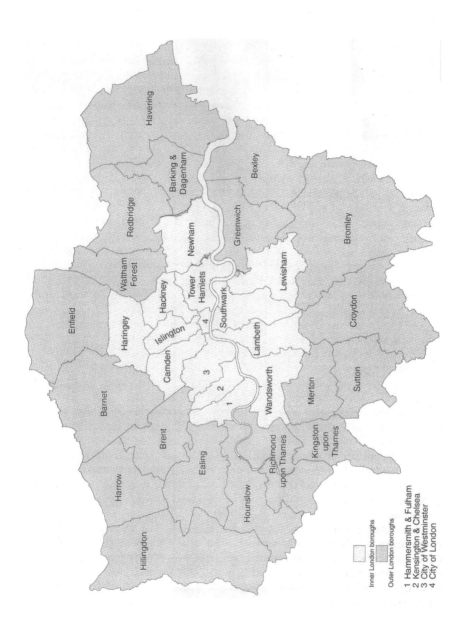

Figure 10.1 Local authorities in London

there have been recent attempts to bring Somali community organisations groups together and factionalism seems to be decreasing. There are also at least 30 Somali women's groups in the UK, many of them founded by women who were active in civil society in Somalia. Some of these women's groups have pioneered work across clan, regional and ethnic boundaries.

There is evidence of some secondary migration out of London by northern Somalis – to Sheffield, Birmingham, Leicester and Liverpool. This process started in 1999 and extended family groups have been reconstituted by this migration. In Birmingham, Somalis have purchased vacant business and residential properties in the Stratford Road area. Some of the entrepreneurial spirit of Somalis has been revived in an area where property prices are lower than London. Here Somalis have also set up their own school. Some commentators have been critical of this process which they interpret as lack of integration and community cohesion, conditions that the Government views as a social problem (Home Office, 2001). Certainly, Somalis who live in Stratford Road or in the 'Granby triangle' of Liverpool experience greater housing segregation than in London. But is the formation of a Somali 'enclave' such an undesirable social problem? This clustering of Somalis in 'enclaves' may have benefits, with families able to offer support to each other. Sellen's research gives an example of such support: his study of nutritional status of refugee children, noted that Somali children were better nourished than non-refugee families on a similar low income. Somali mothers often shared food purchasing, enabling discount purchases in bulk. Mothers too, cooked together, enabling a better diet on a low income (Sellen, 2000).

Most Somali children leave school with few qualifications. Somalis have been largely excluded from employment in the UK. Racial harassment is a universal experience. House searches[65] and street stop-and-search are causing growing anger among the Somali community. Not surprisingly, many young Somalis feel a sense of rejection by mainstream British society. In this respect Stratford Road represents a restoration of pride and self-help and an affirmation of Somali culture. If US experiences of segmented assimilation have any relevance in the UK, the presence of enclaves such as Stratford Road may provide the means by which Somali values are transmitted (Portes and Zhou, 1993). Children who grow up in the presence of moderate Somali success, in the presence of employed role models, may have more positive educational experiences. Greater 'integration' may be achieved through a period of greater separation.

While clan relations are the driving force behind the organisation of community, Griffiths (2002) suggests that new identities are emerging in exile, particularly among the young. An educated elite is emerging; a group who see themselves as successful, young, British and black. Orientation towards 'home' is also changing, with growing numbers of young Somali adults seeing their future in the UK, albeit with strong transnational links to

---

[65] In London and Manchester there have been a number of house searches made under anti-terrorist legislation. A raid on a Somali household in Manchester in late 2004 almost led to serious unrest.

Somalis in other states. Kahin, himself Somali, also looks at shifts in identity among Somali children. Unlike Harris, he concludes that most children are not troubled by living in 'two different worlds', and they learn to switch between the cultural norms of the home and school (Kahin, 1997: 41).

Religion is another component of Somali identity. Almost all Somalis are Sunni Muslims of the Shafii sect. The majority of Somalis are observant, visiting the mosque and keeping the Ramadan fast. However, some Somalis are abandoning regular religious practice – as a result of challenges faced in school or the workplace:

> I ought to pray five times a day, but I don't . . . I don't always eat halal food.

> ('Mohamed')

Conversely, a small number of Somalis have embraced Islamic fundamentalism. They may have lived in Saudi Arabia or its neighbouring states before migration to the UK and have been influenced by Wahhabiism. There is some evidence that shows some younger Somalis, brought up in the UK, turning to more fundamentalist forms of Islam, in their search for answers and self-worth.

Griffiths also analyses gender identity, suggesting that unemployment among Somali men and the perceived emancipation of Somali women has provoked a crisis in male identity in some households. This uncertainty is sometimes played out in school, with Somali boys being unwilling to accept female authority (Griffiths, 1997: 14; Kahin, 1997).

Somali children: what is known

Minutes of the Steering Group on Refugee Education, a London-based issue network, noted concerns about Somali children by the early 1990s, namely concerns about psychiatric morbidity, with children being described as 'traumatised' by teachers. A number of writers also identify the disproportionate numbers of Somali boys excluded from school (see, for example, Jones and Ali, 2000; Kahin, 1997). Both authors suggest this is a consequence of war: Somali children may see violence as the normal way of dealing with dissent and fight in schools when things do not go their way. Surprisingly, neither Jones and Ali nor Kahin examine previous research on disproportionate levels of school exclusion for African–Caribbean students (see Gillborn, 1995; Mac an Ghaill, 1988; Osler et al., 2002; Sewell, 1997). This omission gives further support to the separation of refugee research from that relating to older established minority ethnic communities.

By 1997 there was disquiet about Somali children's underachievement at GCSE and in national tests. In 1999 just one Somali child out of 330 gained five grades A*–C at GCSE in six London local authorities. In the same year, the London Borough of Camden undertook research that showed 3.1 per cent of Somali children attained five grades A*–C at GCSE, compared with 47.7 per cent of all children in that local authority (Jones and Ali, 2000). Existing literature attributes Somali children's underachievement to a number of factors, including interrupted or non-existent prior education, traumatic experiences in the home country, bullying, poor school attendance, poverty, parental illiteracy and poor home–school liaison (Jones and Ali, 2000; Kahin, 1997: 75; Mohamud, 1996; Tower Hamlets, London Borough of, 1992).

More recent quantitative data on Somali educational achievement give 22 per cent of Somali children gaining five grade A*–C at GCSE in 2003, compared with 51 per cent of all English children. However, less than 25 local authorities collected and submitted data on Somali children's achievement (DfES, 2005). Indeed, school statistics on Somali achievement were not well processed by a number of local authorities with large Somali populations. Here, as with the Congolese, school data on Somali children's achievement were subsumed within the category 'Black African' and failed to highlight significant under-achievement. There is some evidence to suggest that this practice is deliberate in its deception:

> We collect the data on Somali achievement; schools send it in, but the man in the statistics office says that he had been told to include Somalis' statistics with the Nigerians and Ghanaians.
>
> (Refugee support teacher, London)

Somali achievement at GCSE has increased since 1999, although there has been no significant improvement in test results at 7, 11 and 14 years. The numbers of Somali students progressing on to 'new' universities in London has increased in this period.[66] But most of these students come from middle-class families and most have also come from households where there are working adults. These are students who one would expect to go to university. In analysing data on Somali children's achievement (as well as other minority ethnic communities) it is important not to be seduced by the achievements of the elite.

A more detailed analysis of achievement data at local authority and school level yields more information. Statistics from the six local authorities indicates that:

- In 2003 Somali children secured GCSE results that were 11.6 per cent lower than their local authority average and 24 per cent below the national average. But GCSE performance ranged between 16 per cent of Somali students securing 5 Grade A*–C to 40 per cent.
- In two local authorities, Somali students outperformed white students at GCSE in 2003, although their GCSE results were still 11 per cent below the national average.
- At 14 years Somali children secured test results 18.2 per cent lower than the local authority average in English, mathematics and science. There was not a large range in these results, unlike the GCSE results cited above.
- At 11 years Somali children secured test results 23.3 per cent lower than their local authority average, again there was not a large range across different local authorities.

---

[66] Ethnicity data held at London Metropolitan University suggest this.

- At seven years Somali children secured test results 20.7 per cent lower than their local authority average.
- In the six local authorities Somali students were the lowest or second lowest achieving minority ethnic group in tests at seven, 11 and 14 in the period 1999–2003, although not at GCSE.
- Children who had a fairly complete prior education and had been in the UK between four to six years appeared to secure the best test and examination results. Children who had been in the UK for a longer period usually secured poorer results than those whose residence was between four and six years.
- Individual schools and a small number of local authorities had obtained a sustained increases in GCSE results of Somali children – by focusing interventions on that community.
- There was no significant difference in levels of male and female achievement in school. This result was unexpected, given a national gender gap, as well as the problematisation of Somali boys.

New evidence

The above data indicate a complex picture in relation to Somali children's school achievement. The remainder of the chapter draws on research on Somali children undertaken in five schools and includes an analysis of interviews with eight Somali children.

'Mohamed' was one of the students who was observed and interviewed. He was 12 years old and was born in northern Somalia. He had six siblings who also lived in the family home. His father was a shopkeeper in Somalia, but since arrival neither of his parents had worked. Mohamed's mother had a very basic education, although his father had completed secondary school. Like many Somali refugees, Mohamed had a difficult journey to the UK. As a baby he had spent nearly a year living with his mother and siblings in a refugee camp in Ethiopia, after the aerial bombing of Hargeisa.

Mohamed's poverty was apparent; his trousers were much too short, his shoes were in poor condition and he came to school without socks. His teacher said he played truant on the days he had physical education; she thought he did not possess the required clothing. Another teacher suggested that Mohamed did not possess underwear, causing his absence from PE lessons as he would be required to undress. A visit to his house indicated his sitting room was bare apart from basic furniture and ornaments from a relative's Haj pilgrimage. When asked, the family said they had no books other than the Qu'ran. Despite their poverty, the family were making remittance payments to relatives in Somaliland.[67]

At school Mohamed was not part of any friendship group. He was judged to have special educational needs because of language and literacy difficulties. However, his oral skills were superior to most other students in his class. He

----

[67] For a discussion of Somali remittance payments see Lindley (2005).

was able to talk about his uncle's Haj pilgrimage, his parents' memories of Hargeisa (their home town) and a primary school residential trip. He appeared an articulate boy, but unable to express his ideas in writing.

'Hassan' was another boy who was observed and interviewed. Now 13 years old, he was nine or ten when he arrived in the UK. No teacher knew of his home circumstances, although he lived with both parents. The school intended to use a Somali home–school liaison worker to meet the parents and talk about Hassan's progress. This should have happened some months previously, but staff changes delayed this.

His reading age was 6.01 years. When observed, Hassan had little conceptual understanding of learning tasks, merely copied text from books or the work of his friends. For example, he had no understanding of maps. Asked to colour in member states of the EU from a list, using the atlas to guide him, Hassan was unable to distinguish between land and sea. Hassan had been identified for a mentoring programme, although this had not started. This was all the additional support he was receiving. The special educational needs coordinator said he was 'traumatised', although she knew nothing about his home circumstances or life in Somalia. She did not think he had learning difficulties.

In class, 'Hassan' sat with three other boys. He tried to gain their acceptance and was easily led by their behaviour. When they worked, he tried to work, when they fooled around, he did so. They did not reciprocate his attentions and on a number of occasions referred to him not as 'Hassan' but as 'the black Arab'.

'Hassan' was uncommunicative in class. Outside the class he was much more articulate. He explained that he did not attend school in Somalia. He recounted memories of time spent in the countryside with relatives who owned livestock. He asked for an opinion on 'shit catchers' – baggy trousers favoured by some of the African-Caribbean boys in the school – which he found a ridiculous garment. Hassan also talked of his worries about leaving school – he did not know what work he might find.

Mohamed and Hassan's stories are unique, but they illustrate issues that affect many of the Somali students encountered in the research. Economic stresses, isolation, the desire for acceptance and specific difficulties with reading and writing featured in the life histories of many of the young Somalis.

Pre-migration experiences: prior education

Many of the Somali children had an interrupted prior education (five of the eight children whose life history data were collected experienced interruptions to their schooling). One child had received some home tuition from her mother, previously a teacher. The other children had received no education in Somalia, or their countries of first asylum. (Lack of money may have prevented children from receiving schooling in Kenya, Ethiopia and Yemen.) Such interruptions, coupled with a lack of appropriate learning support in the UK, were crucial in limiting Somali children's progress.

Parental employment and social class

Data were collected on parental employment in the home country and in the UK. The Somali families had diverse prior employment experiences and were not solely a public sector elite. Of the children interviewed, five families had businesses, including a garage, cattle and a grocery. Two children came from fairly wealthy families, including a Bravanese family who owned a number of businesses, and an ethnic Somali family with business and livestock interests. Female employment was high: four of the Somali children stated that their mothers worked in Somalia, and one child's mother held a senior teaching post. Despite comparative economic success in Somalia, the Somali families had been less successful in securing employment in the UK: only two families had parents who were in employment. One child's father was working as an interpreter and another child's father worked as a bus driver, with the mother working for a community organisation. Poverty was a real issue for most of the children.

Psychological stressors

Data on potential stressors and potentially traumatic events were collected, as well as observation and interview data on children's adaptation in the UK. All the children had direct exposure to armed conflict. However, the impact of the conflict on the families was varied. Some families had remained intact and uninjured, but one child had lost his father in the bombing of Hargeisa. Another child had been separated from family during fighting, and not reunited with them.

Two of the eight Somali children were not functioning at school. Their behaviour was unpredictable and often aggressive. Another child appeared unhappy and withdrawn at times. Their educational progress was being limited by their current mental health. All three children had seen breakdown of family relationships during flight and exile, suggesting that family breakdown is a more significant stressor than exposure to armed conflict. But observation data and interviews indicated that the remainder of the Somali children had adapted well. Special needs data supported this finding: in the five schools that were visited about 3.7 per cent of Somali children were listed as having emotional and behavioural difficulties, compared with 14 per cent of white British children. Somali children were not uniformly 'traumatised' as suggested in much policy text.

Use of language

Children were asked about their home language use and access to Somali books, magazines and videos. One child was Bravanese and spoke Brava as his home language. The remainder of the children spoke Somali at home but only two of them could read and write in Somali. One child had received some education in Somalia, the other had been taught Somali by her mother.

None of the Somali students attended community schools, although there are an estimated 49 Somali schools in London alone (Resource Unit for Supplementary and Mother Tongue Schools, 2000). These teach the Somali language, sometimes with other subjects including Qu'ranic Arabic, mathematics, English and Somali history. One boy had attended a Somali community school on a few Saturdays, but stated that he did not enjoy it. None of the Somali children had access to Somali books, magazines or videos, although one girl had borrowed some Somali children's books from her local library, complaining that they were 'for babies'.

Children's home language skills were primarily oral, with a vocabulary focusing on the home. However, children did discuss academic concepts in Somali. It is important to acknowledge this and not to assume that children's academic thinking is solely in English, while basic communication and thinking is undertaken in Somali. (Cummins's separation of basic interpersonal communication skills (BICS) and academic English (termed cognitive academic language proficiency (CALP) may be partly responsible for this notion (Cummins, 1981b)). Issa's study of home language use among Turkish children challenges the assumption that academic concepts are only processed in English, with the Turkish children in his study able to discuss complex ideas in Turkish (Issa, 2005).

Unlike many other minority communities, some of smaller size, Somali children are not able to study their language at GCSE. The Department for Education and Skills has maintained a view that home language teaching is 'the responsibility of communities'. Recently, civil servants in several government departments have asserted that the teaching of community languages in mainstream schools reinforces cultural differences, acts as a barrier to integration and the forging of a common sense of belonging. Despite continual lobbying, the Qualifications and Curriculum Authority[68] has refused to grant an examination board permission to develop a Somali GCSE course.[69] Arguably, Somali children would be afforded greater integration and a greater sense of belonging to British society by the development of GCSE and A-Level Somali. Such a course would help develop children writing in Somali and thus their reading and writing skills in English. It would also grant status to the Somali language.

Many of the Somali children had English-language oral skills that were superior to their UK-born peers. Not all of the children were talkative in class, but in small groups or more supportive situations, most of the Somali children were articulate and were able to offer sophisticated opinions on current affairs among other topics. Their oracy challenges Bernstein's theory that

---

[68] The Qualifications and Curriculum Authority oversees the examination system in England.
[69] A number of academics based at the School of Oriental and African studies, University of London have offered to help develop the course.

poorer children's educational success is limited by their linguistic register – their use of 'restricted codes' rather than the 'elaborated' codes of the middle classes (Bernstein, 1971).[70] However, oral competencies were not matched by reading and writing skills.

Somali children were generally over-represented on schools' special educational needs registers.[71] Some of the Somali children on schools special needs registers had medical needs, including war injuries. Around 3.7 per cent of Somali children had 'social, emotional or behavioural difficulties', less than might be expected from a population described as traumatised in much writing about them.

What was unexpected was the high proportions of Somali children who were diagnosed with 'language and literacy difficulties' (overall 45 per cent). Like 'Mohamed' and 'Hassan' many of these children, while having very good oral skills, had poorly developed writing and reading skills. All of these children with literacy difficulties had limited exposure to the written word, either in Somali or English, as well as limited help in developing their academic English at school or at home. None of the schools afforded extra help to children who were no longer English-language beginners. Parental illiteracy, lack of disposable income with which to purchase books and the greater emphasis placed on the spoken word may have contributed to the lack of exposure to the written word at home. Thus language and literacy difficulties had multiple causes, but probably represent the most significant limitation to children's educational progress.

Support for children's learning in school

Somali children are more likely to have experienced an interrupted prior education than any other refugee group. All the Somali children were asked about the additional learning support they had received in schools in the UK. Of the five children with an interrupted prior education, three had received some small group teaching in addition to classroom-based support. All of them were pupils at the same school where there was an induction class for new arrivals who have English as an additional language. This programme, lasting six weeks, ran for one day per week, with pupils attending mainstream classes for the remaining four days.

Other Somali children with an interrupted prior education were entirely dependent on in-class support. Children such as 'Huda' and 'Hassan' entered UK schools unable to read and write. The level of small group teaching offered to them and other children with an interrupted prior education was, from the

---

[70] Bernstein has fallen out of favour, particularly with the left. Labov (1969) has been one of the most vocal of his critics, postulating that children can express complex concepts in non-standard English. It should be noted that Bernstein had a real commitment to urban education and believed that education could not compensate for societal inequality.

[71] See Glossary for definitions of special educational needs.

evidence gathered in the schools, insufficient to teach them the skills and concepts that they need to learn and to make educational progress. Even for those Somali children whose prior education was not interrupted, EAL support was limited and appeared to be a major factor in limiting Somali children's eventual educational achievements. Students who had achieved survival English rarely received extra support and help to develop their academic literacy. Consequently their written work contained mistakes or was written in 'street' English. A history teacher and an RE teacher in one school talked of their experiences of EAL support:

> My subject is taken at GCSE. But I have never had any in-class support for children (with English as an additional language) unless they were complete beginners. I was told that that it was not school policy to help children (with English as an additional language) in class after they had been in the school for more than a term.

> I have got lots of Somali children in my class who have been here (in the UK) for quite a time. They speak fluent English, but their written English is poor. I can go some way in improving it, but my time is limited in each lesson.

Teacher stereotyping

In all of the schools that were visited there were negative perceptions of Somalis boys and girls among some (but not all) teaching staff. These perceptions assumed that Somali boys were 'traumatised' or 'aggressive' and therefore could not be expected to learn:

> I put him out of every lesson. He's traumatised, he can't sit still, he can't behave. [This 14-year-old boy was a talented actor in a community arts project.]

The labelling of Somali boys appears to be a reworking of the labelling of African-Caribbean boys discussed by Mac an Ghaill and Sewell among others (Mac an Ghaill, 1988; Sewell, 1997). Somali boys are being constructed as 'mad' rather than 'bad'. School data also indicated that Somali boys were very over-represented among pupils excluded from secondary schools: they were eight times more likely to be permanently excluded than their white peers. However, only one London local authority is presently keeping data on permanent exclusions of Somali pupils.

In all the lessons that were observed there was little teacher-engagement with Somali girls – they were effectively ignored by their teachers and received no personalised help. Some teaching staff talked about Somali girls being 'passive' and oppressed Muslim women, who would be prevented by their parents from progressing to further and higher education. While the majority of adult Somalis are observant Muslims, not all are and the extent of religious practices varies. Not all girls wear the *hijab* at school. Yet Somali girls were viewed by their teachers as being uniformly religious. A PHSE teacher talked about how she dreaded delivering sex education to Somali children because she feared their parents might complain. In one school with a large population of Somali students, a leaflet about out-of school community drama activities was not handed out to Somali children:

> The teacher who handed out the leaflet said that Somali parents would disapprove and make trouble. He said they don't like their daughters to perform, you know.
>
> (EAL teacher in the school)

Many teachers were unaware of the children's backgrounds and origins. That a child's mother held a post-graduate qualification and had a successful career came as a surprise to teachers in one school. That some of the Somali families had considerable cultural capital was a surprise to a number of teachers.

Bullying, friendship and isolation

Children were asked about their experiences of bullying, with all of them stating that they had been bullied. Harassment of children had many forms, from physical abuse, damage to property, spitting and verbal abuse. Young Somalis were exposed to racial harassment within the school and in the home communities.

Children's engagement with their peer groups was observed as part of the classroom observation schedule. During interviews children were also asked about their best friends. An older Somali student said she felt different, unwelcomed and not part of the school and the community. (That their parents and other adults were orientated towards Somalia as being the home may have added to her sense of not belonging.)

Many Somali children appeared isolated at school, with those friendships forged at school often being transient. For one boy, his unpredictable behaviour appeared to isolate him. Arrival at school after friendships groups have been formed may contribute to isolation. English language difficulties, too, prevent some children forming close friendships when new to the UK. There may be economic factors that hinder the development of friendship groups, which are often cemented outside school, at birthday parties, at visits to the cinema. But these out-of-school leisure activities require money – something that is in short supply in many Somali households. The perception among teachers and children's peers that Somalis were observant Muslims, thus 'different', may also have compounded isolation.

Children in longer established Somali communities appeared to have experienced greater acculturation in schools where the predominant culture was 'laddish' and anti-education. Bullying, isolation and rejection by the mainstream has made some Somali children adopt strategies to help gain them greater acceptance. These survival strategies comprised an abandonment of an ethos of hard work and self-improvement through education – their immigrant habitus – followed by attempts to gain the acceptance of dominant peers. Children who had perhaps been highly motivated when they first arrived in the UK manifested ambivalent attitudes to schoolwork. Griffiths (2002) writes about Somali boys attempting to identify with African-

Caribbean street culture in order to gain acceptance, an observation which concurs with my own research. Arguably these are strategies of survival.

Enrichment and play

Having a hobby and participating in leisure activities can be protective factors that promote resilience among children (Richman, 1998a). Enrichment activities such as arts and music education are also components of cultural capital, possession of which has been advanced as an explanation for the greater educational achievement of middle-class children (Bourdieu, 1986). Children who are more able, settled and making progress may be more likely to organise their leisure time. My research showed that among refugee children there is correlation between hobbies and best educational progress: children who were making good progress at school were largely the ones who stated that they had hobbies.

In comparison with Congolese and Sudanese children, Somali children were less likely to state a hobby, with no girls responding positively to questions about hobbies. This may be reflective of the gendered notion of leisure in the home – with girls expected to help their mothers. Children were asked about the places they had visited in London; almost all visits outside their local authority comprised school trips or visits to relatives. 'Hawa', a Somali girl said she liked cartoons, but that she had never been to the cinema in the UK, although she did visit the cinema in Somalia. Outside school few Somali children participated in the free extra-curricular enrichment and play activities run by many local authorities, museums, arts and sports organisations. Perhaps lack of parental knowledge about free enrichment activities also contributed to this lack of participation. Another cause is the severe financial hardship experienced by many Somali families, for while enrichment activities may be free, they may involve travel costs. Lack of money to travel may also limit some Somali children's ability to attend community schools.

Learning and the home

Pupil absenteeism was higher among Somali children than most other ethnic groups in the case study schools. A major cause appeared to be household duties – Somali children interpreting for parents who spoke little English. (Absenteeism may also have been caused by fear of racial harassment and wanting to opt out of PE, as well as genuine illness.)

Parental stress impacted on the well-being of some Somali children in the five schools. Previous exposure to violence, loss of support of the extended family, isolation and lack of financial security may cause stress and trigger mental illness in a small number of parents (East London Schools Fund, 1999). The larger family size of most Somali households may mean that women have less time to support the home learning of each child:

I have seven children, the youngest is four and the oldest is seventeen. When they were smaller, it was really hard just getting them to school. At that time we lived on the fifth floor of a block of flats with no lift. Getting them to the top and bottom was so hard, crossing the road was very hard . . . I did not have enough time to help them all with their reading and homework. But now things are easier. My oldest son is at college and the older children help.

> (Somali mother, South London, who has founded a self-help
> organisation for Somali women)

Parental illiteracy impacts on children's educational experience. Mothers narrated how they felt they could not help their children with homework. They also felt the stigma of being illiterate. Indeed, many Somali children did have difficulty in completing homework: teacher interviews and an examination of homework diaries indicated that six of the eight Somali children had severe problems completing homework.

In much policy text about Somali children home–school relationships have been portrayed as problematic. Many Somalis describe poor relationships with their children's schools (see, for example, London Challenge, 2005; Kahin, 1997). Policy texts from local government construct Somali parents as lacking in agency when it comes to choosing schools and establishing relationships with teachers. But is this a stereotype? Many Somali parents discussed choosing schools, debating nearness and convenience in relation to how supportive and welcoming the school might be to Somali parents. There is evidence to suggest that Somali parents do possess agency and select schools that they perceive as being supportive of their children's needs. (In 2003 a London Somali organisation nominated a London secondary school for an award for its work with Somali children.) There is no evidence to suggest that Somali parents attend school meeting and events less than other populations.

The way forward

The above research findings challenged the hegemonic explanation that traumatic past experiences were the main cause of Somali children's lack of educational progress. Such lack of progress has multiple and complex causes, including:

- an interrupted or non-existent prior education for new arrivals from Somalia, Yemen and east Africa and insufficient school support for this group
- exposure to violence in Somalia and in east Africa and Yemen
- lack of exposure to written language
- schools not developing children's academic literacy
- higher pupil absenteeism caused by illness, family responsibilities and truancy
- negative teacher perceptions, particularly of boys
- acculturation into anti-education cultural forms

- racial harassment leading to unhappiness and disengagement from education
- inability to access enrichment and play activities in the locality
- carer stress – the impact on children of carers who found it difficult to cope in the UK
- poverty and the stress of living in large households
- parental illiteracy among some new arrivals.

Some Somali children are enjoying success and progressing to college and university. But these children are almost always from middle-class families. Policy makers must not be seduced by the achievements of a small elite. It is important to acknowledge class differences within refugee groups.

Nationally, children whose families came from northern Somalia in the period 1988–91 appear to be the least well-achieving group, despite a complete education and having been in the UK for the longest time. There may be localised issues that cause this, but observations also indicated a process of acculturation into an anti-intellectual culture dominant in many schools. This acculturation may be a survival strategy where children face bullying, rejection, isolation and economic exclusion. It does not equate with positive cultural syncretism and the positive development of new ethnic identities. The finding also challenges staged approaches to the study of refugee adaptation that stress the processual nature of integration (see, for example, Al-Rasheed, 1993; Baskauskas, 1980; Eastmond, 1993; Harrell-Bond and Voutira, 1992).

Somali parents and children are not passive victims. They have agency and resilience, and can act to change some of their circumstances. In particular, the Somali community has a strong sense of self-help, as manifest by the energy of community organisations. Many local authorities are not using these resources and not working in partnership with Somali communities.

Despite national concern about the lack of educational progress of many Somali pupils, little has been done to improve the educational opportunities for them, with the DfES disengaging from this issue entirely. A number of local authorities employ Somali teachers or classroom assistants: at the time of writing around 14 local authorities across the UK were doing so. But in England the numbers of Somali teachers and educational support staff appears to have declined in London since the Ethnic Minority Achievement Grant was devolved to schools in 1999. Many local authorities who have substantial Somali populations do not employ a single Somali teacher or classroom assistant.

There seems to be much rhetoric about the problems faced by Somalis, but little by way of monies and long-term support for this community. London Challenge, an initiative to improve the capital's education, convened a Somali parents' forum in 2003–04, but this group no longer meets. A number of northern local authorities have met to discuss Somali children's progress, but there has been little regional coordination of work. Nationally, there is a clear need for local authorities to work collaboratively, perhaps developing cross-authority projects targeted at Somali children

It has been individual schools, local authorities and community organisations that have planned and delivered most support for Somali children. Interventions such as those described below have been developed as a result of the hard work of determined individuals. But a weakness of this bottom-up approach is that it relies on the personal skills and on-going involvement of an individual or a small group of people.

There is still cause for hope, as manifest by interventions that make a difference to Somali children's educational progress. Projects that help parents acquire literacy in English and Somali appear to be successful. A school in east London set up a project called 'Somali Families Learning Together' after Somali parents told teachers that they did not know how to help their children with homework. A computer suite was set aside each week for Somali parents to work with their children alongside a crèche staffed by a classroom assistant who was also a qualified nursery worker. Parents were able to develop IT skills, find out about schooling and homework help and meet other parents, as well as read with their children. The Refugee Education Team in the local authority helped the school select Somali books and tapes.

In another local authority parents were invited along to school meetings in Years 10 and 11 and given details of GCSE coursework demands and deadlines. This improved performance at GCSE. A west London local authority has developed a Somali mentoring project, where Somali students studying at universities work with younger school pupils. There are two Sure Start projects targeting Somali children and their carers, attempting to meet children's needs by helping parents be better parents. All of these interventions are ecological in their approach, building on the resilience of Somali children and their families, and focusing on home and learning needs.

SUCCESS STORIES: THE
SOUTHERN SUDANESE

While Congolese and Somali children are not securing the educational success that the 'average' UK child enjoys, there is evidence to suggest that some groups of refugee children are obtaining better test and GCSE results than their UK-born peers. In the small number of local authorities that collect and analyse ethnicity data, these achieving children include Afghans, Iranians, Iraqi nationals, Sudanese, Tamils and Vietnamese. This chapter examines the educational experiences of southern Sudanese. It argues that definitions of 'success' and 'integration' must encompass long-term labour market experiences.

Background: the Sudanese

The 2001 census lists 10,673 people born in Sudan as resident in the UK (Office of National Statistics, 2002). Approximately 8570 asylum applications from the Sudan were lodged with the Home Office between 1990 and 2005, with the peak years of application being 1991 and 2004 (Refugee Council, 1998a: 85; Home Office, 1999a, 2005a).

Sudan is an ethnically diverse country. Around 40 per cent of the population identify themselves as Arabs, although the claim of Arab descent is more a matter of cultural allegiance than ethnic origin. Most Sudanese Arabs live in northern Sudan. Non-Arab groups living in northern Sudan include the Nile Nubians, Beja, Nuba, Ingessana, Fur and Massalete.

Southern Sudanese form about 30 per cent of the population. The Dinka, Nuer, Shilluk, Azande and Bari are major ethnic groups. The peoples of southern Sudan speak languages from a number of language families and, as in the North, there has been much inter-marriage.

Arabic is the official language of Sudan, spoken by about half the population, mostly in northern Sudan. English is widely spoken in government and academic circles. About 70 per cent of the population are Muslim, 18 per cent animists, 8 per cent Roman Catholic, 0.5 per cent Protestant and 0.5 per cent Coptic Christian. Since 1989, hundreds of Copts have been dismissed from their jobs, simply because they are Christian. About 3000 Sudanese Copts have fled to the UK, with the majority resident in Brighton and Hove (Fyvie-Gauld, 2000).

Sudanese in the UK

Almost all ethnic groups are represented among the Sudanese community in the UK, although northern Arabic speakers and southern Dinka comprise the two largest groups.

Before the 1970s, the Sudanese community was very small, mostly comprising business people and students. The latter came from both northern and southern Sudan. Today, the Sudanese community comprises three groups: business families, students and those who have been asylum-seekers, whether in the UK or in other European countries. There has been a migratory movement to the UK of southern Sudanese refugees from EU states such as Sweden and Germany. The desire to join family and friends, as well as to live in an English-speaking country, are pull factors that have brought Sudanese from mainland Europe to the UK.

The business community is mostly from the urban centres of the Arabic-speaking north. Many live in west-central London, around the Arabic 'enclave' of the Edgware Road, where there are a number of Sudanese restaurants, groceries and businesses. Sudanese students, who comprise elite populations from both north and south are more scattered, studying at universities across the UK. Although having entered the UK with student visas, some of these students may be forced migrants.

Asylum-seekers are a diverse group and include southern Sudanese, Copts, political opposition, trade unionists, politically active university students and other opposition forces. There has been a recent increase in asylum applications, caused by the greater suppression of political opposition in the north and post-peace treaty political changes in southern Sudan. London-based Sudanese have also facilitated the migration of relatives, sending money home to help others make the journey to the UK. A process of chain migration is starting, albeit very recently.

The largest Sudanese refugee communities are resident in Brighton, London, Manchester and Birmingham. Although portrayed in the press as Coptic Christians, the Brighton community comprises about 30 per cent Muslims. Almost all have left the urban centres of the north – Khartoum, Omdurman, Dongola and other cities. Social networks facilitated their migration to Brighton, with a Sudanese property owner (and ex-student of Sussex University) offering rented accommodation to Sudanese refugees. Most male heads of household are well-educated professionals. In London, most Sudanese refugees are from southern Sudan, or the urban centres of the north. The largest numbers of southern Sudanese are resident in inner central London, mostly in Camden and Westminster, although southern Sudanese refugees exhibit much less housing segregation than many other refugee groups.

There is very little written about Sudanese in the UK – they are a small community and they are not constructed as a social problem. But a needs analysis conducted by Brighton and Hove Council suggests that Sudanese refugees share many of the problems of other refugee groups: insecure immigration status and unemployment (Fyvie-Gauld, 2000). This survey indicated that 65 per cent of adult Sudanese refugees lacked fluent English, most notably northern Sudanese women, and thus find difficulty in accessing services. Many Brighton Sudanese cite racial harassment as an issue. Data on the educational achievement of Sudanese children have not been analysed by Brighton and Hove Council.

The children

This chapter examines the experiences of refugee children from southern Sudan. Riak Akuei (2005) suggests that about 1200 southern Sudanese live in the UK, the majority resident in London, although with smaller communities living in Birmingham, Manchester and other university cities. It is likely that Riak Akuei's figure is an underestimate, but compared with many refugee populations, the southern Sudanese are a small community. The small size of this group also indicates that large-scale chain migration had not occurred, and that they are largely an elite group of pioneer migrants.

The Dinka are the dominant southern group living in the UK, although there are a small numbers of Nuer, Shilluk, as well as other groups. There is also intermarriage among southern Sudanese.

Detailed life history and educational data were gathered from six southern Sudanese children aged between 11 and 16 years. The children were largely new arrivals; they had been in the UK for an average of 2.1 years, although one child had lived here for more than five years. Two of children were unaccompanied, and another three children were living in the UK with relatives.

Four children were Dinka and one girl was Nuer. Another boy spoke Mundu as his home language. None of the Sudanese children could read and write in their first language although four could read and write in Arabic. In London, none of the Sudanese attended refugee community schools, although four children said they attended cultural events run by community organisations. A further linguistic difference that distinguished the Sudanese children from many other groups of refugees was that all of them came from homes where English was spoken by one or both parents. Almost all of the Sudanese children had entered a UK school speaking English. (All but one child had arrived in school as a stage 3 or stage 4 learner of English.[72])

The southern Sudanese children were an elite group of migrants. All of the children had parents who had held senior public or NGO jobs in Sudan,

---

[72] See Glossary for an explanation of the English language acquisition stages.

including academia and senior administrative posts in government. Some of the parents also owned substantial amounts of land. However, in coming to the UK, many families experience downward social mobility and found themselves unemployed (Riak Akuei, 2005). Of the four children who were living with parents or relatives, one family had no working adults, one father worked for a community organisation, one was a student and another combined part-time study with work in a food takeaway. One mother was also studying. Among the Sudanese, education and training as seen as long-term strategies to secure future success in the labour market.

Pre-migration experiences: prior education

Two of the children had attended school in Sudan and three children had been to school in Cairo. (There is a large Sudanese community in Cairo, comprising peoples from all parts of Sudan. Egypt is often a country of first asylum, before migration to North America or Europe).

Two children had received an English medium education before coming to the UK. Almost all the older Sudanese children had experienced some interruptions to their education as a result of warfare in southern Sudan and flight to the UK. One boy – 'Luke' – had had little schooling, but remarkably had taught himself to read and write. He was born in Yei, south-central Sudan, but fled as a very young child to Uganda. Here he had a very interrupted education, comprising less than three years in total, but broken as his parents moved or ran out of money. Conflict caused him to flee again when the Lord's Resistance Army attacked the outskirts of the Ugandan town where he lived. He fled to Kampala from where his passage to the UK was arranged. While he did not speak English confidently, his written English was meticulous. He recounted teaching himself English, using the books that he could find. His class teacher said he had made a great deal of progress since arriving in the school eight months before. While his English was good and he had a good general knowledge, he had missed much conceptual learning. He constantly stressed how his lack of a basic education has made his schooling very difficult:

> We did not do electricity at school, now it is so hard for me to do this here ... Sometimes I want to give up and go back to Uganda.

An interrupted prior education is a common experience of many refugee children. However, this issue is rarely discussed in literature about refugee education.

Those who had attended school in Sudan or Egypt often stressed the differences between schools there and their learning experiences in the UK. These differences, often forcefully articulated, concerned teaching and learning styles and classroom behaviour. However, the difficulties encountered by refugee children when entering a new school system are also seldom discussed in policy text on refugee education:

The teachers hit you if you were rude or talked in class. Once a teacher twisted my arm really hard. But that was better than here when the teachers take no notice if you do wrong.

There, the teachers just wrote things on the blackboard. Here you get sent to the library and told to find things out.

We didn't have computers in Uganda and when I came here, I did not know anything about computers. I could not even switch it on and I had to ask Erfan to help me. He just laughed at me and said, 'Didn't you have a computer in your hut?'

Psychological adaptation

Data on potential stressors and trauma-causing events were analysed, to see if the case study children's progress was being limited by psychological consequences of flight and exile.

At least two of the Sudanese children had direct experience of armed conflict. Another girl whose mother had earlier died of natural causes had to contend with the disappearance of her father, a political activist. Separation from parents increases psychological vulnerability among refugee children; two of the older Sudanese boys had arrived in the UK as unaccompanied children and another three children were living with close relatives. But both the unaccompanied children (two older boys) were judged to be happy and well-adjusted by their teachers and both were making excellent progress at school. Both boys were living in a children's home specifically for refugee children. It enjoyed a reputation for giving high quality care and this may have acted as protective factor for these boys.

Neither of the unaccompanied boys had received positive decisions on their asylum applications. Their teachers talked about how unsettled they became when they had to attend interviews about their asylum claim:

'Paul' knows his future in the UK is not certain. He is worried about what will happen after he is 18.[73] Every time he meets his solicitor or even his social worker it reminds him that his future is uncertain. Last time he was really wound up and tense for days and was short tempered with his friends and abusive to a teacher. He would not apologise. That is really unlike him.

(Paul's class teacher)

'Luke', the other unaccompanied refugee, was also anxious about proposed changes to his care arrangements. He had received notification that his children's home placement would cease at 16 and he would have to find his own rented accommodation. This worry affected his career planning – he felt

[73] At the time of writing many unaccompanied asylum-seeking children received discretionary leave to remain until their 18th birthday. At the age of majority they can lodge another asylum application, or be faced with removal to the home country.

he had to earn a living at the soonest opportunity, to ensure his survival in London. Plans to go to college were shelved.

One child appeared to have more persistent adaptation problems. This was 'Sara', a Dinka girl. When observed and interviewed she seemed an isolated, unsmiling and unhappy girl. Her family moved from southern Sudan to Khartoum where Sara's mother died. Her father was involved in opposition politics and later disappeared. Sara came to the UK by air and was now looked after by a paternal aunt, with two younger daughters. The family were living in temporary accommodation and had moved home four times. The present housing was of poor quality and leased from a private landlord. Greater care is given to the aunt's natural daughters according to a report from the previous school and her class teacher stated a lack of love and attention was a real problem for Sara. Her class teacher was also concerned that Sara had many domestic obligations – housework and the care of her younger cousins.

Sara had a complete education in her home country where she attended a private school. When she arrived in the UK she was enrolled at a large comprehensive school in central London. Her teacher said that she was very happy there and had a circle of close friends, including some Sudanese girls. Sara then moved house and started a new school in east London. There were no other Sudanese in that school. She remained at that school for two months before moving to her present school.

Sara was a fluent English speaker and her teacher said she was of above average ability. Her teachers felt she was making excellent progress after 18 months in the UK (they seemed unaware that her previous education was conducted through the medium of English). She enjoyed English and drama and also sings in her school choir, although was very worried about her ability to attend out-of-school choir events. In a library reading period she completed a piece of biology homework and then selected two library reading books. One was for much younger children and the other was a popular piece of teenage fiction. Sara talked of how much she enjoyed reading girls' magazines but her aunt could not (or would not) buy them for her.

The data above indicate that there is not a clear relationship between exposure to organised violence and armed conflict (the most frequently cited traumatic experience for refugees) and ability to function in the country of exile. Other factors such as loss of parental love and care, isolation and uncertain immigration status all influence children's psychological adaptation.

Identity

One of the most striking observations was the quiet social confidence exhibited by many of the male students and an expressed pride in being southern Sudanese. The boys were confident in talking about the southern Sudanese community in London, both with their peers and with adults. This is unusual among refugee children – the desire not to be different, the media portrayal of refugees, as well as the pressures to keep secrets means that many refugee children are reticent about talking about their communities.

The children's height may have granted them confidence – all but one of the older boys were over six feet tall. Their height and features made them a very visible group of students. As they could not hide their difference they might as well celebrate it. One boy believed that his height had protected him from being bullied:

> They did use to tease me, but they know if I hit them I would really hurt them, so they stopped.

They boys also delighted in recounting the sporting success of Manute Bol and Luol Deng. (Luol Deng, the son of a Sudanese parliamentarian, was granted refugee status in the UK, before gaining an American sports scholarship. He had recently been signed to play for the Chicago Bulls.)

The boys also adopted 'British' and non-Sudanese cultural forms with ease. They followed Premier League football teams and read Harry Potter. New hybrid identities seemed to be developing in London.

However, the girls did not seem to be undergoing this process of cultural syncretisation to such an extent. They had little interest in boy bands, or other concerns of their peers. The girls stated fewer hobbies or leisure activities, although visiting relatives and attending community events were important. The success of Arek Deng, a female basketball player and sister of Luol Deng, had little resonance. Lack of money may limit access to fashion and leisure activities. Additionally, girls' household duties may also restrict leisure opportunities. Southern Sudanese society tends to confine women to the private sphere – the home is a woman's responsibility – while men take public roles. (It is notable that there are far fewer female community activists in southern Sudanese refugee organisations than in the Somali community.) One teacher stated that it was always Sudanese children's fathers rather than their mothers who attended parents' evenings and dealt with school matters.

Some of the Sudanese children talked about relatives who owned land or livestock (as did a number of Somali children whose experiences are discussed in the preceding chapter). In Sudan the children had often stayed with these relatives. For one Sudanese child, although the son of civil servant, 'home' was definitely a settlement in the countryside, although he had never lived there. The boy talked about 'my village'. A number of the Sudanese children had some knowledge of animal and crop husbandry, not information that many London children possess. (One Sudanese child was a keen gardener.) Their relationship with the rural was very different from that of most urban school children in London. Yet refugee populations are viewed as an urban issue in the UK. Although not explored in academic writing, some refugees' loss of their rural roots features among the losses that exile brings.

Educational progress

Of all the three refugee groups whose educational experiences are discussed in this book, the Sudanese students are the group newest to the UK. But despite their recent arrival, the majority of the Sudanese children (five of the six) were making progress comparable to, or better than the targets expected of average

British children. Five children secured higher than average test and GCSE results, including 'Paul' who gained seven GCSEs at Grade A*–C, after just two years in the UK.

One of the students unlikely to do well in GCSE examinations was 'Luke', a student who had had very little schooling before arrival in the UK. He was self-taught, but despite this was an excellent writer. His teachers stated that he had made good progress since arriving in the UK – validating the notion that data on progress, rather than naked summative achievement data, is what teachers of refugee children need to measure.

None of the Sudanese children were on their schools' special needs registers. School attendance was notably higher among Sudanese children than among other refugee groups such as Congolese and Somali children. During the previous six weeks, Sudanese children had secured 97 per cent attendance. That their parents and carers spoke English may have meant that they missed less school because of domestic interpreting duties.

Where available, children's homework diaries were examined. All of the children completed homework on most occasions. In structured classroom observation also all the Sudanese students were engaged in learning tasks at most times during lessons. They were a well-motivated group of students. Many of the children were forthcoming in their frustration with their peers' behaviour and lack of respect for teachers. They often made negative comparisons of their schools, and felt they learned more in Egypt and Sudan where their teachers were stricter.

One teacher described the Sudanese children as being 'well-behaved, well-motivated and a pleasure to teach'. Others used similar descriptors. Unlike some Congolese and Somali students, the older Sudanese children were not described as being disaffected. In one school where disproportionate numbers of African-Caribbean and African students were being excluded, the Sudanese appeared to have escaped a racialised school discipline system.

It was also noticeable that teachers did not invoke discourses of trauma when discussing Sudanese children – none of them was described as 'traumatised'. Yet half of the Sudanese children had been exposed to organised violence. Somalis are described as traumatised, sometimes irrespective of their adaptation in school, but Sudanese children are not. Their labelling as hard-working and well-adapted on the one hand, or traumatised and thus uneducable on the other may influence teacher expectations, as well as any psycho-social intervention.

Conclusions

Sudanese children are enjoying some educational success in the UK. This may have a number of causes. One factor that appeared to contribute to high levels of educational progress was children's confidence in a distinctly southern Sudanese identity and their maintenance of cultural forms that valued education. They had remained committed to school work even in secondary schools where the dominant youth culture did not favour academic success. Sudanese children had resisted acculturation in schools where male behaviour was largely 'laddish'. Like Tamils and Vietnamese, many Sudanese children possess embodied cultural capital – dispositions or habitus that favour self-improvement through education (Bourdieu, 1986).

In this respect southern Sudanese educational experiences support the segmented assimilation model discussed in Chapter 3. Sudanese children have followed the trajectory of enjoying educational success and maintenance of values and cultural forms of their community (Portes and Rumbaut, 2001; Portes and Zhou, 1993; Rumbaut and Portes, 2001).

But resistance to acculturation is not the only factor that appears to account for their comparative educational success. First, the southern Sudanese children are an elite group of migrants. Second, southern Sudanese children came from homes where fluent English was spoken and all of the children had entered school able to speak some English. High teacher expectations also contributed to children's achievement, as did escaping the label of traumatised and thus uneducable.

Long-term data on Luke and Paul's progress were available, as both men had kept in contact with Sudanese community organisations. Paul gained seven good GCSEs and had the ability to secure a university place. But at 16 he left school and undertook a vocational course in hotel management at his local college. He then moved to work and live in a hotel in the West End of London. Paul talks about going to university when he is older, but, alone in the UK, is acutely conscious of the need to earn his living. At 22 years of age, Paul has still not received a decision on his application for asylum. With this uncertainty, he feels he has to continue earning money.

Luke took English, mathematics and carpentry courses at college. He now works as a bus driver. He is keen to marry and settle down and has had a number of girlfriends, but does not know whether he should marry a Sudanese girl or not.

Both Paul and Luke were very able students. Had they been born in the UK in all likelihood they would gone to university. Paul gained good GCSEs and Luke has secure employment. But do their educational and labour market experiences comprise successful integration? And what will Paul and Luke be doing in ten years? Will Paul have fulfilled his ambition to go to university or will he be trapped in a low paid job? And what of the Sudanese girls? Will they progress to college and secure employment? Or will traditional expectations of marriage and home making come before higher education and employment?

Sudanese children have secured success at school. But there is little long-term data on their experiences in further and higher education and in the labour market. This is a powerful argument for a longitudinal study of young refugees' adaptation, educational progression and eventual employment. The integration research agenda should not end with the completion of GCSEs. Definitions of successful settlement must encompass the long-term experiences of young refugees.

PART FOUR:
NEW VISIONS FOR
REFUGEE CHILDREN

NEW VISIONS FOR REFUGEE CHILDREN

The past 15 years have seen an increase in the numbers of forced migrants in UK schools. From 1989 until very recently, most of these children entered the asylum determination system. Today increasing numbers of children whose families have experiences of forced migration are remaining in the UK as children of work permit holders, overseas students or as irregular migrants. This trend is likely to continue. Policy interventions targeted at children who are forced migrants should not exclude a group purely on the basis of immigration status. It is also important for educationalists to note that the distinctions between voluntary and forced migrants are blurred.

Refugee children have very mixed experiences of the UK education system. In the world's fifth richest nation, many refugee children have great difficulty finding a school place. Education is a basic human right, yet schools, local authorities and central government invoke procedural and bureaucratic arguments to try and escape fulfilling a legal and moral duty.

Some refugee children are enjoying a measure of success at school. Others are not, including many Congolese, Somali, Turkish and Kurdish children. Racist bullying of refugees is an all too common occurrence in schools. Many factors contribute to this, including unbalanced and inaccurate media reporting. Sadly, schools are rarely successful in challenging commonly held beliefs about refugees.

The migration of refugees often involves children losing much of their educational cultural capital – habitus or dispositions that value learning. In this respect, UK refugee experiences support the segmented assimilation model discussed in Chapter 3 (Portes and Rumbaut, 2001; Portes and Zhou, 1993; Rumbaut and Portes, 2001). But maintenance or loss of the immigrant habitus is not the only factor that accounts for differential educational progress. Hard work alone may not compensate for racism, economic deprivation or the specific linguistic problems experienced by many Congolese refugees.

Many other factors contribute to the lack of progress of refugee children.

Some relate to their pre-migration experiences. Others are associated with post-migration conditions – within the child's inner micro-system as well as the school, community and nation. Research into refugee children's achievement needs to be ecological in its approach, examining pre-migration and post-migration experiences, and including home, community and school factors.

Policy texts tend to construct refugee children as a homogeneous group, in ways that impede in-depth analysis of the multiple actors that may limit children's progress. Such homogenisation also impedes focused interventions to promote the progress of different groups of refugee children. Additionally, refugee children's needs have largely been framed in terms of trauma and post-traumatic stress disorder. But there is little evidence to suggest that refugee children are a universally traumatised group: most of the children in this research were happy and had adapted well to their new surroundings. A few refugee children have had horrific pre-migration experiences, usually of armed conflict, and do manifest disturbed behaviour. Yet they are a minority among refugee children, and family breakdown, changes in care arrangements or extreme parental stress also contribute to these children's psychiatric morbidity. Educationalists, therefore, must be critical of trauma discourses. Their dominance in research and policy text again labels and homogenises refugee children, preventing a rigorous analysis of other pre-migration or post-migration issues that influence children's adaptation in the UK.

But while many educationalists invoke discourses of trauma, interventions for refugee children comprise limited English as an additional language support and little more. Indeed, trauma talk camouflages this shabby service, as it is difficult to be critical in the face of such expressed compassion.

So how should refugee children be supported? What are my new visions for refugee children? First, as a nation we need to build an asylum system that is fair and fulfils the UK's commitments under the 1951 UN Convention Relating to the Status of Refugees and its 1967 Protocol. Human rights organisations such as Amnesty International and the Joint Council for the Welfare of Immigrants continue to lobby for a just and humanitarian asylum system, arguing for asylum applications to be determined by an independent body. All asylum-seekers should have access to good quality legal advice to assist them in their initial applications and appeals and the strict time limits on submitting evidence should be abolished. Human rights organisations also argue for the minimum use of detention, the right of detainees to be bailed and meaningful in-country appeals against negative asylum decisions (Amnesty International (UK), 2004, 2005; Joint Council for the Welfare of Immigrants, 2001). The right of asylum-seekers to work is also a key demand of human rights organisations

Second, central government needs to engage coherently with debates about inequality and social class. As argued in earlier chapters, educational policy on equality is marginalised and distinctly 'add on' in its approach. As an appendage to the mainstream of education policy, planning on equality, including refugee education, often runs contrary to it. All parts of central government need to recognise that the causes of educational underachievement lie with the school *and* the family, the community and wider society. While poor teaching is undesirable, central government needs to acknowledge that children's educational under-achievement also has causes that lie outside the school. Projects to support refugee children must meet their needs holistically, supporting theirs and their carers' welfare needs, as well as their schooling. Support should be in the form of casework, not advice leaflets and services that refer refugees to other agencies. Chapter 8 gives a case study of one school that has considered children's ecological needs, and has seen a small but sustained improvement in children's educational achievement.

Third, I remain convinced that a cultural acceptance of violence within schools is a major cause of racist behaviour, and also limits the success of educational interventions. Central government needs to focus on violence within secondary schools, rather than fan moral panics about bad behaviour.

Education policy has been characterised by reified and essentialist notions of race. I believe that central and local government needs to discard their essentialist notions of 'race' and that studies of racisms and racialised life experiences must be ecological in their approach.

There are some specific interventions that would make a difference to the lives of refugee children. Central government should take a more robust approach with schools and local authorities that fail to provide school places for children.

Debate about the real costs of providing English as an additional language support is needed. Other funding reforms are necessary, including contingency funding within targeted support such as the English Ethnic Minority Achievement Grant. This would enable assistance to new groups of migrants whose arrival may be sudden and unplanned. Targeted funding for refugee children should also enable more schools and local authorities to employ home–school support workers who would offer parents casework support.

Many refugees have organised their own community schools. These institutions have a key role in providing peer support for young people. Community schools can also help in the transmission of educational cultural capital – habitus or values that support learning. Yet many community schools are under-funded and operate in isolation from mainstream education. Training of community teachers and the sharing of premises are initiatives that support community schools. Central government and a greater number of local authorities need to see community schools as partners.

Somalis are a particularly marginalised refugee group. Their numbers include many young people who have undertaken most or all of their education in the UK and speak fluent English. Despite this, many leave school with few qualifications and are unsuccessful in finding work. A Somali GCSE examination would afford greater integration and a greater sense of belonging to British society, as well as developing Somali children's home language literacy and thus their reading and writing skills in English. Programmes to help young Somalis find work – job clubs offering long-term support rather than short-term courses – are also needed for a community where less than 15 per cent of adults are in work (Greater London Authority, 2005).

In planning interventions for refugees, a child's background and experiences in their home country need to be considered; different national groups of children have different linguistic, educational and social experiences. Educational interventions need to focus on particular groups, such as the Somalis, rather than refugee children as a whole.

Two policy initiatives offer real opportunities to support refugee children. The development of extended schools in England, and their equivalents in Scotland and Wales, may enable schools to offer broad-ranging support for refugee children and their parents. By 2010 all schools in England will be expected to offer a range of activities that might include additional schooling, homework clubs, arts and leisure activities for pupils, community learning opportunities for people living in the environs of the school and for parents, childcare and welfare support for children and their parents and carers. But evaluations of pilot extended schools have highlighted two important issues. First, there is little agreement as to what should be included in the extended schools programmes. Related to this there is an unresolved tension – whether extended schools should promote achievement or promote child welfare. It is now up to refugee advocacy organisation and their supporters to argue for projects that support children and their parents, meeting their holistic needs.

The reform of 14–19 education is also essential. There is a long-standing divide between academic and vocational qualifications in all parts of the UK, with the former being afforded much higher status. This rift, and that many children still leave school with no qualifications, prompted a review of 14–19 education, led by Mike Tomlinson, the former Chief Inspector of Schools in England. His report proposed a single school leavers' diploma to be awarded at four levels: Entry (pre-GCSE), Foundation, Intermediate and Advanced (A-Level equivalent). The diploma would replace GCSEs, A-Levels and the myriad of occupational and vocational qualifications. Students would study 'core' subjects – information technology, mathematics, English language. Volunteering, community activities, work experience and citizenship education would also be included in the core. Outside the core would be a choice of optional subjects and students would be able to take a mixture of academic and vocational subjects if they desired. The diploma would be assessed by examinations and the submission of a single piece of coursework (DfES, 2004b).

The proposed 14–19 diploma offered real opportunities for refugee children. The original proposals would let young people progress through education at their own rate; mixed-age classes would be an outcome of this reform. Refugee children would be afforded the chance to catch up with new curricular concepts, as well as develop language fluency in mixed-age classes. They would also be able to study different subjects at different levels. Children who arrived in the UK with little or no prior education would be more likely to leave school with a qualification. The requirement for a single piece of coursework would also benefit refugee children. For many children who arrive in the UK mid-way through a GCSE course, the demands of completing multiple pieces of coursework prevent good GCSE grades.

Tomlinson's proposals attracted broad support, from industry, academia and the teaching unions, as well as those concerned with social justice.

Despite universal support, in early 2005 the Goverrnment failed to adopt them, due to concerns about how middle England would react to the abolition of A-Levels. Once more, fear of the *Daily Mail* determined Government policy. But lobbying continues and hopefully the single 14–19 diploma will eventually be realised.

Finally, my new vision for refugee children encompasses a rethink of what we mean by integration and citizenship. Much writing about refugee children has focused on the notion of 'culture clash' – refugee children living and moving between two different and separate cultural worlds. This culture clash is usually presented as a clash between UK and 'backward' minority values with gender relations and sexual mores almost always cited as examples of the alleged backwardness. Integration into cultural forms of the majority community is always presented as a desirable process. But as previously discussed, the 'culture clash' for some refugees is often between a community that values education and a majority community that places less value on learning.

Government should reject its present construction of integration outlined in Chapter 5. Present policy models of integration have assimilative associations of 'them' becoming like 'us'. Home Office policy also makes strong connections between educational achievement, economic advancement and cultural integration – suggesting that you cannot progress educationally and economically without a considerable degree of cultural assimilation into the mainstream (Ager and Strang, 2004; Home Office, 2004b). The experiences of many refugees, including the southern Sudanese prove this otherwise.

Definitions of successful integration must encompass the long-term experiences of young refugees. The integration agenda should not end with the completion of GCSEs. But there are no longitudinal studies of young refugees in the UK. There is no data on UK-educated refugee children's eventual experiences in further and higher education and in the labour market. This is a powerful argument for a longitudinal study of young refugees' adaptation, educational progression and eventual employment.

Migration and citizenship are central themes that run through this book.

The migration of refugees is part of a larger international movement of people. As Chapter 2 argues, there is an asylum–migration nexus. All countries are affected by migration, whether as countries of origin, transit nations or countries of destination. Both forced and voluntary migration have their roots in conflict, injustice and poverty. There are no easy solutions to poverty; similarly, there are no easy answers when it comes to considering the causes and effects of migration. Although I have some personal sympathies with the Open Borders movement, their policies are presently an unrealisable ideal and have unforeseen short-term social consequences.

Most policies that deal with migration are national policies, yet migration is transnational in its character. A transnational social issue such as migration requires international governance, as well as transnational cooperation involving individuals and the agencies of civil society. In summary, international migration requires global citizenship.

Citizenship enshrines the relationship between the individual and the collective. It carries with it legal, political and social rights, as well as responsibilities. It is 55 years since T. H. Marshall wrote *Citizenship and Social Class* (1950). His understanding of citizenship was equated with formal membership of the nation-state. Since then, European societies have experienced increased international migration, as well as the development of the supernational institutions of the European community. National citizenship, with its rights and responsibilities, is increasingly mediated by membership of other collectives: political, social, ethnic, local, regional, supernational, as well as transnational. Yet European societies often seem unable to acknowledge multiple and multi-layered citizenship. Cultural difference and transnational belongings are under attack from politicians and the press. Perhaps the answer is to include both difference *and* equality into our construct of citizenship, and to build global citizenship.

Much of this book describes the removal of citizenship rights – legal, political and social – from asylum-seekers, refugees and other migrants. Yet I believe that the responsibilities of all citizens include the constructive and peaceful criticism of political life, as well as participating in action to improve the quality of life for all, including new migrants. Those who are concerned about migrants' rights have a duty to take action. In an essay on urban unrest, Stuart Hall provides a pertinent reflection:

> I have a reluctance about entering once again into what seems to me a terribly familiar and recurring cycle. The cycle goes something like this. There is a problem that is followed by a conference; the conference is followed by research; the research reinforces what we already know, but in elegant and scholarly language. Then nothing happens.
>
> (Hall, 1987: 45)

I hope that some of the readers of this book may join with others to work for justice and equality, a world without violent conflict and poverty, and a world where education liberates the minds of children.

BIBLIOGRAPHY

Aboud, F. (1988) *Children and Prejudice*, Oxford: Blackwell.

Adorno, T., Frenkel-Brunswik, E., Levison, D., and Sanford, R. (1950) *The Authoritarian Personality*, New York: Harper.

Ager, A. and Strang, A. (2004) *Indicators of Integration*, London: Home Office.

Ahmed, E. (1991) The Educational and Training Needs of the Somali Community in South Glamorgan, unpublished report, Welsh Refugee Council.

Ahmed, I. (1998) Feeling Exclusion? A survey of the Somali community in Lewisham, unpublished report, London Borough of Lewisham..

Al-Ali, N. and Koser, K. (eds) (2003) *New Approaches to Migration: Transnational Communities and the Transformation of Home*, London: Routledge.

Alba, R. and Farley, R. (2002) 'The New Second Generation in the United States' *International Migration Review* 36: 669–701.

Allodi, F (1989) 'The Children of Victims of Political Persecution and Torture: Psychological Study of a Latin American community' *International Journal of Mental Health* 18 (2).

Al-Rasheed, M. (1993) 'The Meaning of Marriage and Status in Exile: The Experience of Iraqi women' *Journal of Refugee Studies* 6 (2).

American Psychiatric Association (1980) *Diagnostic and Statistical Manual of Mental Disorders,* 3rd edition, Washington, DC: APA.

American Psychiatric Association (1994) *Diagnostic and Statistical Manual of Mental Disorders*, 4th edition, Washington, DC: APA.

Amnesty International (UK) (2004) *Get It Right: How Home Office Decision Making Fails Refugees*, London: Amnesty International (UK).

Amnesty International (UK) (2005) *Seeking Asylum is Not a Crime: Detention of People who Have Sought Asylum*, London: Amnesty International (UK).

Anderson, A. (2004) 'Resilience' in R. Hamilton and D. Moore, (eds) *Educational Interventions for Refugee Children*, London: Routledge Falmer.

Anderson, B. and Rogaly, B. (2005) *Forced Labour and Migration to the UK*, Oxford: Centre for Migration, Policy and Society, University of Oxford.

Anthias, F. and Yuval-Davies, N. (1992) *Racialized Boundaries: Race, Nation, Gender, Colour and Class and the Anti-racist Struggle*, London: Routledge.

Archer, L. and Francis. B. (2003) *Negotiating the Dichotomy of Boffin and Triad: British–Chinese Pupils' Constructions of 'Laddism'*, London: Institute for Policy Studies in Education, London Metropolitan University.

Arroyo, W. (1985) 'Children Traumatized by Central American Warfare' in S. Eth and R. Pynoos (eds) *Post Traumatic Stress Disorder in Children*, Washington, DC: American Psychiatric Press.

Arshad, R, Closs, A. and Stead, J. (1999) *Doing Our Best: Scottish School Education, Refugee Pupils and Parents – a Strategy for Social Inclusion*, Edinburgh: Centre for Education in Racial Equality in Scotland.

Association of London Government (ALG) (2005) *Breaking Point: Examining the Disruption Caused by Pupil Mobility*, London: ALG.

Association of Teachers and Lecturers (ATL) (2002) Letter from Peter Smith to Home Secretary on Asylum Children, unpublished correspondence .

Back, L. (1996) *New Ethnicities and Urban Culture: Racisms and Multiculture in Young Lives*, London: UCL Press.

Baker, C. (1996) *Foundations of Bilingual Education and Bilingualism*, Clevedon: Multilingual Matters.

Baker, R. (1983) 'Refugees – an Overview of an International Problem' in R. Baker (ed) *The Psychosocial Problems of Refugees*, London: Refugee Council.

Balibar, E. (1991) 'Is There a Neo-racism?' in E. Balibar and I. Wallenstein (eds) *Race, Nation, Class: Ambiguous Identities*, London: Verso.

Ball, S. (1994) *Education Reform: A Critical and Post-structural Approach*, Buckingham: Open University Press.

Ballard, C. and Driver, G. (1977) 'The Ethnic Approach' *New Society* 16 June.

Banafunzi, B. (1996) 'The Education of the Bravanese Community' *Race, Ethnicity and Education* 1 (1).

Barker, M. (1981) *The New Racism*, London: Junction Books.

Barsh, R. and Marlor, C. (2000) 'Grounded, Experiential Teaching about Violence' *HFG Review* 4 (1): 27–38.

Baskauskas, L. (1980) 'The Lithuanian Refugee Experience and Grief' *International Migration Review* 15 (1): 276–291.

Bell, J. (1993) *Ugandan Refugees: A Study of Housing Conditions and the Circumstances of Children*, London: Community Development Foundation.

Benn, C. and Chitty, C. (eds) (1997) *Rethinking Education and Democracy: A Socialist Alternative for the 21st Century*, London: Tuffnell Press.

Bernstein, B. (1971) *Class, Codes and Control, Volume One*, London: Routledge.

Berry, J. (2001) 'A Psychology of Immigration' *Journal of Social Issues* 57: 615–631.

Berry, J., Kim. V., Minde, T. and Mok, J. (1987) 'Comparative Studies of Acculturative Stress' *International Migration Review* 21 (3): 491–511.

Bhattacharya, G., Ison, L. and Blair, M. (2003) *Minority Ethnic Attainment and Participation in Education and Training: the evidence*, London: DfES.

Bhavnani, K. and Phoenix, A. (1994) 'Shifting Identities, Shifting Racisms: An Introduction' *Feminism and Psychology* 1 (1): 5–18.

Black, G. (1998) *JFS: The History of the Jews' Free School, London since 1732*, London: Tymsder Publishing.

Bloch, A. (1999) 'Carrying Out a Survey of Refugees: Some Methodological Considerations and Guidelines' *Journal of Refugee Studies* 12 (4): 367–383.

Bolloten, B. and Spafford, T. (1996) Brava: An Educational Resource Pack, unpublished report, London Borough of Newham.

Bolloten, B. and Spafford, T. (1998) 'Supporting Refugee Children in East London Primary Schools' J. Rutter and C. Jones (eds) *Refugee Education: Mapping the Field*, Stoke on Trent: Trentham Books.

Bourdieu, P. (1986) 'The Forms of Capital' in J. Richardson (ed.) *Handbook of Theory and Research for the Sociology of Education*, New York: Greenwood Press.

Bourdieu, P. and Passeron, J.–C. (1977) *Reproduction in Education, Society and Culture*, Los Angeles: Sage.

Bourhis, R., Moiese, L., Perreault, S. and Senecal, S. (1997) 'Towards an Inter-active Acculturation Model: A Social Psychological Approach' *International Journal of Psychology* 32: 369–386.

Bourne, J. and Blair, M. (1998) *Making the Difference: Teaching and Learning Strategies in Successful Multi-ethnic Schools*, London: DfEE.

Bowe, R. and Ball, S. (1992) *Reforming Education and Changing Schools*, London: Routledge.

Boyd, M. (1989) 'Family and Personal Networks in International Migration: Recent Developments and New Agendas' *International Migration Review* 23 (3) 635–70.

Boyd, M. (2003) 'Educational Attainments of Immigrant Offspring: Success or Segmented Assimilation?' *International Migration Review* 36: 1037–1060.

Boyden, J. and De Berry, J. (2004) *Children and Youth on the Front Line: Ethnography, Armed Conflict and Displacement*, Oxford: Berghahn Books.

Boyden, J. and Ryder, P. (1996) The Provision of Education to Children Affected by Armed Conflict, unpublished paper, Refugee Studies Centre, University of Oxford.

Bracken, P. (1998) 'Hidden agendas: Deconstructing Post Traumatic Stressdisorder' in P. Bracken and C. Petty (eds) *Rethinking the Trauma of War*, London: Save the Children.

British Council for Aid to Refugees (BCAR) (1969) *One Year Later, A Report on Czechoslovak Arrivals*, London: BCAR.

British Council for Aid to Refugees (BCAR) (1973) *Annual Report 1972*, London: BCAR.

British Council for Aid to Refugees (BCAR) (1974) *Annual Report 1973*, London: BCAR.

British Council for Aid to Refugees (BCAR) (1980) *Annual Report 1979*. London: BCAR.

British Refugee Council (1989a) *Asylum Statistics 1979–1988*. London: British Refugee Council.

British Refugee Council (1989b) Submission to Home Office Section 11 Scrutiny, unpublished report.

British Refugee Council (1989c) Minutes of the Education and Training Working Group, March 1989, unpublished minutes.

Bronfenbrenner, U. (1992) 'Ecological Systems Theory' in R. Vasta (ed) *Six Theories of Child Development: Revised Formulations and Current Issues*, London: Jessica Kingsley Publishers.

Brooks-Gunn J. (2001) 'Children in Families in Communities: Risk and Intervention in the Bronfenbrenner Tradition' in P. Moen, G. Elder and K. Lusher (eds) *Examining Lives in Context: Perspectives on the Ecology of Human Development*, Washington, DC: American Psychological Association.

Brown, R. (1995) *Prejudice: Its Social Psychology*, Cambridge, MA: Blackwell.

Buijs, G. (ed.) (1993) *Migrant Women: Crossing Boundaries and Changing Identities*, Oxford: Berg Publishers.

Burnett, A. and Peel, M. (2001) 'The Health Needs of Asylum-seekers and Refugees' *British Medical Journal* 322: 544–547.

Bush, K. and Saltarelli, D. (2000) *Two Faces of Education in Ethnic Conflict: Towards Peace Building Education for Children*, New York: UNICEF.

Cahalan, P. (1982) *Belgian Refugee Relief in England During the Great War*, New York: Garland.

Camden, London Borough of (1996) Refugee Educational Policy, unpublished policy document..

Camino, L. and Krulfeld,R. (eds) (1994) *Reconstructing Lives, Recapturing Meaning: Refugee Identity, Gender and Cultural Change*, New York: Gordon and Breach.

Caplan, N., Choy, M. and Whitmore, J. (1991) *Children of the Boat People: A Study of Educational Success*, Ann Arbor, MI: University of Michigan Press.

Carey-Wood, J., Duke, K., Karn, V. and Marshall, T. (1995) *The Settlement of Refugees in Britain, Home Office Study 141*, London: HMSO.

Cassanelli, L. (1994) *Victims and Vulnerable Groups in Southern Somalia*, Ottawa: Canadian Immigration Board Research Directorate.

Castles, S. and Kosack, G. (1973) *Immigrant Workers and the Class Structure*, London: Institute of Race Relations, in association with Oxford University Press.

Castles, S. and Loughna, S. (2002) Trends in Asylum Migration to Industrialised Countries 1990–2001, unpublished paper for UN University, World Institute for Development Economic Research.

Castles, S. and Miller, M. (1998), *The Age of Migration: International Population Movements in the Modern World*, 2nd edition, Basingstoke: Macmillan.

Chatty, D. and Hundt, G. (2004) 'Advocating Multidisciplinarity in Studying Complex Emergencies: The Limitations of a Psychological Approach to Understanding How Young People Cope with Prolonged Conflict in Gaza' *Journal of Biosocial Science* 36 (4): 417–431.

Children of the Storm (1998) *Invisible Students: Practical and Peer-led Approaches to Enhancing the Educational and Emotional Support for Refugee Children in Schools*, London: Children of the Storm.

Chimienti, G., Nasr, J. and Khaliffeh, I. (1989) 'Children's reactions to war-related stresses' *Social Psychiatry and Psychiatic Epidemiology'* 24 (6)

Chitty, C. (1992) *The Education System Transformed: A Guide to School Reforms*, Manchester: Baseline Books.

Clarke, J., Dobson, J., Koser, K. and Salt, J. (2003) *The Ins and Outs of Migration*, London: Commission for Racial Equality, available at: www.cre.gov.uk.

Cline, T., de Abreu, G., Fihosy, C., Gray, H., Lambert, H. and Neale, J. (2002) *Minority Ethnic Children in Mainly White Schools*, London: DfES.

Cohen, P. (1989) *The Cultural Geography of Adolescent Racism*, London: UCL Press.

Cohen, R. (1997) *Global Diasporas: An Introduction*, London: UCL Press.

Commission for Racial Equality (CRE) (1983) *Vietnamese Refugees in Britain*, London: CRE.

Commission for Racial Equality (CRE) (1986) *Teaching English as a Second Language: Report of a Formal Investigation in Calderdale LEA*, London: CRE.

Commission for Racial Equality (CRE) (1992) *Set to Fail?*, London: CRE.

Commission for Racial Equality (CRE) (2000) *Learning for All: Standards for Racial Equality in Schools*, London: CRE.

Committee of Inquiry into the Education of Children from Ethnic Minority Groups (1985) *Education for All: The Report of the Committee of Inquiry into the Education of Children from Ethnic Minority Groups (Swann Report)*, London: HMSO.

Community of Congolese Students in UK (CCS UK) (2002) *Annual Report 2001–02*, London: CCS UK.

Community Relations Commission (CRC) (1974) *One Year on: A Report on the Resettlement of Refugees from Uganda in Britain*, London: CRC.

Crisp, J. (ed.) (2002) *Learning for a Future: Refugee Education in Developing Countries*, Geneva: UNHCR.

Crozier, G. (2000) *Parents and School: Partners or Protagonists?* Stoke on Trent: Trentham Books.

Cummins, J. (1977) 'Cognitive Factors Associated with Attainment of Intermediate Levels of Bilingual Skills' *Modern Language Journal* 61: 3–12.

Cummins, J. (1981a) 'The Role of Primary Language Development in Promoting Educational Success for Language Minority Students' in California State Department of Education (ed.) *Schooling and Language Minority Students: A Theoretical Framework*, Los Angeles: California State University.

Cummins, J. (1891b) *Bilingualism and Minority Language Children*, Ontario: Ontario Institute for Studies in Education.

Cummins. J. (1996) *Negotiating Identities: Education for Empowerment in a Diverse Society*, Ontario: Canada Association for Bilingual Education.

Cummins, J. and Swain, M. (1986) *Bilingualism in Education*, New York: Longman.

Dalby, A. (1998) *Dictionary of Languages*, London: Bloomsbury.

Danish Refugee Council and European Council on Refugees and Exiles (ECRE) (2003) *European Asylum Systems: Legal and Social Conditions for Asylum Seekers and Refugees in Western Europe*, London: ECRE.

Dedezade, K. (1994) Turkish Pupils are Underachieving in British Schools. Fact or Myth? MA dissertation, University of North London.

de Jastrzebski, T. (1916) 'The Register of Belgian Refugees' *Journal of the Statistical Society*, 79: 133–153.

de Kisshazy, C. (1979) The Hungarians. Internal Memorandum of the British Council for Aid to Refugees, unpublished report.

de Kisshazy, C. (1981) Hungarians in Britain. Internal report of the British Refugee Council, unpublished report..

Department for Education (DfE) (1991) *Partnership Teaching*, London: DfE.

Department for Education and Skills (DfES) (2001) *Code of Practice on Special Educational Needs*, London: DfES.

Department for Education and Skills (DfES) (2003a) *On the Move: Guidance on Managing Pupil Mobility*, London: DfES.

Department for Education and Skills (DfES) (2003b) *The Standards Fund 2003–04: Guidance*, London: DfES.

Department for Education and Skills (DfES) (2003c) *Vulnerable Children Grant:: Guidance for Financial Year 2004/05*, London: DfES.

Department for Education and Skills (DfES) (2004a) *Aiming High: Guidance on Supporting the Education of Asylum-seeking and Refugee Children*, London: DfES.

Department for Education and Skills (DfES) (2004b) *14–19 Curriculum and Qualifications Reform: Final Report of the Working Group on 14–19 Reform*, London: DfES.

Department for Education and Skills (DfES) (2005) *Ethnicity and Education: The Evidence on Minority Ethnic Pupils*, London: DfES.

Department of Health (2003) *Guidance on Accommodation: Children in Need and Their Families LAC 13*, London: Department of Health.

Department of Health (2004) *Proposals to Exclude Overseas Visitors from Eligibility to Free NHS Primary Medical Services: A Consultation*, London: Department of Health.

Desforges, C. (2003) *The Impact of Parental Involvement, Parental Support and Family Education on Pupil Achievement and Adjustment*, London: DfES.

Dobson, J. and Pooley, C. (2004) *Mobility, Equality, Diversity: A Study of Pupil Mobility in the Secondary School System*, London: Migration Research Unit, University College London.

Dobson, J., Henthorne, K. and Lynas, Z. (2000) *Pupil Mobility in Schools, Final Report,* London: Migration Research Unit, University College London.

Dobson, J., Koser, K., Mclaughan, G. and Salt, J. (2001) *International Migration and the United Kingdom: Recent Patterns and Trends,* London: Home Office.

Dorkenoo, E. and Elworthy, S. (1994) *Female Genital Mutilation: Proposals for Change,* London: Minority Rights Group.

Duevell, F. (1998) *Undocumented Migrant Workers in the UK,* Report One, Exeter: University of Exeter Department of Social Work.

Duke, K. and Marshall, T. (1995) *Vietnamese Refugees since 1982,* London: HMSO.

Dyer, R. (1997) *White,* London: Routledge.

Dyregov, A. (1991) *Grief in Children: A Handbook for Adults,* London: Jessica Kingsley Publishers.

East London Schools Fund (1999) *Somalis in London,* London: East London Schools Fund.

Eastmond, M. (1993) 'Reconstructing Life: Chilean Refugee Women and the Dilemmas of Exile' in G. Buijs, (ed.) *Migrant Women: Crossing Boudaries and Changing Identities,* Oxford: Berg Publishers.

Eggleston, J., Dunn, D. and Anjali, M. (1986) *Education for Some: The Educational and Vocational Experiences of 15–18 Year Old Members of Minority Ethnic Groups,* Stoke on Trent: Trentham Books.

Elbedour, S., ten Bensel, R. and Bastien, D. (1993) 'Ecological Integrated Model of Children of War' *Child Abuse and Neglect,* 17: 805–819.

El-Solh, C. (1991) 'Somalis in London's East End: A Community Striving for Recognition' *New Community* 17: 539–552.

Enneli, P., Modood, T. and Bradley, H. (2005) *Young Turks and Kurds: A Set of Invisible Disadvantaged Groups,* York: Joseph Rowntree Foundation.

Enfield, London Borough of (1999) *Refugee Education Handbook,* London: London Borough of Enfield.

Eriksen, T. (2002) *Ethnicity and Nationalism,* London: Pluto.

Espino, C. (1991) 'Trauma and adaption: The Case of Central American Children' in F. Ahearn and J. Athey, (eds) *Refugee Children: Theory, Research and Services,* Baltimore, MD: Johns Hopkins University Press.

Eth, S. and Pynoos, R. (1985) (eds) *Post Traumatic Stress Disorder in Children,* Washington, DC: American Psychiatric Press.

Etzioni, A. (1996) *The New Golden Rule: Community and Morality in a Democratic Society,* New York: Basic Books.

European Council (2003a) *Council Directive 2003/9/EC of 27 January 2003: Laying Down Minimum Standards for the Reception of Asylum-seekers,* Brussels: European Council.

European Council (2003b) *Council Directive 2003/86/EC of 22 September 2003 on the Right to Family Reunification,* Brussels: European Council.

European Council for Refugees and Exiles (ECRE) (1997) *Position Paper on Temporary Protection,* London: ECRE.

European Council for Refugees and Exiles (ECRE) (2004) *Asylum Applications and Country of Origin Information in Europe, 2004,* London: ECRE.

European Roma Rights Centre (ERRC) (1997) *In the Time of the Skinheads: Denial and Exclusion of Roma in Slovakia,* Budapest: ERRC.

Fairclough, N. (1989) *Language and Power,* London: Longman.

Fairclough, N. (1995) *Critical Discourse Analysis,* Harlow: Longman.

Faist, T. (2000) *The Volume and Dynamics of International Migration and Transnational Social Spaces,* Oxford: Oxford University Press.

Fazel, M. and Stein. A. (2002) 'Mental Health of Refugee Children' *Archives of Disease in Childhood* 87 (5): 366–370 .

Fekete, L. (2001) *The Dispersal of Xenophobia*, London: Institute of Race Relations.

Fischer, G. (1996) 'Hungary for Freedom or Just Hungry?' *The Times* 22 October.

Foucault, M. (1972) *The Archaeology of Knowledge and Discourse on Language*, New York: Pantheon.

Frazer, E. (1999) *The Problem of Communitarian Politics: Unity and Conflict*, Oxford: Oxford University Press.

Free, E. (2005) *Young Refugees: A Guide to the Rights and Entitlements of Separated Refugee Children*, London: Save the Children.

Freire, M. (1990) 'Refugees, ESL and Literacy' *Refuge* 10: 3–6.

Freud, A. and Burlingham, D. (1943) *War and Children*, New York: Ernst Willard.

Furedi, F. (2003) *Therapy Culture: Cultivating Vulnerability in an Anxious Age*, London: Routledge.

Fyvie-Gauld, M. (2000) *Hard to Reach Groups in Brighton and Hove*, Brighton: Brighton and Hove Council.

Galtung, J. (1996) *Peace by Peaceful Means*, London: Sage.

Gartner, L. (1960) *The Jewish Immigrant in England, 1870–1914*, London: George Allen and Unwin.

Gewirtz, S., Ball, S. and Bowe, R. (1995) *Markets, Choice and Equity in Education*, Buckingham: Open University Press.

Giddens, A. (1984) *The Constitution of Society*, Berkeley, CA: University of California Press.

Gigler, M. (1983) *The Czechs in Australia*, Melbourne: Australian Ethnic Heritage Series.

Gillborn, D. (1995) *Racism and Anti-Racism in Real Schools: Theory, Policy and Practice*, Buckingham: Open University Press.

Gillborn, D. and Gipps. C. (1996) *Recent Research on the Achievement of Ethnic Minority Pupils*, London: Office for Standards in Education.

Gillborn, D. and Mirza, H. (1998) *Educational Inequality: Mapping Race, Class and Gender*, London: OFSTED.

Gillborn, D. and Youdell, D. (2000*) Rationing Education*, Buckingham: Open University Press.

Goodhart, D. (2004) 'Too Much Diversity?' *Prospect* February.

Government Office for London (GOL) (2003) Social Cohesion: A Presentation, unpublished conference presentation.

Greater London Authority (GLA) (2004) *Destitution by Design – Withdrawal of Support for In-country Asylum Applicants, an Impact Assessment for London*, London: GLA.

Greater London Authority (GLA) (2005) *Country of Birth and Labour Market Outcomes in London*, London: GLA.

Griffiths, D. (1997) 'Somali Refugees in Tower Hamlets: Clanship and New Identity' *New Community*, 23 (1) 5–24.

Griffiths, D. (2002) *Somali and Kurdish Refugees in London: New Identities in the Diaspora*, Aldershot: Ashgate Books.

Griffiths, D., Sigona, N. and Zetter, R. (2005) *Refugee Community Organisations and Dispersal*, Bristol: Policy Press

Hall, S. (1987) 'Urban Unrest in Britain' in J. Benyon and J. Solomos (eds) *The Roots of Urban Unrest*, Oxford: Pergamon Press.

Hall, S. (1991) 'The Local and the Global' in A. King (ed.) *Culture, Globalisation and the World System*, London: Macmillan.

Hall, S. (1992) 'New Ethnicities' in J. Donald and A. Tatansi (eds) *'Race', Culture and Difference*, London: Open University Press/Sage.

Hamblen, J. (1998) 'Practice Parameters for the Assessment and Treatment of Children and Adolescents with PTSD' *Journal of the American Academy of Child and Adolescent Psychiatry* 37 (10).

Hamilton, R. and Moore, D. (2004) *Educational Interventions for Refugee Children*, London: Routledge Falmer.

Hammar, T. (1990) *Democracy and the Nation State: Aliens, Denizens and Citizens in a World of International Migration*, Aldershot: Avebury.

Haringey, London Borough of (1997) *Refugees and Asylum-seekers in Haringey*, London: London Borough of Haringey.

Harrell-Bond, B. (1986) *Imposing Aid: Emergency Assistance to Refugees*, Oxford: Oxford University Press.

Harrell-Bond, B. (2002) Refugee Children in Cairo: An Invisible 'at Risk' Group in the City, unpublished paper, American University in Cairo.

Harrell-Bond, B. and Voutira, E. (1992) 'Anthropology and the Study of Refugees' *Anthropology Today* 8 (4).

Harris, H. (2004) *The Somali Community in the UK*, London: Information Centre about Asylum and Refugees.

Harrow, London Borough of (1999) *Listening to Somali Pupils and Their Parents*, London: London Borough of Harrow.

Healthy Islington 2000 (1994a) The Islington Zairean Refugee Survey Report. London: Healthy Islington 2000, unpublished report.

Healthy Islington 2000 (1994b) The Islington Somali Refugee Survey Report. London: Healthy Islington 2000, unpublished report.

Her Majesty's Government (2005a) *Controlling our Borders: Making Migration Work for Britain*, London: Home Office.

Her Majesty's Government (2005b) *Higher Standards, Better Schools for All*, London: Stationery Office.

Hewitt, R. (1996) *Routes of Racism: The Social Basis of Racist Action*, Stoke on Trent: Trentham Books.

Hewitt, R. (2003) *Asylum-Seeker Dispersal and Community Relations*, Swindon: Report to Economic and Social Research Council.

Hickman, M. and Walter, B. (1995) 'Deconstructing Whiteness: Irish Women in Britain' *Feminist Review* 50: 5–19.

Hicks, D. (1988) *Education for Peace: Issues, Principles and Practice in the Classroom*, London: Routledge.

Hill, M. (1997) *The Policy Process in the Modern State*, Harlow: Prentice Hall.

Hill, M. and Hupe, P. (2002) *Implementing Public Policy: Governance in Theory and Practice*, London: Sage.

Hodes, M. (2000) 'Psychologically Distressed Refugee Children in the UK' *Child and Adolescent Mental Health* 5 (2).

Hollins, K., Heydari, H. and Leavey, G. (2003) *Refugee Adolescents without Parents*, London: Barnet, Enfield and Haringey Mental Health Trust.

Holmes, C. (1988) *John Bull's Island: Immigration and British Society 1871–1971*, London: Macmillan.

Home Office (1988) *A Scrutiny of Grants under Section 11 of the Local Government Act 1966*, London: HMSO.

Home Office (1997) *Consultation on the Future of Section 11 Grants*, London: Home Office.

Home Office (1998) *Fairer, Faster, Firmer: A Modern Approach to Asylum and Immigration*, London: HMSO.

Home Office (1999a) *Asylum Statistics 1998*, London: Home Office.

Home Office (1999b) Special Grant Report No 49 – Special Grant for 1999/2000 for Kosovan Evacuees, unpublished correspondence..

Home Office (2000a) *Asylum Statistics 1999*, London: Home Office.

Home Office (2000b) *Full and Equal Citizens: A Strategy for the Integration of Refugees in the UK*, London: Home Office.

Home Office (2001) *Community Cohesion: A Report of the Independent Review Team Chaired by Ted Cantle*, London: Home Office.

Home Office (2002) *Secure Borders, Save Havens: Integration with Diversity in Modern Britain*, London: Home Office.

Home Office (2003a) *Asylum Statistics 2002*, London: Home Office.

Home Office (2003b) *Control of Immigration Statistics 2002 United Kingdom*, London: Home Office.

Home Office (2004a) *Asylum Statistics 2003*, London: Home Office.

Home Office (2004b) *Integration Matters: A National Strategy for Refugee Integration, Consultation Paper*, London: Home Office.

Home Office (2005a) *Asylum Statistics 2004*, London: Home Office.

Home Office (2005b) *Improving Opportunity, Strengthening Society: The Government's Strategy to Increase Race Equality and Community Cohesion*, London: Home Office.

Humpage, L. (1999) Somali Refugee Adolescents in Christchurch secondary schools, Christchurch, New Zealand: Refugee Resettlement Support, unpublished report.

Information Centre on Asylum and Refugees (ICAR) (2004a) *Media Image, Community Impact*, London: ICAR.

Information Centre on Asylum and Refugees (ICAR) (2004b) *Understanding the Stranger*, London: ICAR.

Inner London Education Authority (ILEA) (1969) *Literacy Survey: Summary of the Interim Results of the Study of Pupils Reading Standards*, London: ILEA.

Issa, T. (2005) *Talking Turkey: The Language, Culture and Identity of Turkish Speaking Children in Britain*, Stoke on Trent: Trentham Books.

Jaine, S. (2000) 'Teaching English as an Additional Language: Time for a Productive Sythesis' in S. Shaw (ed.) *Intercultural Education in European Classrooms*, Stoke on Trent: Trentham Books.

Joint Council for the Welfare of Immigrants (JCWI) (2001) *Manifesto for the Reform of British Immigration Policy*, London: JCWI.

Jones, C. and Ali, E. (2000) *Meeting the Educational Needs of Somali Pupils in Camden Schools*, London: London Borough of Camden.

Jones, P. (1982) *Vietnamese Refugees: A Study of their Reception and Resettlement in the United Kingdom*, Home Office Research and Planning Unit Paper 13, London: HMSO.

Jupp, J. and Luckey, J. (1990) 'Educational Experiences in Australia of Indo–Chinese Adolescent Refugees' in *International Journal of Mental Health* 18.

Kahin, M. (1997) *Educating Somali Children in Britain*, Stoke on Trent: Trentham Books.

Kay, D. (1987) *Chileans in Exile: Private Struggles, Public Lives*, London: Macmillan.

Kay, D. and Miles, R. (1988) 'Refugees or Migrant Workers? The Case of the European Volunteer Workers in Britain (1946–1951)' *Journal of Refugee Studies* 1 (3/4) 214–236.

Kent County Council (1998) Asylum-seeking Education Team (ASET), unpublished minutes of meetings.

Kidane. S. (2001) *Food, Shelter and Half a Chance*, London: British Agencies for Adoption and Fostering.

Kingston on Thames, Royal Borough of (2002) *Educational Development Plan*, London: Royal Borough of Kingston on Thames.

Kinzie, J., Sack, W., Angell, R., Manson, S. and Rath, B. (1986) 'The Psychiatric Effects of Massive Trauma on Cambodian Children, 1. The Children' *Journal of the American Academy of Child Psychiatry*, 25: 370–376.

Klein, G. (1993) *Education Towards Race Equality*, London: Cassell.

Koser, K. (1997) 'Social Networks and the Asylum Cycle: The Case of Iranian Asylum-seekers in the Netherlands' *International Migration Review* 31 (3).

Kumar, K. (2003) *The Making of English National Identity*, Cambridge: Cambridge University Press.

Kunz, E. (1973) 'The Refugee in Flight: Kinetic Models and Forms of Displacement' *International Migration Review* 7 (2), 125–146.

Kunz, E. (1981) 'Exile and Resettlement: Refugee Theory' *International Migration Review* 15 (1): 42–51.

Kushner, T. and Knox, K. (1999) *Refugees in an Age of Genocide*, London: Frank Cass.

Labov, W. (1969) 'The Logic of Non-standard English' in F. Williams (ed.) *Language and Poverty: Perspectives on a Theme*, Chicago: Markham.

Lam, T. and Martin, C. (1994) *Vietnamese in London: 15 Years of Settlement*, Occasional Paper 2, London: South Bank University.

Lambeth, London Borough of (1998) Educational Statistics, 1998. London: Lambeth Research and Statistics Department, unpublished report.

Lambeth, Southwark and Lewisham Health Action Zone (2000) *The Needs of Young Refugees in Lambeth, Southwark and Lewisham*, London: Lambeth, Southwark and Lewisham Health Action Zone.

Landau, R. (1992) *The Nazi Holocaust*, London: IB Tauris.

Legarreta, D. (1984) *The Guernica Generation: Basque Refugee Children of the Spanish Civil War*. Reno, Nevada: University of Nevada Press.

Lemos, G. (2005) *The Search for Tolerance: Challenging Racist Attitudes and Behaviour among Young People*, York: Joseph Rowntree Foundation.

Leonard, D., Epstein, D., Mauthner, M., Hewitt, R. and Watkins, C. (2003) A Violence Like Any Other: Rethinking Sexual Harassment, unpublished paper, Institute of Education, University of London.

Levy, C. (1999) 'Asylum-seekers, Refugees and the Future of Citizenship in Europe' in A. Bloch and C. Levy (eds) *Refugees, Citizenship and Social Policy in Europe*, Basingstoke: Macmillan.

Liebkind, K. (1993) 'Self-reported Ethnic Identity, Depression and Anxiety among Young Vietnamese Refugees and their Parents' *Journal of Refugee Studies* 6 (1): 25–39.

Lindley, A. (2005) *Report on Informal Remittance Systems in Africa, Caribbean and Pacific*, Somalia Country Report, Oxford: COMPAS.

Lipsky, M. (1980) *Street Level Bureaucracy: Dilemmas of the Individual in Public Service*, New York: Russell Sage Foundation.

Local Government Board (1916) Departmental Committee on Belgian Refugees, London: Local Government Board, unpublished report.

Lodge, C. (1998) 'Working with Refugee Children: One School's Experience' in J. Rutter and C. Jones (eds) *Refugee Education: Mapping the Field*, Stoke on Trent: Trentham Books.

London Challenge (2005) Report of the London Challenge Somali Forum, unpublished report, London Challenge.

London Research Centre (1999) Statistics on Asylum-seekers in London, unpublished report, London Research Centre.

Lord Laming (2003) *The Victoria Climbié Inquiry*, London: HMSO.

Loughrey, G. (1997) 'Civil Violence' in D. Black, N.Newman, J. Harris-Hendricks and G. Mezey (eds) *Psychological Trauma: A Developmental Approach*, London: Gaskell.

Lutz, H., Phoenix, A. and Yuval-Davis, N. (eds) (1995) *Crossfires: Nationalism, Racism and Gender in Europe*. London: Pluto Press. .

Mac an Ghaill, M. (1988) *Young, Gifted and Black: Student–Teacher Relations and the Schooling of Black Youth*, Buckingham: Open University Press.

Mac an Ghaill, M. (1999) *Contemporary Racisms and Ethnicities*, Buckingham: Open University Press.

McCallin, M. and Fozzard, S. (1990) *The Impact of Traumatic Events on the Psychological Well-being of Mozambican Refugee Women and Children*, Geneva: International Catholic Child Bureau.

McDonald, J. (1995) *Entitled to Learn? A Report on Young Refugees' Experiences of Access and Progression in the UK Education System*, London: World University Service.

McDonald, J. (1998) The Education of 16–19 Year Olds in the London Borough of Camden, unpublished research report.

McDowell, C. (1996) *A Tamil Asylum Diaspora: Sri Lankan Migration, Settlement and Policy in Switzerland*, Oxford: Berghahn Books.

McLeish, J. (2002) *Mothers in Exile: Maternity Experiences of Asylum Seekers in England*, London: The Maternity Alliance.

Macpherson, W. (1999) *The Stephen Lawrence Inquiry: Report of an Inquiry by Sir William Macpherson of Cluny*. London: HMSO.

Maksoud, M. (1992) 'Assessing War Trauma in Children: A Case Study of Lebanese Children' *Journal of Refugee Studies* 5 (1).

Marrus, M. (1985) *The Unwanted: European Refugees in the Twentieth Century*, Oxford: Oxford University Press.

Marsh, D. and Rhodes, R. (1992) *Policy Networks in British Government*, Oxford: Oxford University Press.

Marshall, T. H. (1950) *Citizenship and Social Class and Other Essays*, Cambridge: Cambridge University Press.

Marshall, T. (1991) *Cultural Aspects of Job-seeking*, London: Refugee Council.

Marshall, T. (1992) *Careers Guidance with Refugees*, London: Refugee Council.

Mashaw, J. (1983) *Bureaucratic Justice*, New Haven, CT: Yale University Press.

Massoud, R. and Dowling, J. (1997) A Report on a Study into the Needs of Refugee Pupils at North Westminster Community School and Arrangements to Meet these Needs. Unpublished report, Westminster Educational Psychology Service.

Masten, A., Best, K. and Garmezy, N. (1991) 'Resilience and Development: Contributions from the Study of Children who Overcome Adversity' *Development and Psychopathology* 2: 425–444.

Mehmet, A. (2001) *No Delight*, London: Fatal Books.

Melzak, S. (1997) Meeting the Needs of Refugee Children, unpublished training material from the Medical Foundation for the Care of Victims of Torture.

Melzak, S. and Warner, R. (1992) *Integrating Refugee Children in Schools*, London: Minority Rights Group.

Minderhoud, P. (1999) 'Asylum-seekers and Access to Social Security: Recent Patterns and Contemporary Realities' in A. Bloch and C. Levy (eds) *Refugees, Citizenship and Social Policy in Europe*, Basingstoke: Macmillan.

Ministry of Education (1956) *Education in Exile: A History of the Committee for the Education of Poles in UK*, London, HMSO.

Mohamud, S. (1996) The Sociolinguistic Problems of Somali Refugees and Their Children in the UK. Brighton: University of Sussex, MA thesis.

Morris, L. (1998) 'Governing at a Distance: The Elaboration of Controls in British Immigration' *International Migration Review* 32 (4): 949–973.

Morris, L. (2004) *The Control of Rights: The Rights of Workers and Asylum-seekers under Managed Migration*, London: Joint Council for the Welfare of Immigrants.

Mott, G. (2000) *Asylum-Seeking and Refugees: The Role of LEAs*, Slough: EMIE.

Munoz, N. (1999) *Other People's Children: An Exploration of the Needs of and the Provision for 16- and 17-Year-Old Unaccompanied Asylum-seekers*, London: Children of the Storm and Guildhall University.

Munroe-Blum, H., Boyle, M., Offord, D. and Kates, N. (1989) 'Immigrant Children: Psychiatric Disorder, School Performance and Service Utilization' *American Journal of Orthopsychiatry* 59 (4): 510–519.

Myers, K. (2001) 'National Identity, Citizenship and Education for Displacement: Spanish Refugee Children in Cambridge, 1937' *History of Education* 28: 3.

Nesdale, D. (1999) 'Social Identity and Ethnic Prejudice in Children' in R. Martin and W. Noble (eds) *Psychology and Society*, Brisbane: Australian Academic Press.

Noll, G. (2003) 'Visions of the Exceptional: Legal and Theoretical Issues Raised by Transit Processing Centres and Protection Zones' *European Journal of Migration and Law* 5 (3).

Nzongola-Ntalaja, G. (2002) *The Congo: from Leopold to Kabila*, London: Zed Press.

Office of National Statistics (ONS) (2002) *Census 2001 Table ES03*, London: ONS.

OFSTED (2002) *The Achievement of Black–Caribbean Pupils: Good Practice in Secondary Schools*, London: OFSTED.

OFSTED (2003a) *More Advanced Learners of English as an Additional Language in Secondary Schools and Colleges*, London: OFSTED.

OFSTED (2003b) *The Education of Asylum-seeking Pupils*, London: OFSTED.

OFSTED (2003c) *Writing in EAL*, London: OFSTED.

Osler, A., Street, C., Lall, M. and Vincent, K. (2002) *Not a Problem: Girls and School Exclusion*, London: National Children's Bureau.

Park, C. (2000) 'Learning Styles: Preferences among South East Asian students' *Urban Education* 35 (3): 245–268.

Peach, C. (1998) 'South Asian and Caribbean ethnic minority housing choice in Britain' *Urban Studies* 35 (10).

Phillips, D. (1998) 'Black Minority Ethnic Concentration, Segregation and Dispersal in Britain' *Urban Studies* 35 (10).

Pollard, S. (2004) *David Blunkett*, London: Hodder and Stoughton.

Portes, A. and Rumbaut, R. (2001) *Legacies: the Story of the Immigrant Second Generation*, Berkeley, CA: University of California Press.

Portes, A. and Zhou, M. (1993) 'The New Second Generation: Segmented Assimilation and its Variants' *Annals of the American Academy of Political and Social Science* 530: 74–97.

Power, S., Whitty, G. and Youdell. D. (1998) 'Refugees, Asylum-seekers and the Housing Crisis: No Place to Learn' in J. Rutter and C. Jones (eds) *Refugee Education: Mapping the Field*, Stoke on Trent: Trentham Books.

Qualifications and Curriculum Authority (QCA) (2000) *Citizenship: the National Curriculum Programme of Study at Key Stage 3 and Key Stage 4*, London: QCA.

Rattansi, A. (1992) 'Changing the Subject? Racism, Culture and Education' in J. Donald and A. Rattansi (eds) *Race, Culture, Difference*, London: Sage.

Reakes, A. and Powell, R. (2005) *The Education of Asylum-seekers in Wales*, Slough: National Foundation for Educational Research.

Refugee Council (1989) *Asylum Statistics 1980–1988*, London: Refugee Council.

Refugee Council (1991a) *Refugee Community Schools Directory*, London: Refugee Council.

Refugee Council (1991b) *Vietnamese Refugee Reception and Resettlement 1979–88*, London: Refugee Council.

Refugee Council (1994) Statistics on Refugee Children 1993, unpublished report.

Refugee Council (1995) Draft Mission Statement, London: Refugee Council, unpublished document.

Refugee Council (1996) Section 11 and Refugee Children, unpublished report.

Refugee Council (1997a) Response to Home Office Consultation on the Future of Section 11, unpublished report.

Refugee Council (1997b) *The Development of a Refugee Settlement Policy in the UK*, London: Refugee Council.

Refugee Council (1998a) *Asylum Statistics 1987–97*, London: Refugee Council.

Refugee Council (1998b) *Refugees: A Primary School Resource*, London: Refugee Council.

Refugee Council (1998c) Statistics on Refugee Children, unpublished report.

Refugee Council (1999a) Submission to the DfEE Consultation on the Ethnic Minority Achievement Grant, unpublished report.

Refugee Council (1999b) *Unwanted Journey: Why Central European Roma are Fleeing to the UK*, London: Refugee Council.

Refugee Council (2000) *Helping Refugee Children in Schools*, London: Refugee Council.

Refugee Council (2001) Statistics on Refugee Children, unpublished report.

Refugee Council (2004) *The Asylum and Immigration Act 2004: Main Issues and Areas of Concern*, London: Refugee Council.

Refugee Council (2005a) *Donate*, London: Refugee Council.

Refugee Council (2005b) *Tell It Like It Is*, London: Refugee Council.

Refugee Council (2005c) *The Refugee Council's Submission to the Campaign Against Legal Aid Cuts about the Impact of Changes to Legal Aid*, London: Refugee Council.

Refugee Council and Oxfam (2002) *Poverty and Asylum in the UK*, Oxford: Oxfam.

Refugee Council and World University Service (1990) *Refugee Education into the 1990s*, London: Refugee Council and World University Service.

Resource Unit for Supplementary and Mother Tongue Schools (2000) *Directory of Supplementary and Mother Tongue Classes 2000*, London: Resource Unit for Supplementary and Mother Tongue Schools.

Retamal, G. and Aedo-Richmond, R. (1998) *Education as a Humanitarian Response*, London: Cassell.

Rex, J. (1973) *Race, Colonialism and the City*, London: Routledge.

Rex, J. and Tomlinson, S. (1979) *Colonial Immigrants in a British City*, London: Routledge.

Riak Akuei, S. (2005) *Remittances as an Unforeseen Burden: The Livelihoods and Social Obligations of Sudanese Refugees*, Geneva: Global Commission on International Migration.

Richman, N. (1995) *They Don't Recognise Our Dignity: a Study of the Psychosocial Needs of Refugee Children and Families in Hackney*. London: City and Hackney Community NHS Trust.

Richman, N. (1998a) *In the Midst of a Whirlwind: A Manual for Helping Refugee Children*, Stoke On Trent: Trentham Books.

Richman, N. (1998b) 'Looking Before and After: Refugees and Asylum-seekers in the West' in P. Bracken and C. Petty (eds) *Rethinking the Trauma of War*, London: Save the Children.

Richmond, A. (1993) 'Reactive Migration: Sociological Perspectives on Refugee Movements' *Journal of Refugee Studies*, 6 (1): 7–24.

Robinson, V. and Hale, S. (1989) *The Geography of Vietnamese Secondary Migration in the UK, Research Paper 10*, Warwick: Centre for Research in Ethnic Relations.

Robinson, V., Andeson, R. and Musterd, S. (2003) *Spreading the Burden: A Review of Policies to Disperse Asylum-seekers and Refugees*, London: Policy Press.

Rousseau, C. and Drapeau, A. (2003) 'Are Refugee Children an At-risk Group: A Longitudinal Study of Cambodian Adolescents' *Journal of Refugee Studies* 16 (1): 67–81.

Rousseau, C., Drapeau, A. and Corin E. (1996) 'School Performance and Emotional Problems in Refugee Children' *American Journal of Orthopsychiatry* 66 (2).

Royal College of Paediatrics and Child Health (1999) *The Health of Refugee Children*, London: Royal College of Paediatrics and Child Health.

Rumbaut, R. (1991) 'The Agony of Exile: A Study of Migration and Adaptation of Indo–Chinese Refugee Adults and Children' in F. Ahearn and J. Athey (eds) *Refugee Children: Theory, Research and Services*, Baltimore, MD: Johns Hopkins University Press.

Rumbaut, R. and Portes, A. (2001) *Ethnicities: Children of Immigrants in America*, Berkeley, CA: University of California Press.

Runnymede Trust (1993) *Equality Assurance in Schools*, London: Runnymede Trust.

Runnymede Trust (2003) *Complementing Teachers: A Practical Guide to Promoting Race Equality in Schools*, London: Runnymede Trust.

Rutland, A., Milne, A., McGeorge, P. and Cameron, L. (2003) *The Development and Regulation of Prejudice in Children*, Swindon: Economic and Social Research Council.

Rutter, J. (1994) *Refugees in the Classroom*, Stoke on Trent: Trentham Books.

Rutter, J. (1999) Pupil Mobility in School, unpublished report, Refugee Council.

Rutter, J. (2003a) *Supporting Refugee Children in 21st Century Britain*, Stoke on Trent: Trentham Books.

Rutter, J. (2003b) *Working with Refugee Children*, York: Joseph Rowntree Foundation.

Rutter, J. (2004a) Congolese Children in Camden, London: London Borough of Camden, unpublished report.

Rutter, J. (2004b) *Refugees: We Left Because We Had To*, 3rd edition, London: Refugee Council.

Rutter, J. (2006) *Worlds on the Move: Educational and Social Care Responses to Changing Migration Patterns*, Stoke on Trent: Trentham Books.

Rutter, J. and Stanton, R. (2001) 'Refugee Children's Education and the Education Finance System' *Multicultural Teaching* 19 (3): 33–39.

Rutter, M. (1985) 'Resilience in the Face of Adversity – Protective Factors and Resistance to Psychiatric Disorder' *British Journal of Psychiatry*, 147: 598–611.

Sabatier, P. and Jenkins-Smith, H. (eds) (1993) *Policy Change and Learning: An Advocacy Collation Approach*, Boulder, CO: Westview Press.

Save the Children (1997) *Let's Spell It Out: Peer Research by the Horn of Africa Youth Scheme*, London: Save the Children.

Save the Children (2004) *I am Here: Teaching About Identity, Inclusion and the Media*, London: Save the Children.

Save the Children Scotland and Glasgow City Council (2002) *Starting Again*, Glasgow: Save the Children Scotland.

Schatzberg, M. (1988) *Politics and Class in Zaire*, New York: Holmes and Meier.

Schuster, L. (2003) 'Common Sense or Racism: The Treatment of Asylum-seekers in Europe' *Patterns of Prejudice* 37 (3).

Scottish Refugee Integration Forum (2003) *Draft Action Plan*, Edinburgh: Scottish Executive.

Sellen, D. (2000) *Young Refugee Children's Diets and Family Coping Strategies in East London*, London: London School of Hygiene and Tropical Medicine.

Sewell, T. (1997) *Black Masculinities and Schooling*, Stoke on Trent: Trentham Books.

Shelter (1995) *No Place to Learn: Homelessness and Education*, London: Shelter.

Sivanandan, A. (1976) *Race, Class and State*, London: Institute of Race Relations.

Sivanandan, A. (1982) *A Different Hunger*, London: Pluto Press.

Skutnabb-Kangas, T. (1981) *Bilingualism or Not: The Education of Minorities*, Clevedon: Multilingual Matters.

Smith, D., Ray, L. and Wastell, L. (2003) *Racial Violence in Greater Manchester*, Swindon: Economic and Social Research Council Research Findings.

Solomos, J. (1993) *Race and Racism in Britain*, Basingstoke: Macmillan.

Sommers, M. (2002) 'Peace Education and Refugee Youth' in J. Crisp (ed.) *Learning for a Future: Refugee Education in Developing Countries*, Geneva: UNHCR.

Southwark, London Borough of (2002) *Educational Statistics 2001*, London: London Borough of Southwark.

Stanley, K. (2002) *Cold Comfort: The Lottery of Care for Young Separated Refugees in England*, London: Save the Children.

Statham, P. (2003) 'Understanding the Anti-asylum Rhetoric: Restrictive Policies or Racist Publics' *Political Quarterly* 74 (1): 163–177.

Steen, A.-B. (1993) *Varieties of the Tamil Refugee Experience in Denmark and England*, Copenhagen: University of Copenhagen and the Danish Centre for Human Rights.

Stewart, E. (2004) 'Deficiencies in UK Asylum Data: Practical and Theoretical Challenges' *Journal of Refugee Studies* 17 (1).

Stornfay-Stitz, A. (1993) *Peace Education in America 1828–1990*, London: Scarecrow Press.

Styan, D. (2003) 'La Nouvelle Vague: Recent Francophone African Settlement in London' in K. Koser (ed.) *New African Diasporas*, London: Routledge.

Summerfield, D. (1998) 'The Social Experience of War' in P. Bracken and C. Petty (eds) *Rethinking the Trauma of War*, London: Save the Children.

Summerfield, D. (2000) 'Childhood, War, Refugeedom and Trauma' *Transcultural Psychiatry* 37 (3).

Swann Report (1985) see Committee of Inquiry into the Education of Children from Ethnic Minority Groups.

Sword, K. (ed.) (1989) *The Formation of the Polish Community in UK*, London: School of Slavonic Studies, University of London.

Tajfel, H. (1978) *Differentiation between Social Groups: Studies in Social Psychology*, Cambridge: Cambridge University Press.

Tamil Information Centre (1998) *Tamil Education in the UK*, London: Tamil Information Centre.

Taylor, M. (1988) *Worlds Apart – A Review of Research into the Education of Pupils of Cypriot, Italian, Ukrainian and Vietnamese Origin, Liverpool Blacks and Gypsies*, Windsor: NFER Nelson.

Timm, J., Chiang, B. and Finn, B. (1998) 'Acculturation in the Learning Styles of Laotian Hmong Students' *Equity and Excellence in Education* 31 (1): 29–35.

Tolfree, D. (1996) *Restoring Playfulness: Different Approaches to Assisting Children Who Are Psychologically Affected by War or Displacement*, Stockholm: Radda.

Toukomaa, P. and Skutnabb-Kangas, T. (1977) *The Intensive Teaching of the Mother Tongue to Migrant Children of Pre-school Age, Research Report 26*, Tampere: Department of Sociology, University of Tampere.

Tower Hamlets, London Borough of (1992) The Somali Community in Tower Hamlets: A Demographic Survey, London: London Borough of Tower Hamlets (council minutes).

Troyna, B. (ed.) (1987) *Race Inequality in Education*, London: Tavistock.

Troyna, B. and Hatcher, R. (1992) *Racism in Children's Lives: Primary Pupils Attitudes to and Understanding of Race*, London: Routledge.

United Nations High Commissioner for Refugees (UNHCR) (1992) *Handbook on Procedures and Criteria for Determining Refugee Status under the 1951 Convention and 1967 Protocol Relating to the Status of Refugees*, Geneva: UNHCR.

United Nations High Commissioner for Refugees (UNHCR) (1994) *Refugee Children: Guidelines on Protection and Care*, Geneva: UNHCR.

United Nations High Commissioner for Refugees (UNHCR) (2005) *Refugees, Asylum-Seekers and Others of Concern to UNHCR, Statistics 1st January 2005* available on www.unhcr.ch.

US Committee for Refugees (USCR) (2004) *Refugee Report 2003*, Washington DC: US Committee for Refugees.

US Department of State (2002) *Congo: Country Briefing*, Washington, DC: US Department of State.

University of East Anglia (UEA) (2004) *Children's Trusts, Developing Integrated Services for Children in England, Phase 1 Interim Report*, Norwich: UEA.

Valverde, M. (1996) 'Despotism and Ethical Liberal Governance' *Economy and Society* 25: 357–372.

Van der Veer, G. (1992) *Counselling and Therapy with Refugees*. New York: John Wiley & Sons.

Van Hear, N. (2003) *I Went as Far as my Money Would Take Me: Conflict, Forced Migration and Class*, Oxford: Centre on Migration, Policy and Society, University of Oxford.

Vasquez, A. and Arayo, A. (1989) 'The Process of Transculturation: Exiles and Institutions in France' in D. Joly and R. Cohen (eds) *Reluctant Hosts: Europe and Its Refugees*, Aldershot: Gower.

Vertovec, S. (1999) 'Introduction' in *Migration and Social Cohesion*, Aldershot: Edward Elgar.

Vincent, C. and Warren, S. (1998) Supporting Refugee Children: A Focus on Home–school Liaison. Unpublished report of a research project conducted by the University of Warwick.

Waldinger, R. and Feliciano, C. (2003) *Will the New Second Generation Experience Downward Mobility? Paper Four*, Los Angeles: Department of Sociology, University of California at Los Angeles.

Watters, C. and Ingleby, D. (2004) 'Locations of Care: Meeting the Mental Health and Social Care Needs of Refugees in Europe' *International Journal of Law and Psychiatry* 27: 549–570.

Werbner, P. (1997) 'Essentialising Essentialism, Essentialising Silence: Ambivalence and Multiplicity in the Construction of Racism and Ethnicity' in P. Werbner and T. Modood (eds) *Debating Cultural Hybridity, Multicultural Identities and the Politics of Anti-racism*, London: Zed Press.

Westermeyer, J. and Her, C. (1996) 'Predictors of English Fluency among Hmong

Refugees in Minnesota: A Longitudinal Study' *Cultural Diversity and Mental Health* 2: 125–132.

Wetherell, M. and Potter, J. (1992) *Mapping the Language of Racism: Discourse and the Legitimation of Exploitation*, London: Harvester Press.

G. White and A. Marsella (1982) 'Introduction' in A. Marsella and G. White (eds) *Cultural Conceptions of Mental Health and Therapy*, Dordrecht: Reidal Publishing.

Williamson, L. (2000) 'Unaccompanied Refugee Children: Legal Framework and Local Application in Britain' in A. Bloch and C. Levy (eds) *Refugees, Citizenship and Social Policy in Europe*, London: Macmillan.

Willis, P. (1977) *Learning to Labour: How Working Class Kids Get Working Class Jobs*, Farnborough: Saxon House.

Witmer, T. and Culver, S. (2001) 'Trauma and Resilience among Bosnian Refugee Families: A Critical Review of the Literature' *Journal of Social Work Research and Evaluation* 2: 173–187.

World University Service (UK) (1974) *Reception and Resettlement of Refugees from Chile*, London: World University Service (UK).

Young, A. (1995) *The Harmony of Illusions: Inventing Post Traumatic Stress Disorder*, Princeton, NJ: Princeton University Press.

Yule, W. (1998) 'The psychological adaption of refugee children' in J. Rutter and C. Jones (eds) *Refugee Education: Mapping the Field*, Stoke on Trent: Trentham Books.

Yuval-Davies, N. (1999) Institutional Racism, Cultural Diversity and Citizenship: Some Reflections on Reading the Stephen Lawrence Inquiry Report, unpublished essay.

Yuval-Davies, N. and Werbner, P. (eds) (1999) *Women, Citizenship and Difference*, London: Zed Books.

Zetter, R. (1991) 'Labelling Refugees: Forming and Transforming a Bureaucratic Identity' *Journal of Refugee Studies*, 4 (1).

Zhou, M. and Bankston, C. (1998) *Growing Up American: How Vietnamese Children Adapt to Life in the United States*, New York: Russell Sage.

Policy texts used in thematic analysis

Appa, V. (2005) *A Study of How Asylum-seekers and Refugees Access Education in Four Local Authorities in England*, London: NCB.

Blackwell, D. and Melzak, S. (1999, reprinted 2000) *Far from the Battle but Still at War: Troubled Refugee Children in School*, London: Child Psychotherapy Trust.

Bristol City Council (1998) Refugee Action Plan, unpublished document from Bristol City Council.

Camden, London Borough of (1992b) *Camden Education Department Policy Statement on Refugees*, London: Camden Education.

Camden, London Borough of (1994) *A Corporate Refugee Policy for Camden*, London: London Borough of Camden, Director of Corporate Services.

Camden, London Borough of (1996a) *Meeting the Needs of Refugee Children: A Checklist for All Staff Who Work with Refugee Children in Schools*, London: London Borough of Camden and Camden and Islington Community NHS Trust.

Camden, London Borough of (1996b) *Refugee Education Policy*, London: Camden Education. Unpublished document.

Camden, London Borough of (1998b) A Report on a Survey of the Education and Training Needs of 15–19 Year Olds in the London Borough of Camden. Unpublished report.

Children of the Storm (1998) *Invisible Students: Practical and Peer-led Approaches to Enhancing the Educational and Emotional Support for Refugee Children in Schools*, London: Children of the Storm.

Children of the Storm (1999) *Other People's Children: An Exploration of the Needs of and Provision for 16 and 17 Year Old Unaccompanied Asylum Seekers*, London: Children of the Storm.

City and County of Cardiff (1999) *Refugee Strategy*, Cardiff: City and County of Cardiff.

Daycare Trust (1995) *Reaching First Base: Guidelines of Good Practice on Meeting the Needs of Refugee Children from the Horn of Africa*, London: Daycare Trust.

Department for Education and Employment (DfEE) (1998) *Draft Circular on the Education of Traveller and Displaced Persons*, London: DfEE.

Department for Education and Skills (DfES) (2004) *Aiming High: Guidance on Supporting the Education of Asylum-seeking and refugee Pupils*, London: DfES.

Department of Heath Social Services Inspectorate (1995) *Unaccompanied Asylum-Seeking Children: A Practice Guide*, London: Department of Heath Social Services Inspectorate.

Ealing, London Borough of (1999) *Refugee Corporate Strategy*, London: London Borough of Ealing.

Enfield, London Borough of (1999) *Refugee Education Handbook*, London: London Borough of Enfield.

Gloucestershire County Council (2000) *A Policy for the Education of Refugees and Asylum-Seekers: Information for Schools*, Gloucester: Gloucestershire County Council .

Haringey, London Borough of (1998a) Haringey Primary Schools Parental and Community Partnership Project.

Haringey, London Borough of (1998b) *Refugees and Asylum-seekers in Haringey*, London: London Borough of Haringey.

Harrow, London Borough of (1994) Refugee Children in Harrow Schools, Report of the Director of Education to the Education Management Sub–Committee.

Home Office (1988) *A Scrutiny of Grants Under Section 11 of the Local Government Act 1966*, London: Home Office.

Home Office (1999) Special Grant Report No 49 – Special Grant for 1999/2000 for Kosovan Evacuees. Unpublished correspondence..

Kensington and Chelsea, London Borough of (1999) Documents from the Leaving Care Outcomes Database.

Kent County Council (1999) Asylum-seeking Education Team (ASET), unpublished minutes of meetings.

Lea, A. (1999) New Arrivals: Access to Education in Lewisham, unpublished report from Lewisham Refugee Network.

Lewisham Education and Community Services (1997) Receiving Asylum-seekers and Refugee Children.

Lewisham Education and Community Services (1998) New Arrival Current Initiatives.

Lothian Refugee Strategy (1990) Corporate Strategy for Support for Refugees in Lothian. Unpublished Policy Report.

McDonald, J. (1995) *Entitled to Learn? A Report on Young Refugees' Experiences of Access and Progression in the UK Education System*, London: World University Service.

Melzak, S. and Warner, R. (1992) *Integrating Refugee Children in Schools*, London: Minority Rights Group.

Midlands Refugee Council (1999) Memo: Educational advice for asylum seekers for finding schools.

Mott, G. (2000) *Refugees and Asylum-seekers: The Role of LEAs*, Slough: EMIE.

OFSTED (2003) *The Education of Asylum-seeking Pupils*, London: OFSTED.

Refugee Council (1990) *Refugee Education Charter: A Policy for the 1990s*, London: Refugee Council.

Refugee Council (1991) *Refugees in the Classroom*, London: Refugee Council.

Refugee Council (1993) *Helping Refugee Children in Schools*, London: Refugee Council.

Refugee Council (1997) *The Development of a Refugee Settlement Policy in the UK*, London: Refugee Council.

Refugee Council (1999) Submission to the DfEE Consultation on the Ethnic Minority Achievement Grant, unpublished reort.

Refugee Council and World University Service (1990) *Refugee Education into the 1990s*, London: Refugee Council and World University Service.

Remsbury, N. (2003) *The Education of Refugee Children*, London: National Children's Bureau.

Rutter, J. (1994) *Refugee Children in the Classroom*, Stoke on Trent: Trentham Books.

Tickell, D. (1991) *An Educational Perspective on the Needs of Children with a Refugee Experience*, Oxford: Refugees in Oxford.

Also examined were annual reports from the Community of Congolese Students in the UK, Halkevi, the Iranian Cultural Centre, the Kurdish Community Centre, The Kurdistan Workers Association, Zaca-Lisanga.

INDEX

UNIVERSITY OF CHICHESTER